D0041717

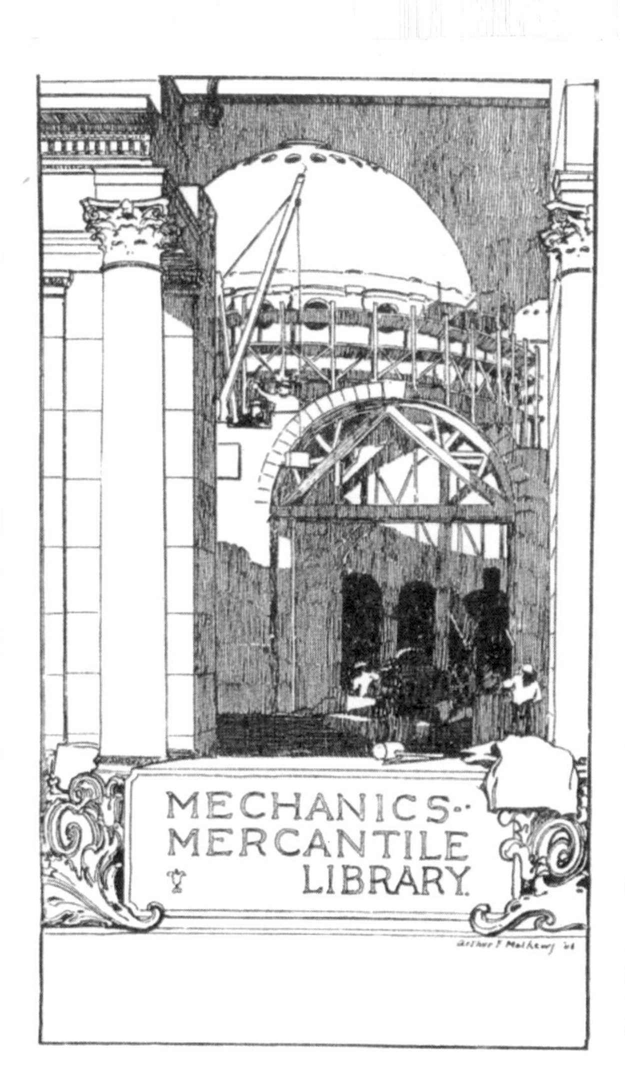
MECHANICS-
MERCANTILE
LIBRARY

Sincerity

Also by R. Jay Magill, Jr.
Chic Ironic Bitterness

Sincerity : How a *moral ideal* born five hundred years ago inspired religious wars | modern art | hipster chic | and the curious notion that we ALL have something to say (*no matter how dull*)

R. Jay Magill Jr.

W. W. NORTON & COMPANY
NEW YORK • LONDON

Printed in the United States of America
First Edition

For information about special discounts for bulk purchases, please contact W. W. Norton Special Sales at specialsales@wwnorton.com or 800-233-4830

Manufacturing by Courier Westford
Book design by Susanna Dulkinys
Production manager: Anna Oler

Library of Congress Cataloging-in-Publication Data

Magill, R. Jay (Ronald Jay), 1972-
Sincerity : how a moral ideal born five hundred years ago inspired religious wars, modern art, hipster chic, and the curious notion that we all have something to say (no matter how dull) / R. Jay Magill, Jr. — 1st ed.
p. cm.
Includes bibliographical references (p.) and index.
ISBN 978-0-393-08098-8 (hardcover)
1. Sincerity. I. Title.
BJ1533.S55M34 2012
179'.9—dc23
2012010360

W. W. Norton & Company, Inc.
500 Fifth Avenue, New York, N.Y. 10110
www.wwnorton.com

W. W. Norton & Company Ltd.
Castle House, 75/76 Wells Street, London W1T 3QT

1 2 3 4 5 6 7 8 9 0

for Tanja & Jasper

Contents

Sincerity

Introduction

It is dangerous to be sincere,
unless you are also stupid.

- George Bernard Shaw,
"Maxims for Revolutionists," 1903

NOT SO VERY LONG AGO, in the Year of Our LORD Two Thousand and Ten, Sarah Palin descended upon the Fox News Channel's *Glenn Beck Program* with a warning. "It's very, very dangerous to trust people in this business of politics," she said, twice. "There's so much doubt as to whom you can trust." Dressed in a smart black jacket, a sassy black skirt, and knee-high black boots, Palin sat chummily with her host in a mushroom beige living-room studio overlooking the Statue of Liberty. "I picked this spot because of that statue, and what it means," Beck said. He then urged Palin to recount her stint as an insider privy to the sundry machinations of American power jockeying when she was chosen as Senator John McCain's running mate in 2008:

> Well, Glenn, there were those who were [sharks], and there were others who were so amazing and awesome and sincere. And I

> thank God for the people who were surrounding the campaign who fit that description! . . . Had it not been for those who were sincere and wanted to see our ticket win, to serve for the right reasons, I would have lost all hope in this political system. . . . The generation of today that is of voting age . . . can see through the insincerity. . . . We have to get the real people, the sincere people.[1]

She went on to rue "these days [when] you can't put your trust in anybody—except your spouse." And looking back to the attitudes of the Founding Fathers and "seeing the sincerity there," she said, "I don't think in recent days we can find those kinds of politicians." Beck concurred: "I have learned over the last year that I just cannot trust *anybody*." All hope of America's future greatness had died with the election of the man Beck and Palin were determined to portray as a foreign-born socialist usurper, Barack Hussein Obama.

In Palin's footsteps, competitors for the position of the most powerful person in the world have continued to vie for the badge of sincerity—to be seen as the candidate who not only means what he says, but who means it the most. And despite what many voters believe to be true about the calculating quality of politics, they still demand that candidates' avowal and action align; that the inner should match the outer; and that political strategists and politicians should say what they really believe instead of manipulating people with what they think voters want to hear.

While admiration for sincerity is understandable, the absence of the trait in politicians is perhaps the age-oldest lament, not exactly worthy of breaking-news status, and it isn't likely to go away soon. And actually, perhaps it shouldn't. Sincerity, after all, is not the same thing as honesty, which means saying what you know to be the truth about objective things or events, regardless of how you feel about them. Sincerity is also not the same as frankness, which means revealing one's judgment about someone or something, even though that judgment might offend. Being sincere is a rather more tricky state of affairs: it means confronting one's innermost thoughts or emotions and relaying them to others straightforwardly, no matter how relevant to the topic, injurious to one's own reputation, or embarrassing—or however correct or incorrect. Sincerity, in other words, is a subjective state that need not have anything to do with reality.

But because self-presentation and impression management are necessary for people dependent on the approval of others, political leaders often resort to saying things they don't mean. In 2007 a team of political psychologists set out to measure the sincerity of that species of publicly elected persons who "extol peace while preparing to start a war, promise tax relief while planning tax increases, express concern and sympathy on issues they care nothing about, oppose a policy in public while pursuing it secretly (or vice versa)." In such situations, say the researchers, it would be useful "for everyone to be in possession of a truth detector." Fortunately, science may now have one.

Siphoning through a bundle of metrics called Thematic Content Analysis (TCA), which measures "integrative complexity," "non-immediacy," and "motive imagery," the researchers set out to assess the sincerity of President George W. Bush. After analyzing micro-gestures and emotional output and tics of verbal expression, they concluded that the former president's remarks about the case for the Iraq war "showed complete consistency among cognitive, emotional, and motivational indices; all . . . markers, show [Bush] to have been very sincere in his remarks."[2] And so, while we may want leaders to really mean what they say, heightened attention to a speaker's sincerity can lead to overlooking more important criteria—such as foresight, accuracy, judgment, and competence. Perhaps it's true, as the great American sociologist David Riesman wrote in *The Lonely Crowd* (1950), that "concern for sincerity in political personalities [is] a vice."

For better or worse, national polls hint at our contradictory feeling that sincerity is both desirable in political figures and a criterion that misses the mark. In the run-up to the 2008 presidential election, *Forbes.com* published a list of the "Most Sincere Presidential Candidates." Beating out, among others, Barack Obama, Dennis Kucinich, Bill Richardson, Hillary Clinton, John McCain, Mitt Romney, Newt Gingrich, and Michael Bloomberg was . . . "Fred Thompson, the most sincere of the 14 presidential candidates of both political parties."[3] The survey attributed the *Law and Order* district attorney's high ranking both to his real-life courtroom experience and, more so, to his "honing sincerity on television." More recently, the second question on a January 30, 2012, *USA Today* / Gallup poll about the frontrunners for the GOP presidential nomination asked whether each was "sincere and authentic," an evaluative category that coexists with "leadership qualities" and the "ability to manage government effectively." Perhaps it's no wonder that in a number of past polls about the most sincere president in history, former actor Ronald Reagan is often the winner. Yet "sincerity is not necessarily a central requirement for a president," *Forbes* wrote in the 2008 poll. "Still, any president who expects to use the power of that office effectively should present at least an appearance of sincerity in dealing with his administration, Congress, or voters."[4]

Niccolò Machiavelli—no surprise—had exactly the same advice for his imaginary prince in 1513, writing that sincerity is indeed useful when you want to appear moral to the people who support you. But actually being sincere is inadvisable: "Those princes who have accomplished great deeds are those who have thought little about keeping faith and who have known how cunningly to manipulate men's minds," Machiavelli counseled. "They have surpassed those who have laid their foundations upon sincerity."[5] Amoral, ruthless politics underneath the cover of smiling innocence was the key to advantage and power. Rule number one: Do not appear as you are.

Machiavelli was drawing on a long tradition, of course: Thucydides' *History of the Peloponnesian War* observes, "The strong do what they can and the weak suffer what they must." Plato himself justified the "noble lie," which placed lofty public goals ahead of personal morality. Aristotle observed the same in the *Rhetoric,* and the *raison d'état* (reason of state) has long been creed among the powerful, from Richelieu, Clausewitz, and Metternich to Kissinger, Rumsfeld, and Rove. In fact, the use of sincerity as a ruse has been so integrated into political life over the last five centuries that not to engage in deceptive tactics or to recognize their utility has become a sign of political immaturity or lack of worldliness. It's what separates old hawks from young doves.

Even in America, "the only country in the world which was founded in explicit opposition to Machiavellian principles," as political theorist Leo Strauss believed, sincerity might have been more promoted than practiced.[6] John Dickinson, author of *Letters from a Farmer in Pennsylvania* (1768), insisted that colonists set out to discover the distinction between men of "sincerity" and men of "policy," and suggested the latter be fought in kind. John Adams, for all his Founding Father sincerity, confided in his diary and other writings that deception and strategy were nonnegotiable parts of political statesmanship. "Dissimulation," he wrote, "is the first Maxim of worldly Wisdom." Benjamin Franklin balanced his forays into grand strategy with the overt promotion of sincerity, ranking it second in his "Thirteen Virtues" (1730), directly after silence. Even our Honest Abe, that earnest Kentucky darling, was maligned by his opponent in the 1858 debates for having sneak-attacked the audience with his "usual artless sincerity." Stephen Douglas begged the crowd "not to be deceived by his seeming innocence, his carefully cultivated spirit of goodwill!" In each of Abe's little homilies, Douglas warned, "lurk concealed weapons."

Sophisticated thinkers have long vacillated between ridiculing sincerity when it appears (e.g., George Bernard Shaw's observation that sincerity was dangerous unless one was stupid) and complaining that others don't take the virtue quite seriously enough. The esteemed Columbia University professor and literary critic Lionel Trilling, for one, cared enough about sincerity to trace its swift decline as a political, moral, and literary value in our own time. "The word sincerity has lost most of its former high dignity," he observed in his compact and commanding book *Sincerity and Authenticity* (1971), based on the Charles Eliot Norton Lectures he delivered at Harvard in 1969–70. "When we hear it, we are conscious of the anachronism which touches it with quaintness," he wrote. "If we speak it, we are likely to do so with either discomfort or irony."[7]

Trilling's contemporary, the critic Patricia M. Ball, had signaled its decline even earlier, in an influential 1964 essay in the *Modern Language Review*, writing that sincerity, once the critical benchmark of the finest Romantic and Victorian literature, was "in its sadder days of exile."[8] Critics like Herbert Read, Marshall Berman, and Henri Peyre had all likewise seen the writing on the wall and took an extended view of sincerity's travails: Read's *Cult of Sincerity* (1968) lamented the rise of a noisy nineteenth-century industrialism that drowned out the inner voice and instigated the decline of sincerity as a critical standard for literature; Berman's Marxist-inspired *Politics of Authenticity* (1970) delineated the French political theory that he thought birthed our obsession with being fully ourselves; and Peyre's *Literature and Sincerity* (1963) traced the rise and fall of sincerity as a literary and moral demand since the sixteenth-century *Essays* of Michel de Montaigne, arguably the first author with a burning desire to show himself as he really was, faults and all.

All of these scholars were thinking about sincerity and authenticity during the 1960s, when, as Trilling put it, "moral life [was] in the process of revising itself." Droves of newly cynical citizens, searching for sincerity, were becoming allergic to politics after a decade of hyperpolitical protest, three horrific assassinations, and an undefined war in Southeast Asia, all of which had led to a "credibility gap" between voters and the federal government that has never really closed. *Sincerity and Authenticity* was published five months prior to the Watergate break-in.

Like it or not, Americans' perception of their fellow citizens' morality and honesty has fallen dramatically since then. A 2006 update to the authoritative Saguaro Report, a study of American social life led by the Harvard social psychologist Robert Putnam (author of *Bowling Alone*), revealed that less than a third of Americans felt that they could trust one another. And while there has been an increase in social trust in the last half-decade (more often than not among Internet users), a widely cited study found that almost half of the American population only had either one person or no one to talk to.[9] The number of Americans lacking someone with whom to discuss important matters had nearly tripled since 1985. (A follow-up Pew Report in 2009 contested these findings but acknowledged that the "diversity of core discussion networks has markedly declined.")[10]

More alone, more suspicious of the motives of our fellow citizens and public servants, and more doubting of others' sincerity, we habitually debunk high-minded rhetoric (on both sides of the political divide) and believe that peeling off the public face reveals a rotten core of disingenuousness, cynical manipulation, and hypocrisy. The truths of these revelations are confirmed nearly every day by *The Daily Show* and *The Colbert Report*, by *South Park* and *The*

Onion, which showcase unsurprising transgressions against the public trust and basic moral standards (Anthony Weiner, Bernie Madoff, Eliot Spitzer, John Edwards, and so on). But these observations, which almost inevitably seem to be delivered in a comic format, are not just facile markers of some chuckling hip awareness or postmodern blasé knowingness. Rather, these judgments of insincerity, hypocrisy, and fake authenticity float like hypercharged electrons around the ancient moral nucleus of sincerity, nodding to its decline with a kind of resentful remorse.

The intriguing thing about our repeated moral letdowns is not that insincerity continues to exist, but that we continue to insist we are outraged by it. In many ways our frustration with insincerity is itself disingenuous—a kind of performance of an upright moral sensibility. Most of us actually do recognize how things get done in the world, for better or worse. Power and money matter. Who you know matters. Public and private do not need to align in political matters. This is called pragmatism, or realism, or realpolitik, or Machiavellianism, or, since Machiavelli, simply politics. WikiLeaks and the Occupy movement may have been arguing against the ways of the world for high-minded moral reasons, but as the intellectual historian Martin Jay recently wrote in his *Virtues of Mendacity* (2010), the political hypocrisy Americans so passionately decry "may be the best alternative to the violence justified by those who claim to know the truth." Many a Communist dictator, Jay notes, regularly enforced the citizenry's total transparency by spying on and slaughtering or banishing dissenters to Siberia. Like it or not, liberty includes the right to lie; freedom allows for deceit. Given the alternatives, insincerity hardly seems disagreeable.

But Americans, more than any other people, it seems, still demand the appearance of sincerity. They have long liked to imagine themselves as more down-to-earth and real than people from other countries. From the framing idea that the United

States is based on a *fundamental* human freedom to the Straight Talk Express, among other "no-bullshit" outlets, Americans often aim to "tell it like it is" and "keep it real." Today's political talk show hosts take us to the "no spin zone," where they play "hardball." Even MTV's *The Real World* asked us at the dawn of our cool age (1992) what would happen if we "stopped being polite . . . and started getting real?" This is so because Americans feel that formality and social distance (both social constructs) are, at the end of the day, unnecessary. Formality is just a bunch of rules that ultimately cover up the real, authentic person, some fundamental being who exists prior to society rather than through it. Some more libertarian Americans believe that they would be much better off if society would just go away and leave them alone altogether so they could enjoy their freedom in peace.

Given these antisocial leanings, American demands for sincerity, it might be argued, are an attempt to surmount our otherwise weak social bonds, our lack of credence in social rituals—our lack of what Alexis de Tocqueville once termed the "sense of society." One might even see sincerity as a fundamentally democratic demand: the person seeking it assumes he or she has the right to know even a superior's innermost thoughts and feelings beyond his or her public mask. The person answering the demand assumes that he or she is valuable enough to warrant interest in his or her subjective world. Seen in this context, sincerity attempts to make intimates of strangers by breaking down social conventions and insisting, "We're all in this together." (Irony, on the other hand, is more aristocratic; it pulls away and says, "Good luck.")

But here it is important to ask: does sincerity mean revealing one's intentions openly and avoiding deceit (as in, "I mean this sincerely"), or does it mean pursuing one's goals in accordance with one's true beliefs (as in, "I sincerely believe that X is the right thing to do and will stop at nothing to do it")? The former sees sincerity as a bond that demands openness of intention with others.

The latter is about the principle of authentic self-sameness: do not stand against yourself, or "To thine own self be true," as Shakespeare's Polonius reminded Laertes in *Hamlet*. It must not follow, however, that if you adhere to sincerity as an honest relationship to your interests that "thou canst not then be false to any man." This kind of sincerity, in fact, as Machiavelli advised his prince, can lead to ever more clever ways of being deceptive.

Given its ethical implications, sincerity has found its most reliable champions and commentators in spheres other than politics: religion, art, literature, and philosophy.

Puritan theology held that without the believer's sincere repentance and genuine spiritual transformation, not only was heaven impossible but so was belonging to the church. Believers were given the opportunity to explain to church elders the details of their "sincere conversion experience"—or else be damned to a life of wandering outside of grace. Under such existential angst, more and more people learned to feign sincerity. Some observant contemporary English and French satirists thus disparaged the trait of sincerity for its perfect ability to cover up lying and deception. The detection of hypocrisy became something of a sport in the seventeenth century, exemplified by Molière's poisonous jab at fake religion, *Tartuffe, or the Imposter* (1664). A century later the eighteenth-century French philosopher Jean-Jacques Rousseau, himself an odd kind of Calvinist, held true to sincerity, believing it was the sole quality that delivered man back to his state of original purity, freed from the false and oppressive protocols of social life. Rousseau's sentiments helped to motivate not only the French Revolution, but also what would become Romantic thought in Europe and America, a movement in art and music that lasted for five decades and urged individuals to see themselves outside of their inherited roles, and outside of society altogether, as unique beings standing on the precipice of the world.

Over the decades, this ethos of sincerity evolved from seeking the truth of oneself to sharing the whole of that truth with others with unabashed pride, a trait that would come to be called, in modern times, authenticity. This insistence on being who one feels oneself to be at all times eventually found a home in modern art and literature. Artists and writers well into the twentieth century, following Rousseau, declared the importance of the self's authenticity against the inauthenticity of modern consumer society, which many critics believed had enslaved individuals in a capitalist system and then offered them illusory freedom through the purchase of its products.

This line of criticism and rebellious self-expressiveness has rolled into our own time, of course, through art, music, fashion, and literature—through Beats and hippies and punk and rap—and eventually through the messages of some of the world's largest advertising agencies and corporations themselves, such as Apple's "Think Different" and other variations of blazing your own trail, flying your own flag, having it your way, thinking outside the box, and other corporate pabulum. Alas, even today's "counterculture" fashions—beards, wacky eyeglasses, piercings, tattoos—play perfectly into this old Romantic logic of showing the authentic self to the world, into being an advertisement for oneself, into trumpeting one's inner uniqueness—one's irreplaceable soul, immortal or not.

Even irony, once the weapon of choice for the necessary lampooning of moral and political hypocrisy, now seems old. It surfaces in any television commercial with "edge," as a quaint rhetorical trick printed on snarky t-shirts, as front-and-center "zingers" on middlebrow sitcoms, or even as tired punch lines of *New Yorker* cartoons. Since the election of Obama in 2008, actually, irony has seemed to become an easy way to showcase rebelliousness and critical thought without having to do anything at all. The best kind of irony, of course, continues to remind us of our sincerity. Importantly, as this book will argue, the two are not opposite.

In fact, morally vigorous irony may be the only form of spin that can jar us into recognizing the itchings of conscience, to get us to see through the fake display of sincerity, to return us to seriousness through jokes.

Moral ideals have histories. They come from somewhere and are pushed forward by the winds of religion and politics, by individuals and mass movements. And though people have always made use of ideals and then killed them off when they were no longer useful, some ideals echo into our own time as a sort of philosophical afterimage, their continuing liveliness made apparent by our own lingering moral feelings.

The ideals of sincerity and authenticity—twin ideals that insist you say what you feel and be true to who you are in order to live a satisfying life—continue to hold enormous and undeniable sway over our lives, even absent their religious origins. They are ideals, as the philosopher Charles Taylor has written, "unrepudiable by moderns." The ideal of sincerity, born five hundred years ago as a moral imperative, abides in us in ways silent and compelling, drawing the secular mind inward like a strange magnetic north.

Chapter I : REFORM THYSELF!

The Church, through ambition & pride . . .
was much altered from the simple sinceritie
of the Primitive tyme.

- John Foxe, *The Book of Martyrs* (1563)

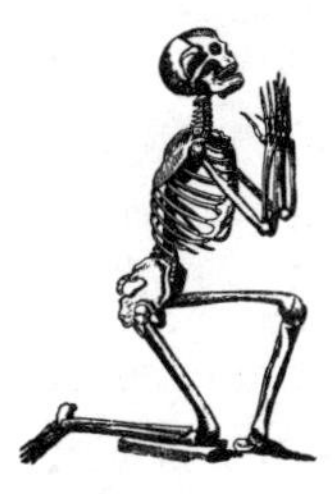

A FEW MONTHS BEFORE being tied to a stake and burnt for heresy, in July 1533, an English Protestant reformer named John Frith summoned a word that had never before been recorded in the English language. In one of his last written exchanges with Sir Thomas More, chancellor to King Henry VIII and author of *Utopia* (1516), Frith described an Oxford scholar named John Wycliffe as a person who had lived "a very sincere life." The *Oxford English Dictionary* still cites Frith's flattering 1533 usage of "sincere" as the first time the word was intended to describe a person as "honest and straightforward."[1]

Sir Thomas was incensed at the description: John Wycliffe, who had been dead for nearly two centuries, was a vilified fourteenth-century heretic. He clandestinely translated the Vulgate (Latin) Bible into English in 1382, advocated a sharp distinction between secular and church power, and called the very notion of a pope essentially ridiculous. Though Wycliffe was tremendously influential among the laity, he was so loathed by the Vatican that a full fifty years after he died of a stroke, in 1384, his rotting remains were exhumed—on the order of Pope Martin V himself—and entirely incinerated, along with all copies of his books that could found. Church authorities then cast Wycliffe's ashes into the river Swift, intending to wash away his existence—and influence—forever.

No such luck. By the middle of the fifteenth century the movement Wycliffe had led, Lollardy, had seeped across southern England, wreaked political havoc, and further ignited anticlerical sentiments throughout western and central Europe, leading the diminutive John Wycliffe, contrary to all papal plans, to be baptized "the Morning Star of the Reformation."

John Frith's choice of the word "sincere" to describe the besmirched Oxford heretic was thus its own act of dissent—a deliberate praising of the damned—in the face of someone like Thomas More, an earnest defender of the Catholic faith against the heresy weaving its way throughout sixteenth-century Europe. Figures in Germany such as Martin Luther, Johannes Oecolampadius, and Philipp Melanchthon, in addition to those in Switzerland such as Ulrich Zwingli and John Calvin, were relentless in their zeal for reforming the Church, utilizing back channels, clandestine printings, and an underground distribution network to get their message out to Europeans near and far.

More had become so disgusted with the Reform movement that he had made eradicating it his personal mission. "These diabolical people!" he wrote of the spreading threat. "[They] print their books at great expense, notwithstanding the great danger . . . they fear no labor, no journey, no expense, no pain, no danger, no blows, no injury . . . they take a malicious pleasure in seeking the destruction of others, and these disciples of the devil think only how they may cast the souls of the simple into hell-fire."[2]

Reform-minded intellectuals were raising the same kinds of ecclesiastical complaints as Wycliffe had a century and a half prior, and they were starting to have far-reaching political consequences—namely, undercutting the very legitimacy of the Church in England. They had to be stopped.

On the morning of July 4, 1533, Frith and his cellmate, Andrew Hewett, a kindred religious dissenter, were taken from their cells, shackled back to back to wooden stakes, and set on fire. As the flames licked his flesh, Frith had the presence of mind to sneak in one final word of defiance: "I am going to die!" he shouted. "But I condemn neither those who follow Luther nor those who follow Oecolampadius, since both reject transubstantiation!"[3] And then the flames dissolved John Frith. He was thirty years old.

Among the ideas that so infuriated Thomas More was the Reform movement's emphasis on the primacy of individual conscience over church dogma. "He sins against God that wounds another man's conscience," Frith had written shortly before he died, in a tract called *A Mirror, or Looking Glass, Wherein You May Behold the Sacrament of Baptism Described* (1533). The manifold "outward signs" of the Church (such as baptism), he argued, were poor attempts to guarantee a sincere faith in the word of God. The sacraments were merely outward signs of belief:

> That every man receives not this treasure in baptism, it is evident; for, put the case, that a Jew or an infidel should say that he did believe, and believed not indeed, and upon his words were baptized indeed (for no man can judge what his heart is, but we must receive him unto baptism if he confess our faith with his mouth, albeit his heart be far from thence), this miscreant, now thus baptized, has received this outward sign and sacrament, as well the most faithful man believing. Howbeit, he neither received the Spirit of God, neither yet any grace, but rather, condemnation.

As with baptism, so with communion, thought Frith: the Eucharist was a symbolic act, not an actual physical transformation of bread into flesh and wine into blood (transubstantiation). But if you didn't really believe that this change happened, why should you pretend that you did? At the pre-dawn of modern science, with its renewed emphasis on empiricism, and with Lutheranism's insistence that you must personally experience faith, what you actually experienced, thought, and believed about the world was beginning to become more important than what Church dogma told you to think and believe. Experience, intelligence, and conscience were becoming revivified guides to individual moral belief after centuries of dogmatic oppression.

Plentiful commentary on the conscience stretches back to the Indian *Upanishads, Bhagavad-Gita,* Buddhist texts, and to the concept of *taqwa,* in Islam, but Western reformers would have been reading ancient Greek and Latin texts—newly discovered during the Renaissance—that spoke of the Greek notion of συνέδρτον, or *sundeidesis*: "to know with something else," or "to know something about one's self." The Roman emperor and philosopher Marcus Aurelius, the Stoic author of the *Meditations* (c. 170 BCE), had observed that the conscience directs us to move from "one unselfish action to another with God in mind." Medieval Scholastics, who from the eleventh to fourteenth centuries justified Christian theology with rigorous dialectical reasoning, wrote of an "intuitive calling to do good." One of them, St. Bonaventure, said that conscience was unexplainable by any rational faculty. St. Thomas Aquinas regarded the conscience as "reason attempting to make right decisions" with the help of *synderesis,* a Latin word designating an echo of awareness of the absolute good implanted by God but corrupted by society and tradition. Only the truly godly, Aquinas wrote in the *Summa Theologiae* (c. 1273), could keep their consciences pure and within reach.

For the religious person of the mid-sixteenth century, professing beliefs outside the dominant credo of Christian theology was heresy, pure and simple. To abide by your conscience—to hold your sincere beliefs and thoughts about God as authoritative, to trust that your judgment about the world and salvation was reliable—was to skirt tradition, power, authority, and to risk your own salvation. The Reformation had set such a logic in motion by unleashing the idea that every man was a king, that everyone had the right to depend on his or her hard-won judgment, that no one could judge your personal relationship with God but you. It was a pretty big gamble—but one that increasing numbers of believers were willing to make.

Richard Bayfield, a former Benedictine monk, was burned alive in 1531 for distributing copies of the first English translation of the New Testament. His death is described in excruciating detail in John Foxe's *Book of Martyrs* (1563): "The bishop . . . took his crosier-staff and smote him on the breast [and then] brake his head." After being flogged, "Bayfield thanked God that he had been delivered from the malignant church of antichrist," and "come into the true sincere church of Jesus Christ, militant here in earth." For lack of a speedy fire, Bayfield remained conscious for the next two hours. When his left arm caught on fire, Foxe writes, "He rubbed it with his right hand, and it fell from his body, but he continued in prayer to the end without moving."

Three years later, the esteemed translator of that English Bible, William Tyndale, who had found refuge all across Europe and who had worked alongside John Frith in Marburg, was arrested and jailed for sixteen months in the castle of Vilvoorde, just outside Brussels. On the brisk morning of October 6, 1535, Tyndale was summarily tried for heresy, found guilty, and publicly garrotted. His beaten body was then set ablaze in the town square to discourage sympathizers. "Lord, open the King of England's eyes," Tyndale is said to have uttered as he burned. His assistant, William Roye, a destitute Franciscan friar who had helped him tease the New Testament out of the original Greek and Hebrew, had also been burned alive, in the city of Portyngale, in 1531, at the personal behest of Thomas More.

Another three years later, Thomas More himself was executed—not for heresy, of course, but for taking the wrong side in Henry VIII's contentious divorce proceedings with Catherine of Aragon and refusing to take the oath of the First Succession Act, which made Anne Boleyn Henry's lawful wife and their unborn princess daughter, Elizabeth, the true successor to the Crown. This act, part of the more sweeping Act of Supremacy, further severed ties with the Catholic Church to which More had dedicated his life and heart. Caught between the identities of loyal servant and devout believer, More chose the latter and was promptly thrown into the Tower of London on April 17, 1534, and subsequently found guilty of high treason.[4] "Through the clearness of my own conscience," he wrote to his daughter, Margaret, on June 3, 1534, "though I might have pain I could not have harm, for a man may in such a case lose his head and not have harm."[5] Sincerity wasn't just for Protestants anymore.

Sincerity was not an entirely new concept in 1533. The French cognates upon which it is based, *sincère* and *sincérité,* appeared much earlier: the Middle French word *sincérité* is first recorded in 1237; and *sincère* in 1475. Both words stem from the Latin *sincerus,* which means clean, pure, or sound. That Latin word is built from the prefix *sem-* or *sim-,* which means "one," as in "simple" or "single," and the root *crescere,* which means "to grow," as in "crescendo" or "crescent." *Crescere* itself is derived from the Roman goddess of grain, Ceres, from which we get the word "cereal." The Latin word *sincerus* denotes a thing of one growth: something honest, whole, unadulterated, and pure.

There is also an explanation of the word's origins in the Old Greek term for wax, *keros.* This word becomes in Latin *cera,* as in "ceramics." Roman quarrymen, the tale goes, pinned *cera* to the prefix *sine-* ("without") to create the phrase *sine cera*, or "without wax." This supposedly advertised the high quality of the quarry's product; lesser-quality marble contained cracks that were patched with wax to disguise natural impurities. Sculptors did the same with their own works, using wax to cover up mistakes, and so the presence of wax implied cover-up or deceit. The Roman senate passed a law declaring that any marble bought by the government must be flawless and therefore *sine cera*, or without wax. From this, "sincere": without deceit.

It is a great story, but the *Oxford English Dictionary* writes, "There is no probability in the old explanation from *sine cera* 'without wax.'" There was, however, an actual Greek word that approximates what we mean today by sincerity: *eilikrineia* (εἰλικρίνεια), which Aristotle had employed in the *Nicomachean Ethics* (350 BCE) to describe "a desirable mean-state between the deficiency of irony or self-deprecation and the excess of boastfulness." *Eilikrineia* implied truthfulness toward oneself and frankness with others, and it was a quality, Aristotle believed, of moral excellence. *Eilikrineia* designated a "lover of truth, who is truthful even when nothing depends on it."[6]

This little foray into Latin and French says something quite remarkable about Frith's use of the word "sincere" in 1533: previously, it did not apply to people. *Sincerus*, the Latin term, had been used to describe physical things—wine, glass, precious stones, honey—substances that were unaltered, pure, and whole if they were to be of any value. The French cognates maintained this meaning. Doctrines, scripture, and laws were described as sincere: authentic, genuine, bona fide, the real thing.

The physical basis of the word can still be seen at the outset of the sixteenth century, when Frith's usage fascinatingly foreshadows the word's linguistic explosion into the realm of people and society. In the midst of great clashes between religion and the state during the first third of the sixteenth century, the words "sincere," "sincerity," and "sincerely" all enter the English language through Reformation tracts, poems, parliamentary acts, and sermons. The English reformer Thomas Starkey, for example, in his *Dialogue Between Reginald Pole and Thomas Lupset* (c. 1534), writes, "The lawys, wyche be syncere and pure reson, [are] wythout any spot or blot of affection." In Act 31, section 14, of English parliamentary law of 1539, one reads, "Almightie god, the very author and fountaine of al true vnitie and sincer concorde"; and in Act 27, "The syncere and pure doctrine of Goddes worde," in both cases describing the veracity of Christian doctrine. It was also used as a metaphor for wholesomeness, as in a famed 1557 New Testament translation of St. Paul: "As newe borne babes desire the sincere mylke of the worde."[7]

For Henry VIII's sixth and final wife, the independent-minded Catherine Parr, a discreet but unmistakable Lutheran, lacking sincerity had already come to be a human deficiency, as she cast aspersions upon Anglican religious figures in her autobiographical *Lamentations of A Sinner* (1548). Writing of her complicity in the torture of a "heretic" named Anne Askew (a political hunt to bring down Parr herself), Parr accuses the clergy surrounding the royal court of "[making] not Christ their chief foundation; professing his doctrine of a sincere, pure, and zealous mind; but . . . to procure some credit and good opinion."[8] They faked a faith in Christ to win the king's good political graces.

The adverb "sincerely" makes its appearance in 1535 in a contemporary account of Tudor England called *Wriothesley's Chronicle*: "This yeare was commaunded by the King that all bishops Injunctions to and curates should preach the gospell of Christe syncerlye."[9] The noun "sincerity" eventually makes its way onto the very tongue of Henry VIII, who capitulates in 1546, a decade after burning heretics at the stake for translating the Bible into English: "The Holy Bible should be set forth in our tongue, to the end that England might the better attain to the sincerity of Christ's doctrine."[10]

By the middle of the sixteenth century the word "sincerity" was becoming moral shorthand for what the reformed faith claimed to offer: a return to simplicity, honesty, forthrightness, purity, an adherence to Christ's original message. After centuries of ecclesiastical abuse, Protestant reformers believed, the true church of Jesus was returning to its original errand: living the word of God with innermost conviction. They would restore Christ's original doctrine of love and faith to those who accepted him with a sincere and pure heart, unsullied by the avarice of the world. "More than anything," wrote the British historian J. M. Roberts, "the Reformation displaced so many values with the one supreme value of sincerity."[11] To be sincere was to be reformed.

Reformers and their predecessors were reacting against the Papacy's long history of making a mockery of basic Church tenets.* Pope Alexander VI (reigned 1492-1503), the "abstinent" Borgia pope, sired at least six children with at least two mistresses, all of whom he beat, and kept a harem of prostitutes in the Vatican. His parties at the papal palace rivaled even those of Caligula: after a long night of drink and feast, guests would strip down and have sex with the Vatican prostitutes in the gilded banquet room, while

* Movements for Church reform, with the implication of regaining sincerity of belief in contrast to its ritualization, had been underway in Europe for at least two centuries prior to the Reformation. Aside from John Wycliffe, there were other figures worthy of the venerable title "Morning Star of the Reformation": the Frenchman Pierre Vaudès (1140-1218; also known as Peter Waldo) argued against papal excesses and the reality of transubstantiation, and promoted the forbidden practice of lay preaching. The Bohemian priest Jan Hus (1369-1415) had long argued against transubstantiation, along with Jerome of Prague (1379-1416). When Hus was burned for heresy, the Hussite wars convulsed eastern Europe for the next two decades. The Dutch theologian Wessel Gansfort (1419-89) lamented the "paganizing" of the church and its use of "magical" sacraments, as well as appealing for the authority of the ecclesiastical tradition over the Church. And the anonymous author of the German *Reformatio Sigismundi* urged radical church reform—including through "force and pain of punishment"—in his appeal of 1438. A good source of primary documents on the forerunners to reform in Germany is Strauss, ed., *Manifestations of Discontent in Germany.*

servants kept track of how many orgasms each man spurted: Alexander liked to reward virility with expensive gifts bought with the money collected from his parishes. Pope Innocent VIII (reigned 1484-92) fathered sixteen illegitimate children, sold Church offices, bribed cardinals to acquire his own, and established a Vatican bank for the sale of pardons. He also mortgaged the papal tiara and entire treasury to pay for the wedding of his illegitimate son, Franceschetto Cybo, a gang-rapist who liked to sodomize nuns and leave them unconscious in the street. Franceschetto married Maddalena de' Medici, the sister of the future Pope Leo X.

Not to be outdone by the Papacy, the clergy, apparently insatiable in sexual appetite, comprised such a high percentage of brothel clientele across Europe that, beginning under Pope Sixtus IV (reigned 1471-84), the Church began collecting part of brothel revenues. It was also under Pope Sixtus IV that the sale of those famed indulgences—an established practice for saving Christians from purgatory via cold hard cash—was extended to include saving relatives (in addition to oneself) from an eternity of waiting in God's holding grounds.[12] These indulgences, of course, were what would unleash the rage of an Augustinian monk named Martin Luther. Money was not necessary to get into heaven, Luther said; that was God's choice alone. Priests, bishops, and friars who demanded they be paid were therefore committing "barefaced robbery, trickery, and tyranny appropriate to the nether regions, a destruction of the body and soul of Christendom."[13] Indulgences were simply theft, and Luther's rebellion against them would lead to his being issued a papal bull, called to trial, and ultimately excommunicated from the Church—by Leo X.

The new kind of Christianity Luther was attempting to forge from the rubble of Vatican abuses was going to completely counteract the Papacy, which he believed had been taken over by the Antichrist. "We are *all* Christians," he wrote in *An Appeal to the Ruling Class of German Nationality as to the Amelioration of the State of*

Christendom (1520). "Why then should we not be entitled to taste or test, and to judge what is right or wrong in the faith?"[14] He continued in the *Appeal* to assail the Church for its underhanded ways. "Proposals have often been made at councils but have been cunningly deferred by the guile of certain men," he writes. "Their artifices and wickedness I intend with God's help to lay bare."[15] The Romanist clergy had succeeded so long because it had managed to awe kings and princes, "in spite of all the deceitful and cunning dodges." Each successive accusation implies a deeper transgression against the ideal of showing oneself openly and transparently, how one really is. Revealing intentions honestly was in keeping with the spirit of universal Christian brotherhood and mutual respect.

Luther took to using common language to address students and congregations. Though he used the word "shit" *(Scheiss)* to describe what the devil had thrown at him, in his sermons Luther employed the word "sincerity" (*Aufrichtigkeit* or *Ernsthaftigkeit*) to denote the necessary quality of belief. It appears four times in the *Ninety-Five Theses* (1517), always in conjunction with *Reue,* or contrition. Why did "contrition" require "sincere" to modify it? In contrast to the ritual of oral confession perpetuated by the Catholic Church, which stressed atonement, Luther concentrates instead on the subjective experience of contrition—true repentance for sins that was motivated by the love of God alone, rather than the payment of lip service to Church authority or a confession motivated by fear of hell. (The latter is known in Catholic terminology as "attrition," or "imperfect contrition.") Was contrition truly felt or was it simply acknowledged for pragmatic ends? Is there real repentance before God, real remorse? Was it somehow personal? As the German-American psychiatrist Erik Erikson would later write, Luther was a theologian obsessed "with the meaning of meaning it."[16]

Luther justified his criticism of the Church with detailed

passages of Scripture. In 1513 he had read in St. Paul's Second Letter to the Corinthians, "Unlike so many, we do not peddle the word of God for profit. On the contrary, in Christ we speak before God with sincerity, like men sent from God" (2:17); and, "Now this is our boast: our conscience testifies that we have conducted ourselves in the world, and especially in our relations with you, in the holiness and sincerity that are from God" (1:12).* It was also in St. Paul that Luther discovered a new entry into faith and the character of God's love as deeply personal. In his Letter to the Romans, Paul describes Christ as *pro me* ("for me"), which posited God's love as a fact, as grace to be accepted (*sola gratia*) rather than something to be earned. God was always for you; this was no test. You simply had to open yourself to being loved by God. It changed forever the way Luther, half-crazed for mercy, understood God and his duty to reform Christianity.

This sense of righteousness would reach its zenith in Luther's pious sense of self-reliance: "I am more afraid of my own heart than of the Pope and all his cardinals," he wrote. "I have within me the great pope, Self." The personal experience of inward transformation was more important than the abstractions of theology because, as Luther wrote in his *Exposition of the Magnificat* (1521), "No one can understand God or God's word unless he has it directly from the Holy Spirit, and no one has it unless he experiences and is conscious of it." Such sentiments hurl the believer back on himself. They promote self-reflection and a consciousness perceptive of its own experience of God. This is also why Luther advocated, as would other Reformation leaders, the silent reading of Scripture—an uncommon and mostly impossible practice prior to the vernacular translation of the Bible from Latin, Greek, Aramaic, and Hebrew. Reading in his native language, the layperson could

* Luther would have been reading the original languages of the Bible, which used words that would come to be translated as aufrigtichkeit and "sincerity": *sincerus* (Latin); *eilikrineia* (Greek); *tamiym* (Hebrew); and *peshitta* (Aramaic/Syric).

experience God's penetrating omnipotence firsthand; the Holy Spirit's actual words were transported inside the believer.[17] The Reformation's encouragement of private reading of the Bible as an article of faith (*sola scriptura*) would eventually foster, as literacy spread, a Protestant culture of religious inwardness that emphasized feeling, reflection, and self-examination.[18]

Martin Luther was by no means alone in his frustrations with the Church and the spiritual condition of "Babylonian" captivity it inspired. Indeed, conditions across Europe during the early sixteenth century had promoted the general feeling that society needed to shed frivolities and get back to basics. There was a belief that the world was very old and that it would soon come to an end with the rapturous Second Coming of Christ. The traditional social order was breaking up, and a distant Church bureaucracy in Rome was infusing daily life with confusing intricacies. Capitalist expansion caused economic and material gluts, often brought on by, as many in the lower orders believed, dodgy business practices at the top. Complaints about the rich were widespread, and peasants were driven from their lands, leading to increasingly bloody social rebellions, such as the Peasants' War of 1524-25, in Germany, which saw 100,000 people killed for a mix of social and religious reasons. The sixteenth century was a time of incredible social change, widespread death by disease and starvation, sectarian religious violence, and dramatic political upheaval, all the while filled with the rueful sense that a golden age had recently passed away.

Add to this confusion the emergence of greater social mobility by the end of the century, which created a new degree of social anonymity. Men and women alike, especially in England and France, were beginning to leave their inherited classes to better their social status in an emerging mercantile society in urban centers. London had 60,000 inhabitants in 1550, a number that more than doubled by the end of the century. As people lived increasingly among strangers, the idea that one should represent oneself honestly became an emblem of reformed Christian identity.

This situation of increased social camouflage was made more confusing by the gradual disappearance of sumptuary laws, which had regulated European appearances for hundreds of years. These Church-derived policies detailed the kinds of clothing or distinctive markers that were permitted or forbidden to be worn by members of various groups. They aided in the easy identification of station or profession, as did the required clothing worn by criminals, lepers, prostitutes, and Jews. There were laws that regulated the length of swords, the size of ruffles around the neck, the use of fabrics, the color of buttons, hair length, and materials used to make shoes. The goal was to keep society transparent and social station fixed. Always difficult to enforce, by the late sixteenth century sumptuary laws began to fall out of favor. (In England, James I would repeal nearly all of them during his rule, 1603-25.) Their disappearance spelled the loss of clear, immediately discernible class and social boundaries, and a fear arose of novel social types: the "impostor," the "dissembler," and the "villain," figures who dressed other than they were, who through disguise misinformed the public about who and what their intentions—and they—really were.

Shakespeare's plays attest to how much the times were consumed by ideas of the impostor, the false self, the undisclosed. A favored dramatic technique was to allow the audience to know what was going on while keeping the secret hidden from the characters on stage. Masks and costumes hid characters' "true" identity, and false presentation was commonplace, such as Falstaff's complex character—a fat and bumbling knight who hides a deep and modern subjectivity—in *Henry IV*. The use of deceptive (yet audience-shared) language in *Much Ado About Nothing* and *Othello* reveals both the trickery of others and the deceptive potential of language itself, whether in lying or irony. The value of holding true to one's identity in order to be a whole person is evidenced in Polonius's famed lines, "To thine own self be true, and it must follow, as the night the day / Thou canst not then be false to any man." While this advice denotes a new kind of moral ideal, Shakespeare's view of sincerity was far more complex than simply encouraging the cultivation of the trait; Polonius is pitched as a bit out of touch and unworldly. Those with more experience knew that Christian sincerity was sometimes welcome and sometimes hurtful to one's selfish interests.

Despite the popularity of poets and playwrights like Shakespeare (who may have been a Catholic) and Christopher Marlowe, the more stringent Protestant thinkers during the sixteenth century were resistant to poetry, which they felt was artificial and showy. They preferred instead the direct address of sermons or hymns that said exactly what they meant in plain language. John Frith's *A Mirror or Glass to Know Thyself* (1532) caricatures his intellectual sparring partner Thomas More mockingly: "Mr. More with hys painted poetrie and crafty conveyance doe call a mist before your eyes, that you might wander out of the right way." He offers an antidote of plain language "to dispel his mist and vaine Poetrie."[19] German Protestant poets like Hans Sachs (1494–1576) attracted a large and devoted following. Sachs promoted Lutheranism in verse, plays, and hymns, all admired for their simple and direct style. His "Fair Melody: To Be Sung by Good Christians," gently warns:

Trust thou in flattering tongues no more,
Though many they may be;
All human teachings dread thou sore,
Though good they seem to thee;
But put thy whole affiance
In God's good-will and holy Word,
There is our one reliance.

While Catholicism at the end of the sixteenth century was hurtling headlong into the Baroque—that ornate style which would successfully embody the Counter-Reformation—Protestant aesthetics were in slim-down mode, thoroughly set against all forms that were artificial, staged, theatrical, illusionary, or magical. Some were against images of saints and Jesus in paintings or stained glass. There was a great routing of things that were not what they seemed to be. This new Reformed person—along with his art and literature—was to be dedicated to presenting himself as he really was.

Shakespeare's tricksters and deceivers had real-life counterparts, and because of the Protestant vilification of deception and false presentation, they often met inglorious fates if they were caught. Nuremberg's state executioner from 1578 to 1617, Meister Franz Schmidt, a Protestant convert from the southern city of Bamberg, reserved his harshest retribution not for murderers, common thieves, or rapists, but rather for criminals who pretended to be someone else or broke a promise, such as fraudsters or counterfeiters. (Death was also the sentence for a man who literally stabbed a person in the back—that is to say, dishonestly, the origin of our metaphor for betrayal.) On October 11, 1593, Schmidt records in his ledger:

> Gabriel Wolff, of a citizen family here, also known as Glazier, who called himself Georg Windholz, Secretary to the Elector at Berlin; also took the name of Jacob Führer, Ernst Haller, and Joachim Fürnberger. Borrowed 1,500 ducats from the Honorable Council here in Nuremberg by means of a forged letter in the Elector's name and under the seal of the Margrave Johann Georg in Berlin. Was arrested at Regensburg and delivered over to Nuremberg. Besides this he practiced many forgeries. . . . Also practiced many other frauds over twenty-four years, causing false seals of gentlemen to be cut, wrote many forged documents and was fluent

> in seven languages. Executed with the sword as a favor here at Nuremberg, the body being afterwards burnt. Should have had his right hand cut off first. . . [20]

But what is deception? Is false presentation only something that can occur in public? Don't we deceive ourselves, too? And, if so, is there really somewhere inside us where we can rest with finality upon the truth of who we are? The urge to plunge into the self in search of answers to questions like this would find expression in the writings of a non-Protestant Frenchman, Michel de Montaigne (1533–92), who appears on the world stage as perhaps the first modern sensibility—a figure self-ironizing of his social role. Montaigne, a prominent politician by his late thirties, comes to sense a definite split between his public and private selves and is the first author obsessed with wishing to portray himself as he really is.

In book three of his famed *Essays* (1588), in the essay "Of Presumption," he describes himself as "extremely idle," and lacking in "adroitness and agility." He self-deprecatingly analyzes each of his perceived faults: he is "delicate and hard to please"; he is too earnest and fast to say all the things that he knows; he is bad at small talk. His handwriting is sloppy, he does not read well, does not know how to close a letter, "carve at table," or "saddle a horse," all things that a gentleman should know how to do. Regardless of his many faults, however, Montaigne praises himself because he has "a soul all its own, accustomed to conducting itself in its own way." He celebrates his inner freedom, saying, "Having had neither governor nor master forced upon me to this day, I have gone just so far as I pleased, and at my own pace."[21]

Like Luther, Montaigne condemned outward ceremony because it "forbids our expressing in words that are permissible and natural." This included "bows and salutations, by which men gain credit, mostly wrongfully, for being very humble and courteous." Instead, one should stick to the urgings of inner conscience, for "it is a craven and servile idea to disguise ourselves and hide under a mask, and not to dare to show ourselves as we are. . . . A generous heart should not belie its thoughts; it wants to reveal itself even to its inmost depths. There everything is good, or at least everything is human."[22] Montaigne was morally set against "incessant feigning and dissimulating," which he says is "a newfangled virtue . . . so highly honored at present." And yet this sentiment was tempered with Shakespearean reserve: "We must not say everything, for that would be folly," he writes, "but what we say must be what we think; otherwise it is wickedness."[23]

Montaigne represents a turning point in the history of Western self-reflection; indeed, his work is the most revealing of inner turmoil since St. Augustine's late fourth-century *Confessions*. But when Montaigne initially set sail for the safe harbors of the soul, he expected to reach an unshakable stoic shore. This is what the ancients he so admired—Lucretius, Marcus Aurelius, Cicero—had found. For these Romans, reason provided an unwavering foundation amidst the shifting desires of the unwise and the fluctuating fortunes of the external world. The inner reality that Montaigne discovered was altogether different: he found a self that seemed never to be in the same place. It was fickle, terrifyingly unstable, capricious: "My spirit," he writes, "playing the skittish and loose-broken jade . . . begets in me so many extravagant chimeras, and fantastical monsters, so orderless, and without any reason, one huddling upon another."[24]

Throughout this tumult Montaigne braves on, analyzing himself with a judgmental scalpel usually reserved for others. He claims that his honesty with himself is the very basis not just of sincere self discovery, but of a virtuous social order. "Truth is the first and fundamental part of virtue," he writes in "Apology for Raymond Sebond":

> We are men, and hold together, only by our word. He who breaks his word betrays human society . . . it is the interpreter of our soul. If it fails us, we have no more hold on each other, no more knowledge of each other.[25]

Regardless of their faults, people should express themselves for who they were. Nothing could be more immoral, more antisocial and anti-Christian, Montaigne professed, than lying about the contents of one's own heart.

Unless, of course, your name was Niccolò Machiavelli.

By the time Montaigne's self-revealing literature was published, *The Prince* had been in circulation for just over seventy-five years (thus Montaigne's comment about dissimulation being a "new-fangled virtue"). Published in 1513, one year after Martin Luther finished his doctorate in theology, *The Prince* urged that politics must work not toward a pretend ideal, but rather with the material at hand: namely, the knowledge that all states are selfish and brutal, and that to survive the prince must be so, too. Immediately upon its publication, the Catholic Church denounced *The Prince,* adding the work to its list of prohibited books, the Index Librorum Prohibitorum. Ardent Christian reformers and Northern humanists—including Erasmus of Rotterdam—saw Machiavelli and those who followed his advice as atheists and menaces to the good society. "True and sincere faith and charity [must not be] feigned," Erasmus had attested in his *Manual of a Christian Knight* (1501).[26] The perfect social arrangement must be built, he and all Christian humanists believed, upon ideal virtues to which all should aspire.

Machiavelli encouraged aspiring rulers to do the opposite: they must combine the "courage of the lion and the slyness of the fox." Unlike the average citizen, princes should not be governed by ordinary moral scruples. Moreover, Machiavelli's doctrine of "reason of state" or "national interest" (*raison d'état*) demanded that leaders put the interests of the whole nation ahead of their own moral principles. Princes, as the eyes of the state, should cultivate self-interest, fearlessness, and greed. They should practice calculation and deceit in achieving the ends of state—all the while appearing noble and upright: "To those seeing and hearing him, he should appear a man of compassion, a man of good faith, a man of integrity, a kind and religious man."[27] The common people will hardly get near the prince to actually know him, Machiavelli observed, so "everyone sees what you appear to be; few experience what you really are. And those few dare not gainsay the many who are backed by the majesty of the state."[28] The moral emotions—generosity, empathy, remorse—were for the weak of heart. Pangs of the petty conscience had no business in ruling. "Princes who have achieved great things have been those . . . who have known how to trick men with their cunning," he counseled the Medici. "They have overcome those abiding by honest principles."[29] *Noblesse oblige* and the occasional display of public morality kept commoner minds off the brute force and deception operating behind the scenes.

Curiously, Machiavelli himself was convinced of his own plainness and purity, his lack of artfulness. He suggested to his readers that he was being sincere (even if ruthless): "I have not ornamented this book with rhetorical turns of phrase," he writes,

> or stuffed it with pretentious and magnificent words, or made use of any allurements and embellishments that are irrelevant to my purpose, as many authors do. For my intention has been that my book should be without pretensions, and should rely entirely on the variety of the examples and the importance of the subject to win approval.[30]

For Machiavelli, religion and politics should not cross—the first insisted on good behavior; the second required the opposite.

Cool reserve should characterize ruling minds. Combining this knowingness with moral forthrightness, a new cultural figure appeared in the middle of the sixteenth century: the gentleman. Another Italian, Baldassarre Castiglione, presented his vision of the aristocrat devoted to Christian principles in *The Book of the Courtier* (1528). The gentleman combined Renaissance learning, wit, and tolerance; he was the precursor of the modern cosmopolitan, bourgeois personality. He was to avoid the religious fanaticism causing so much blood to be spilled all across Europe. Setting up the moral opposition between sincerity and duplicity, a conversationalist in *The Courtier* advises the count to "avoid affectation in every way possible as though it were some rough and dangerous reef." The clever count responds, "Do you not see that what you are calling nonchalance in messer Roberto is really affectation? [He makes] every effort to show that he takes no thought of what he is about, which means taking too much thought. . . . Nonchalance is affected, is unbecoming, and results in the opposite of the desired effect, which is to conceal the art."[31]

Castiglione's gentleman readers would take his advice and become models of composure that would influence nobility across Europe by the end of the seventeenth century. The gentleman, however, was anathema to the newly radicalized Protestant mind. Christian principles, Reformers believed, must penetrate all aspects of life, particularly politics, or the entire project was for naught. There could be no duplicity between thought and action, no room for emotional remove when the soul's fate was involved. In this bid for the whole human heart, Reformers demanded that each and every Christian commit himself entirely to loving God and to the project of total moral reform. *Cor meum tibi offero Domine prompte et sincere* was stitched into the personal banner of the Swiss reformer John Calvin: "I offer you my heart, Lord, promptly and sincerely."

In a sea of gentleman deceivers, Reformers—who had once

shunned society's rules and hierarchies in favor of the inward soul's authority—became militant advocates of rules and hierarchies that would reveal the fakers amongst them. In their constant suspicion of motive—made no less intense by Machiavelli's famed strategy and the gentleman's deceptive emotional tranquility—Reformed Christians cultivated a kind of sleuthing universal cynicism: all beings except themselves were suspected of being disingenuous. Though they demanded sincerity and the shedding of false appearance from their adherents, their flipside impulse was to unmask the world in all its falseness: "Beware of a wolf in sheep's clothing." Indeed, for the Protestant, the devil himself was behind all deception. Unmasking true intention was now holy duty.

Chapter II : A SAINT'S HEART

The principal thing—that which God especially requires—is to bring a sincere heart.

- John Calvin, *Institutes of the Christian Religion* (1536)

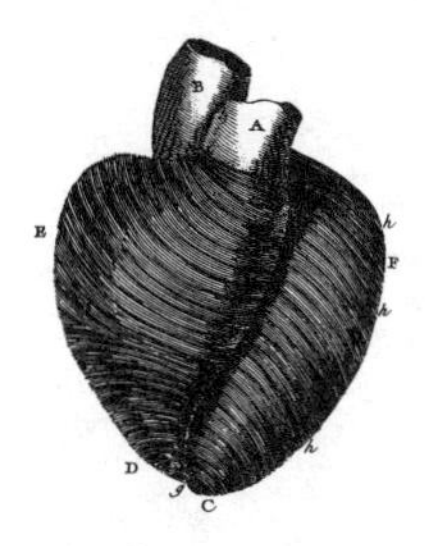

IN 1662, A DEVOUT PURITAN named William Gurnall, rector of the Lavenham Anglican Church of Christ, chose his job and political expediency over his faith. Unlike some two thousand of his fellow clergymen, Gurnall, though begrudgingly, signed the Act of Uniformity, a 1662 parliamentary initiative intended to curtail Puritan efforts at reform. Gurnall's refusenik colleagues had chosen instead to walk away from their congregations and livelihoods, and were immediately branded Nonconformists in what is known as the Great Ejection of 1662.

The Church of England's campaign for ideological purity following the restoration of the Crown after the Civil War (and thus an end to the Puritan dream of a permanent Puritan commonwealth) would continue through other acts of Parliament, each one aimed at hounding troublesome Puritans back into the

Anglican fold—or, as it happened, across the vast and cold Atlantic Ocean to North America. Throughout all of this, however, William Gurnall—outwardly Anglican but inwardly Puritan—managed to keep his employ at the parish of Lavenham, where he would remain for the next thirty-five years.

Between the years 1655 and 1662 rector Gurnall had published three volumes of sermons. This fiery collection, welcomed with great fanfare in London, had a very long title:

THE CHRISTIAN IN COMPLETE ARMOUR:
The Saint's War Against the Devil, wherein a Discovery Is Made of That Grand Enemy of God and His People, in His Policies, Power, Seat of His Empire, Wickedness, and Chief Design He Hath Against the Saints;
A Magazine Opened, From Whence the Christian Is Furnished with Spiritual Arms for the Battle, Helped on with His Armour, and Taught the Use of His Weapon;
Together with the Happy Issue of the Whole War

The Christian in Complete Armour—as the book less breathlessly came to be known—appeared on the scene shortly after around 190,000 people had perished in the English Civil War (1642–51) and countless others had died of related famine and disease.[1] Englishmen were recovering from witnessing the murder of King Charles I, the creation of a military dictatorship under Oliver Cromwell, the marginalization of the national church, the restoration of the king, Charles II, and a number of other social and political upheavals. Gurnall and his countrymen found themselves bereft of solid moral authority, caught between competing political ideologies, awash in conspiracies and new religious sects, and living amidst the most enormous changes that English society had experienced in a millennium.

But for all of this convulsing outward transformation, for Gurnall it was the inner lives of the English that were most in need of help. "What is the killing of bodies compared to the destroying of souls?" he mused in *The Christian in Complete Armour.* "It is a sad meditation . . . to think how many thousands have been sent to the grave by the sword of man; but far more astonishing to consider how many of those may be sent to hell by the sword of God's wrath." *The Christian in Complete Armour* was Gurnall's instruction manual for how the English should get back on the true Christian track, how he and fellow believers might win the holy war being waged between Satan and God on Earth by cultivating a complete suit of moral chain mail.

Of the many virtues that adorn Gurnall's metaphorical Christian armor, sincerity trumps them all: the word appears some 353 times in 938 pages, the word "sincere" 303 times, and "sincerely" twenty-one times—an average instance of the term and its cognates every 1.3 pages.* This notable frequency sets it in high relief above other virtues—courage, faith, trustworthiness, mercy—for all of which sincerity, Gurnall says, is a precondition. "By truth of heart, I understand sincerity," he writes. "It covers all parts of the Christian's uncomeliness." Several questions about sincerity's ambidextrous role follow:

> *FIRST. We shall inquire, which is the truth and sincerity that covers the Christian's uncomeliness. SECOND. We shall inquire, what uncomelinesses they are that sincerity covers. THIRD. How sincerity covers them. FOURTH. Why sincerity doth this; or some account given for all this.*[2]

For readers, *The Christian in Complete Armour* had the effect of elevating their sincerity into a holy realm, into the sole, non-negotiable condition that God sought in his flock. They no doubt

* While "sincerity" does have a grand presence, the word "God" appears 9,241 times in 938 pages—nearly ten times per page.

took the issue of sincerity to heart not just because Gurnall suggested they should, but because they believed, as Gurnall so often lamented, that their day and age "required more care and courage to keep sincerity than formerly." This was so because many things had changed; a new and alienating world was coming into being, and while Gurnall's peculiar focus on sincerity contradicts (or is explained by) his own conflicted religious identity, his spiritual consolations were immensely comforting—not only in his own time but in the generations to come. Over a century later, his writings would make a lasting impression on John Newton, the late eighteenth-century Anglican bishop and abolitionist who composed the hymn "Faith's Review and Expectation"—later known by its opening line, "Amazing Grace"—who wrote of Gurnall's magnum opus, "If I had only one book beside the Bible, I would choose *The Christian in Complete Armour.*"

Even if Gurnall himself was bipolar in his religious identity, his book was representative of consistent Puritan views. Indeed, as inheritors of the Dissenting tradition, Puritans went furthest of their Reforming brethren in condemning what they perceived to be the hypocrisy and luxury of the Church, the failure of Church authorities to be close to the simple needs of the people, and, at root, the idea that religion was a matter of ritual rather than personal conviction and conscience. Their response was to have believers return to the original sincerity of the Christian message. "Many men render to God a formal worship," wrote their spiritual founding father, the Swiss reformer John Calvin, "but very few truly reverence him; while great ostentation in ceremonies is universally displayed, but sincerity of heart is rarely to be found."[3] Dissatisfied with the pace and character of reform, these radical Calvinists saw themselves as the sole inheritors of the Christian tradition, set against both Anglican and Catholic "popish superstitions."

Armed with a conviction that they were closer to God than the ruling Anglican Church, the leaders of the Puritan cause (called divines or saints) were urged in Calvin's fiery instruction to bring religion out of the Church and into the practices of daily life. One's entire existence should be suffused with the Holy Spirit such that all life was life for God, all labor was God's labor. "There is no work, however vile or sordid," Calvin wrote, "that does not glisten before God." Idleness was sin because the world was big (as the age of discovery had revealed), and the work of Reform had far to go before it was complete. Puritans were out to repair what they saw as broken by centuries of church neglect and abuse. While all Protestant splinter groups were drawn to and in some way defined by the ideal of sincerity, it was Puritans in their zeal to reform all things who transformed it from a gentle, admirable quality into a somewhat hysterical and ultimately political demand. As Michael Walzer wrote in his brilliant study *The Revolution of the Saints*, the Puritan was an "active, ideologically committed political radical [who] had never before been known in Europe."[4]

To right the world, a rigorous structuring of society was introduced throughout Calvinist Britain and Holland, and, later, New England: mandatory church attendance, tithing, strict rules of personal and communal behavior, corporal punishment, public inquisitions, and death or banishment to heretics. These were some of the prescriptions; prohibitions numbered far higher. In Essex County in the Massachusetts Bay colony in 1655, activities disallowed included "eavesdropping, meddling, neglecting work, taking tobacco, scolding, naughty speeches, profane dancing, kissing, making love without consent of friends, uncharitableness to a poor man in distress, bad grinding at mill, carelessness about fire, wearing great boots, wearing broad bone lace and ribbons." Between 1656 and 1662, the following seemingly arbitrary prohibitions were added: "Abusing your mother-in-law, wicked speeches against a son-in-law, confessing himself a Quaker, cruelty to animals, drinking tobacco, i.e.

smoking, kicking another in the street, leaving children alone in the house, opprobrious speeches, pulling hair, pushing his wife, riding between two fellows at night (if a woman), selling deer, and sleeping in meeting." In 1670: "Breaking the Ninth commandment (bearing false witness), having a dangerous well, digging up the grave of Sagamore of Agawam, going naked into the meetinghouse, playing cards, rebellious speeches to parents, reporting a scandalous lie, reproaching the minister, selling strong water by small measure, and dissenting from the rest of the jury."[5] The list goes on, but the underlying theme is that each individual was to be committed to the perfectly ordered society, to demanding clarity of intention at all times, to showing uprightness and obedience to authority.

Such a disciplined and earnest vision was also the underpinning, back in England, of Oliver Cromwell's New Model Army, the military dictatorship that kept watch over order in the interregnum period. "I had rather have a plain, russet-coated Captain that knows what he fights for and loves what he knows," Cromwell wrote to Sir William Spring, a fellow Parliamentarian, in September 1643.[6] For Cromwell, his dedicated soldiers, the New England Puritans, and all devout followers of Reform, every obstacle along the way to restoring spiritual and secular order was a mere stumbling block tossed underfoot by Satan. Leading men of faith cautioned fellow believers that they had "never dreamt of reforming a church and state with ease," as John Arrowsmith wrote in his 1643 treatise, *The Covenant-Avenging Sword Brandished*.[7] In their uncompromising push for civic and spiritual revolution Divines were dedicated not only to renewal, but also to a less savory corollary: the total destruction of the old world order. "Reformation must be universal," said the Puritan minister Thomas Case before the House of Commons in 1641:

> Reform all places, all persons and callings; reform the benches of judgment, the inferior magistrates . . . Reform the universities,

> reform the cities, reform the countries, reform inferior schools of learning, reform the Sabbath, reform the ordinances, the worship of God . . . you have more work to do than I can speak . . . Every plant which my heavenly father hath not planted shall be rooted up.[8]

Adherence to God's law in the push for transformation should eclipse even close friendships and family. Neither the individual nor the familial bond mattered most; preeminent was each person's true and unbroken allegiance to the law of God. Calvinism had inspired a particular kind of misanthropic revulsion: if adherents were to truly glorify God, they must first rid themselves and their neighbors of deceit and distractions of the flesh, and condemn the sinful beings they walked among; they must achieve *contemptus mundi,* a contempt for the world. "Cursed is the man who trusteth in man," reads Jeremiah 17:5, the Old Testament author who lends his name to the first American literary genre, the jeremiad, a long and mournful lamentation. There we also find Jeremiah 8:4-6, a Puritan favorite:

> *Beware of your friends;*
> *do not trust your brothers.*
> *For every brother is a deceiver,*
> *and every friend a slanderer.*
> *Friend deceives friend,*
> *and no one speaks the truth.*
> *They have taught their tongues to lie;*
> *they weary themselves with sinning.*
> *You live in the midst of deception;*
> *in their deceit they refuse to acknowledge me,*
> *declares the Lord.*

Deception, slander, lies: each instance implies a detour away from the ideal of sincerity of godly belief. As missionaries of transparency, Puritans became obsessed with the detection of human feigning, deception, and pretense—and with unmasking them as agents of the devil. The Boston Puritan minister John Bailey advised in his *Praxis Pietatis* (1687?) against trusting even one's closest friend, recommending that every morning one should imagine wandering into "a wild forest full of dangers, and to pray God for the cloak of foresight and righteousness."[9] And the Boston Puritan leader John Cotton promoted the idea that goodness was not inherited, writing, "Do not think that you shall be saved because you are the children of Christian parents."[10] Given these hardliner positions, it easy to see why the playwright Ben Jonson satirized the central Puritan contradiction: though advocates of Christian love, they were bitter misanthropes who harbored hatred of their fellow men and who severed familial and personal ties in the name of loving God.

Though Calvinists claimed that only the God-predetermined inner soul was the source of authority, they strove to impose this self-assured will upon others with intense, almost amoral vigor. But in the desperate logic of English Puritanism, to be mercenary in the work of Christ was no contradiction; it was true Christian duty. They believed that a holy war raged, and in their devout determination to overturn all stones, Puritan thinkers happily—if not entirely wittingly—married Machiavelli with Christ. Jonson's 1610 play *The Alchemist* has a devout Puritan character named Tribulation Wholesome utter to his traveling companion, "Good brother, we must bend to all means to give furtherance to the holy cause."[11]

The primary means by which Puritan ministers delivered their messages of enthusiastic Reform and moral condemnation was the sermon. These direct, fiery admonitions were directed at a public seeking not only instruction but also evidence of the speaker's divine election or signs of true moral enlightenment. To this end, Puritan sermons rejected the Anglican practice of reading from a prepared text, or even reading from the sermons of others.

Spontaneity and the first-person voice proved that the minister's message was coming from the heart, from his true, unadorned nature. "The talent on which [Puritan ministers] prided themselves was that of being sincere," Lionel Trilling recounts, "telling the offensive truth to those who had no wish to hear it."[12]

The directness of the appeal set out to counteract the knowledge that language can deceive and that the devil can usurp it to lead believers into evil. Satan was central to the Puritan imagination, of course, and he was chiefly concerned with beating the ministers at their own convincing game. Puritan ministers therefore took "exquisite, almost competitive, pains in laying out the traps and dodges of Satan," writes the intellectual historian Andrew Delbanco in his study of the concept of evil in early America, *The Death of Satan: How Americans Have Lost the Sense of Evil* (1995). The Puritan Satan was a faceless abstract force, slithery, powerful, and formless—somehow more foul and frightening than the image of a fire-breathing, horned beast. The effect of this abstraction, however, was that Satan became "a being without a center, a deceiver," Delbanco writes. "He is falsehood, doubt, despair."[13] Satan, that is, was a self without a core, a shifting surface of faces and motives, the radical opposite of the inwardly-turned, solid self that Puritanism was trying to forge.

These outward orations of Reform and warnings of Satan's wiliness were matched with intense interpersonal interrogations. As seventeenth-century Puritans turned increasingly inward, they were met by a cyclone of inner tumult caused in part by a demanding and paradoxical theology that encouraged believers to try to detect their own state of salvation while insisting that they were powerless to do anything to achieve or change it. This intense obsession with the sincerity of inward discovery was bound up with the primacy of the Puritan conversion experience, which was in many cases actually required for church membership. A prospective joiner had to convince church authorities that

God had dealt with him or her directly, often in terms spelled out in sermons and (in direct contrast to sincerity) accepted theological tropes. Biblical scholar Richard J. Bauckham writes of the standardization of Puritan conversion stories:

> The majority of recorded seventeenth-century testimonies conform to a stereotyped and predictable pattern. This is not to suggest that such testimony is at all insincere, simply that most people asked to give an account of experiences will order and interpret and select experiences according to some sort of recognized pattern. . . . New England made them into tests of whether men had travelled the path. Being a Christian tended to mean: having been through the recognized series of experiences.[14]

Like many other strong-handed Puritan houses of worship, John Cotton's Boston church of the late 1630s did not admit new members until the elders were "convinced in our consciences of the certain and infallible signs of their regeneration."[15] Believers had to withstand cross-examination of their inner journeys and trials with God, accounts often suspected by spiritual authorities to be falsified in order to win the favor of church leaders. The sum total of these interrogations and subsequent pleas led the believer, in both cases, to one big, existentially terrifying question: "Am I one of the elect?" And this question quickly cascaded into a second: "Am I sincere?" Richard Baxter's influential 1654 treatise *The Saints' Everlasting Rest* reflects the worried Puritan's dilemma:

> What shall I do to know my state? How shall I know that God is my Father? That my heart is upright? That my conversion is true? That faith is sincere? I am afraid my sins are unpardoned; that all I do is hypocrisy; that God will reject me; that he does not hear my prayers.[16]

To keep track of the movements of this murky and incalculable self, everyday men and women in seventeenth-century England took to recording their intimate thoughts and feelings, partly to provide detailed evidence of conversion.[17] In the course of the century, this culture of introspection became popularized as a literary form: confessional autobiography.[18]

Prior to the year 1600, there were hardly any autobiographies published in Britain and its colonies. By the end of the century there were well over a hundred, nearly all of them written by Protestants.[19] Puritan writers in particular took aim at sincerity by concentrating on themselves with intense hatred, with an obsessive concern for obliterating the self in order to make way for God's redemptive grace. "Self" for Puritans meant the small, depraved, and rotten core inside each person that longed for all that was seven-sinful and stood in the way of a godly life: vanity, greed, jealousy, sloth, and the like. New England minister Thomas Hooker lamented this depraved self as "the great snare," the "false Christ," "a spider's webbe [spun out] of our bowels," a "figure or type of hell."[20] Egoistic concerns were set against the grandiosity of the believer who proceeded "with a holy kind of violence" back to Christ, who had emptied out his subjectivity and become one of those lucky souls "who be sincere," Hooker wrote in his *Survey of the Summe of Church Discipline* (1648), "for they are truly said to be the mystical body of Christ."[21]

John Bunyan's *Grace Abounding to the Chief of Sinners* (1666) and *The Pilgrim's Progress* (1678–84), the latter widely considered to be the greatest of all English spiritual autobiographies, tell of the author's spiritual journey and serve as handbooks for fellow travelers. "Commune within your heart," Bunyan advises, "look diligently, and leave no corner therein unsearched, for there is treasure hid, even the treasure of your first and second experiences of the grace of God toward you."[22] Other Puritan chronicles—all of which likewise stress the torturous achievement of true belief—were Oliver

Heywood's *Autobiography, Diaries, Anecdote, and Event Books,* George Trosse's *The Life of the Reverend Mr. George Trosse,* Thomas Halyburton's *Memoirs,* John White's *A Way to the Tree of Life,* John Downame's *The Christian Warfare against the Devil, World, and Flesh,* Lewis Bayly's *The Practice of Piety,* and Arthur Dent's *The Plaine Man's Pathway to Heaven: Wherein Every Man May Clearly See Whether He Shall Be Saved or Damned.* Bunyan read the last three of these books during his own spiritual struggle, and they formed a narrative model for his own *Pilgrim's Progress.*

Quakers also wrote many autobiographies. Founded by George Fox, who started preaching in 1647, the Society of Friends insisted, like all Reformed churches, that the true Christian had a direct relationship with God outside of all institutions. Individual conscience, sparked by "inner light," Quakers believed, was the ultimate source and judge of moral action. They had no clergy or church buildings, nor a systematic theology or creed (they did have doctrines). They stressed instead the idea of "continuing revelation," in which God reveals himself to individuals over time with no mediation whatsoever. At their meetings, Quakers spoke (and still do) only when "the Spirit moved them." George Fox's own *Journal* (1694) told readers that he was writing so that "all may know the dealings of the Lord with me, and the various exercises, troubles, and trials through which He led me." Fox's friend and real-estate mogul William Penn extended his private concern for sincerity as a component of the free conscience. His short tract "Truth Exalted" (1668), which landed him in the Tower of London, stressed religious toleration based solely on earnestness of belief: "I love and honor all virtuous persons that differ from me and hope God will have regard to every such one, according to his sincerity."[23]

Ultimately, the Commonwealth that was set up by Oliver Cromwell after the English Civil War was not to last. The restoration of Charles II in 1660 deflated Puritan hopes and represented the loss of a potentially ideal Christian republic on earth (Cromwell was posthumously decapitated). John Milton's *Paradise Lost* (1667) and its aching portrayal of the fall of man via Satan's slithering deceit tells also of the loss of the Puritan dream and takes readers to a new locale of salvation: inside themselves, away from the world of power and politics and toward a life of dwelling internally with one's alienated sincerity: "To leave this Paradise, but shalt possess / A paradise within thee, happier far." All around England, theaters reopened after Puritans had shut them down, and Restoration comedies revivified bawdy, sardonic life. One libertine poet, John Wilmot, Earl of Rochester, wrote of his friend the king:

We have a pretty witty king,
And whose word no man relies on,
He never said a foolish thing,
And never did a wise one.

Puritan New England, however, retained the hope and fervor of an earthly Christian paradise. Of all the tracts that argued for sincerity's heightened role in this new "city upon a hill," a place that would counter England's spiritual decline, perhaps none was more damning (and depressing) than Thomas Shepard's 1641 treatise on the soul-saving precondition of sincerity, entitled:

THE SINCERE CONVERT:
Discovering the Paucity of True Believers and The Great Difficulty of Saving Conversion;
Wherein Is Excellently and Plainly Opened These Choice and Divine Principles:
That There Is A God and This God Is Most Glorious;
That God Made Man in A Blessed State;
Man's Misery by His Fall; Christ the Only Redeemer by Price; That Few Are Saved and That With Difficulty; & That Man's Perdition Is of Himself

The Sincere Convert—as *this* book less breathlessly came to be known—was published in the same year as the first English translation of Machiavelli's *The Prince*, a work immediately seen throughout the Puritan world, on both sides of the Atlantic, as a handiwork of the devil.

The Sincere Convert details the horrors of the unregenerate soul, a being so utterly wrecked by its own depravity that it is nearly impossible for him to experience God's mercy. The only soul that will be truly saved is "the sincere convert," crushed under the heel of God, totally repentant, and utterly eviscerated by his own sense of downtroddenness. Written in the Plain style, *The Sincere Convert* was one of the most widely read doctrinal essays of early congregationalism (the dominant form of church organization in the English Puritan colonies that kept churches autonomous). It was also one of the most heavily employed books in missioning to the unredeemed—among them, naturally, Native Americans.* And like Gurnall's *Christian in Complete Armour*, it was enormously influential.

Not long after arriving in Boston, Shepard helped to found the city of Newtowne, today called Cambridge. While working there on *The Sincere Convert*, he approached a kindred and resourceful young clergyman about helping him start a college that would guide the next generation of believers through the travails of faith and into the arms of Christian salvation. The clergyman—childless and dying of tuberculosis—agreed. In the autumn of 1638 he bequeathed half of his estate—779 pounds, 17 shillings—in

* Contrary to popular images of ignorant Pilgrims traipsing around the virgin woods with Bibles and *The Sincere Convert* in hand, "the Puritan community included a number of serious students of the Indians' religion," writes Andrew Delbanco in *The Death of Satan*, p. 42. These students "found in the natural piety of the wandering tribes no evidence of Satanism, but a resemblance to the ancient Hebrews and even a mirror of themselves. It was chiefly in the South [i.e. Jamestown, Virginia] that the devil seemed a savage stalker outside the stockade rather than a master of disguise who was infiltrating the English community."

addition to the four hundred volumes in his personal library. His name was John Harvard.*

Some scholars have argued that the Puritans' intense inward turn created not just an explosion in the use of the word "self" but a new kind of self altogether, a being that was both God-possessed and possessed of God, a being with a new kind of "internal space." As "men became individuals," in an awkward psycho-historical phrase coined by the French historian Georges Duby, they became aware of having a holy inner life that was solely theirs to cultivate, an interiority accessible to oneself alone and known only to God. One's soul must never bend to worldly hierarchy; it was moved only by God for His purposes. This space was formed by the spiritual practices of reading and praying in solitude, through tireless rumination and attempts at discerning the jagged contours of inner life. These reflective beings were advised by William Gurnall to

> borrow as much time as you can for communion with God, and commune with your own hearts in secret. "The eyes of the Lord are in every place, beholding the evil and the good" (Proverbs 15:3). As he sees when thou shuttest thy closet to pray in secret, and will reward thy sincerity.†

* Not to be outdone in the educational support of sincerity, Yale's original 1701 charter states that its own purpose was the "Sincere Regard & Zeal for upholding & Propagating of the Christian Protestant Religion by a succession of Learned & Orthodox" so that "Youth may be instructed in the Arts and Sciences (and) through the blessing of Almighty God may be fitted for Publick employment both in Church and Civil State." See Franklin Bowditch Dexter, *Documentary History of Yale University, Under the Original Charter of the Collegiate School of Connecticut 1701–1745* (New Haven: Yale University Press, 1916).

† Gurnall, *The Christian in Complete Armour*, vol. II, 205. Of hypocrisy Gurnall also writes, "Hypocrisy is a lie with a fair cover on it. An insincere heart is a half-heart. The inward frame and motion of the heart comports not with the profession and behaviour of the outward man, like a clock, whose wheels within go not as the hand points without."

The shift toward self-possession ran counter to the kind of self that was formed by the traditional building blocks of class, trade, and family. Reformed Christianity urged, regardless of parentage, nationality, or birth, that each person was privileged by the sincerity of his or her belief. Such absolute aloneness with God was unmediated by bishops, prelates, and cardinals, and the believer shuddered at the certainty that his fate would be negotiated between him and the maker of the universe alone.

Under Puritanism, the private self was becoming enshrined at the center of a new kind of security state dedicated to protecting this fragile inner being, the heart of the Saint at the heart of this new society. Believers strove for transparency in themselves and urged it in others, for Christian society would hang or fall together. In their sincerity they aimed to become like God himself: "Sincerity is a most God-like excellency," wrote the Puritan minister John Howe in 1668, "an imitation of His truth, as grounded in his all-sufficiency; which sets him above the necessity or possibility of any advantage by collusion or deceit; and corresponds to his omniciency and heart-searching eye. [Sincerity] heightens a man's spirit to a holy and generous boldness."

Chapter III : THOSE TRICKY BOURGEOIS GENTLEMEN

Sincerity comes from an open heart. It is extremely rare; and what usually passes for sincerity is only an artful pretence designed to win the confidence of others.

- François, duc de La Rochefoucauld (1665)

LIKE MOST NOBILITY OF seventeenth-century Europe, François, duc de La Rochefoucauld, a decorated French soldier from an established Protestant family, understood politics—including personal politics—as an elaborate and cunning game. He had seen plentiful acts of deceit enacted not only by his brothers in arms but also by his archenemy, Cardinal Armand de Richelieu (immortalized for our times by Alexandre Dumas as the villain in *The Three Musketeers*). As Richelieu attempted to further centralize political and religious authority for Louis XIV, he demanded that all privately fortified castles be razed. He stripped all princes, dukes, lords, and other aristocrats of weaponry that might be used against the royal army, and, through a variety of strategic maneuvers, politically neutered the French aristocracy. And because French Protestants in revolt had long stood in the way of national unity under a Catholic king, Richelieu had them twice besieged. When they lost, they were tolerated (under the Peace of Alais) but were stripped of all political rights and protections.

Already embittered by these defeats as both an aristocrat and a Protestant, La Rochefoucauld, who had become a soldier at age ten, was shot in the skull and nearly lost his eyesight in 1652. He also fell in love with the powerful duchesse de Longueville—who eventually betrayed him. Shortly afterward, he fell on hard financial times and came down with a terrible case of gout. Unlucky in love, financially ruined, and in physical pain, La Rochefoucauld decided to devote himself to writing. He moved to Paris and cultivated the role of an *honnête homme*, a world-weary yet honest man of polished speech and manners—in other words, a gentleman.

Deliberate shows of humility and generosity, the worldly and cynical La Rochefoucauld had come to understand, stemmed more often than not from their opposite: an unquenchable desire for power. La Rochefoucauld discovered the crack in sincerity's perfect Christian armor. Things were never what they appeared, as Machiavelli had prescribed, and sincerity of intention was lacking not just in the upper echelons but, as he wrote in 1665, "in every walk of life, men assume the expression and manner which they believe will make them appear as they would wish to be regarded. Thus one might say that our world consists entirely of face values."[1] Though he also engaged in duplicity (using his duchess mistress to get close to her powerful brother), La Rochefoucauld assumed a kind of disdainful, studious remove from the behavior of fellow aristocrats, a distance which permitted him to compose one of the most trenchant collections of social and psychological observations in the history of Western letters: the *Maxims*, comprised of 614 undying truths about human vanity, self-interest, greed, and moral subterfuge.

The *Maxims* still bristle with a peppery wit that elicits pangs of recognition. "When a man's behavior is straightforward, sincere, and honest," reads maxim 170, "it is hard to be sure whether this is due to rectitude or cleverness." Friedrich Nietzsche, Ambrose Bierce, and H. L. Mencken are said to have modeled many of their own pithy aphorisms on the *Maxims,* and many of the sharpest barbs of our own modern sensibility seem to be merely recycled lines of La Rochefoucauld: "When our friends' misfortunes present us with the opportunity of displaying our affection for them," he writes in maxim 235, "we are quickly comforted." Three and a half centuries later, the singer Morrissey's 1992 translation would become an alterna-pop hit: "We hate it when our friends become successful."

For all his suspicion of the true of heart, La Rochefoucauld's observations of women, high society, social strategy, humor, and psychology repeatedly circle back to sincerity—mostly because it is the one trait that provides perfect cover for cunning schemes:

> 62: Sincerity comes from an open heart. It is extremely rare; what usually passes for sincerity is only an artful pretense designed to win the confidence of others.

The force of this maxim blossoms into many others, where one eventually gathers a sense of La Rochefoucauld's entire worldview, common yet often unspoken among the seventeenth-century European aristocracy, that affectation in politics and strategy in life are both acceptable and necessary. Here are echoes of Castiglione and Machiavelli, who shaped the mind-set of an entire class:

> 107: To pose as unaffected is, in itself, a form of affectation.
> 116: Nothing is less sincere than our manner of asking for, and giving, advice.
> 184: We acknowledge our failings; [but] by such patent

sincerity we hope to rectify the harm those failings do us in the eyes of others.
245: A very clever man will know how to hide his cleverness.

But for La Rochefoucauld, sincerity is not always feigned. Though he is ambivalent about the trait, unlike perhaps all of his peers, he gives it a positive spin when it truly appears. This is what makes the *Maxims* so unique: amidst all their sinister observations and uncomfortable truths, there remains a hope of openness between souls of like tenor. Sincerity is valuable because it is so rare. La Rochefoucauld counts himself, of course, among its endangered possessors: "I have studied myself to know myself well," he writes in the introduction, "and I have both sufficient self-assurance to be able to speak openly of those good qualities I may possess and enough sincerity to admit to my defects."[3] He declares that he knows he is witty and does not blush to say it; "Why put any pretense in the matter?" Endless apologetics "smack of vanity hidden beneath a show of modesty." He knows he writes well, that he is invariably polite to women, poorly endowed with curiosity, fond of his friends, and that he has "gone in for love in the past," but not so much anymore. He has also, curiously, "given up flirting . . . a source of astonishment to me that so many honest people should still indulge in it."[4] He indulges a few maxims in the positive:

203: A true gentleman is without pretension.
316: Weak people cannot be sincere.

During the Baroque period, which stretched from 1600 to the beginning of the eighteenth century, the Catholic Church had attempted to win back wanderers from the faith with stunning images, dramatic visual scenes, and soaring architecture that would appeal to an illiterate congregation. Dramatically lit paintings by artists like Georges de La Tour and Caravaggio operatically staged religious parables and powerful moral instruction. In France, the Baroque gently cascaded into the Rococo, or "late Baroque," which gloried in domestic scenes of *joie de vivre* and whimsical ornament. Artists like Boucher, Fragonard, and Watteau epitomized Rococo sugariness with their pastel-colored scenes of flirtation and frolicking. The wealthy displayed the works alongside knick-knacks, the elaborate décor of their houses itself conceived as a total work of art.

The period, not shockingly, saw a change in the concept of manliness, and La Rochefoucauld and other like-minded social observers were reacting in part to how thickly mannered the European aristocracy had become. Throughout the waning of the Middle Ages and even into the beginning of the seventeenth century, the model of manliness remained that of the chivalrous knight or soldier who had achieved prowess on the battlefield. He was respected for his candor, directness, honor, and physical strength. His manner was, he believed, natural and unaffected, his anger openly revealed when spurred, his public role clearly defined: a guardian of the faith who believed that his highest service was preserving tradition.

By the mid-seventeenth century, something strange had happened: the ideal of "courtesy" had taken hold of the European imagination and the role of the nobleman changed forever. Radiating from the glittery hub of Louis XIV's court in Versailles, European courtly life spawned a maze of mannerisms and rules of social etiquette which had to be strictly observed if one was to remain socially agile, to distinguish oneself, and to display clear markers of cultivation and wealth. These new rules extended to how and when one spoke, the kinds of things one revealed or kept hidden, the right turns of phrase, movements, and gestures, and ultimately the proper presentation of the elegantly adorned self to others—the birth of the performative self.

One of the most influential representations and bitter critiques of this new world was Molière's *The Misanthrope* (1666). Competing worldviews jump to the stage via the main character, Alceste—a man deeply cynical of people's motives, and angry at the utter falseness of polite society—and his friend Philinte, who believes that people should always be nice to one another, even if that means being fake. Alceste was a new kind of character. His wholesale rejection of social conventions, while making him unpopular with other characters in the play, garnered audience sympathy. They could identify with Alceste because he was no vulgar hater or uncivilized brute. Rather, he was fundamentally noble in nature yet found himself alienated from and slightly confused by a society that was shot through with a million tiny falsehoods, false avowals, and ingratiating lies.

"When a man comes and embraces you warmly," Philinte says, "you must pay him back in his own coin, respond as best you can to his show of feeling, and return offer for offer, and vow for vow." Alceste resolutely disagrees:

> Not so. I cannot bear so base a method which your fashionable people generally affect; there is nothing I detest so much as the contortions of these great time-and-lip servers, these affable dispensers of meaningless embraces, these obliging utterers of empty words, who view every one in civilities, and treat the man of worth and the fop alike.

Such fake behavior, Alceste believes, leads men and women to act as slaves to others' sensibilities, as perpetual performers in search of an audience. Alceste will have none of it:

> *Philinte.* But when we are of the world, we must conform to the outward civilities which custom demands.
>
> *Alceste.* I deny it. We ought to punish pitilessly that shameful

> pretense of friendly intercourse. I like a man to be a man, and to show on all occasions the bottom of his heart in his discourse. Let that be the thing to speak, and never let our feelings be hidden beneath vain compliments.
>
> *Philinte*. There are many cases in which plain speaking would become ridiculous, and could hardly be tolerated. And, with all due allowance for your unbending honesty, it is as well to conceal your feelings sometimes. Would it be right or decent to tell thousands of people what we think of them? And when we meet with some one whom we hate or who displeases us, must we tell him so openly?
>
> *Alceste*. Yes.

When Philinte desperately asks, "What, then, would you have people do?" Alceste replies, "I would have people be sincere."

Alceste's contempt for the harmless flatteries of everyday life does not keep him from becoming enraptured by the woman who perfectly embodies all the traits he despises: the social-climbing and coquettish Célimène, who shamelessly devotes attention to social appearances and conventions, flirts with multiple suitors, and fancies the gossipy side of polite society. Of course, she ultimately rejects him. Alceste drifts further into disillusionment, exile, and eventually total isolation, the one true place "where one may enjoy the freedom of being an honest man."

Shortly before Molière's *Misanthrope*—and representative of the growing distinction between religious hypocrisy and actual goodness—*Tartuffe, or The Impostor* (1664) exhibited how the perfect show of Christian sincerity made evil scheming much, much easier. A wealthy family man named Orgon takes in a pious-looking stranger dressed as a church cleric, named Tartuffe. Orgon wines and dines him, becomes smitten by Tartuffe's apparent saintliness, and sets the stranger's well-being above that of his wife and children. He even plans to have his daughter marry him and to replace his son with Tartuffe in line for the family inheritance. All of Orgon's family and friends, however, see Tartuffe for what he actually is: a con man who feigns sincerity and righteousness to get what he wants. Tartuffe is the religious hypocrite. Their warnings fall on deaf ears—until Orgon overhears Tartuffe trying to seduce his wife. Ultimately, Tartuffe's deceptive nature is revealed (with the help of the king), and sincerity among the family prevails. "The truly pious people . . . are not the ones who make the biggest show," observes Cléante, Orgon's brother-in-law. "True piety's not hard to recognize." He feels no need to show off his religious devotion to others, because "Heaven sees my heart."

Tartuffe was performed at Versailles in 1664, creating the most trenchant scandal of Molière's career. The depiction of a gullible aristocracy and a hypocritical Christian figure was received with such outrage that actual violence erupted in the theater. On the order of the Archbishop of Paris the play was banned from public performance, and anyone who watched, performed, or read it was to be excommunicated (though the play was still performed in private aristocratic homes). Serious complaints were levied against Molière's politics and personal life. (An influential section of the French aristocracy accused Molière of marrying his own daughter.) But Louis XIV stood by the author, in whom he saw a kindred soul and whose genius at puncturing moral hypocrisy he treasured. Perhaps he also appreciated Molière's spirited defense of comedy, which, he wrote, stemmed from "lying, disguise, cheating, dissimulation, all outward show that is different from reality."[5] Comedy was made from pretended sincerity; Moliere was poking fun at the endeavors and foibles of an entire social class eager to please at the expense of their own integrity. Eventually Louis XIV granted Molière a pension, became the godfather of his first son, and sponsored Molière's reinstated theater troupe. Sincerity at the highest levels of power, beneath all the pomp, was not dead.

—

While French court life was rigidly structured, other enclaves of society had already begun to develop more flowing kinds of relations. Around the year 1610 a young woman who had been born into Roman nobility and bred into courtly life bade it all farewell and set up her own social meeting place in a mansion near the Louvre. Her name was Catherine de Vivonne (1588–1665), the marquise de Rambouillet, and she had had enough of loutish men and King Louis XIII's court intrigue and petulance. In her Hôtel de Rambouillet there were large adjoining reception rooms—salons—that led into the center of the house, ultimately to the "sanctuary of the Temple of Athene," as she called it, or *chambre bleu.* There, Madame de Rambouillet served as waggish doyenne and received visitors from her bed. Her salon was an "alternative space" of writers, philosophers, diplomats, poets, and aristocrats who wanted to discuss the politics and gossip of the day out of earshot of the royal court. In the atmosphere of the proto-Enlightenment, gentlemen and courtly ladies—coquettish, educated—attended salons with a mix of openness and ironic wittiness.[6]

Visitors to salons would regularly run into people they did not know and whom they needed to quickly assess—unlike at court, where social gatherings were predictable and well-ordered. Such interaction spurred a unique blend of earnestness and deflection necessary to cultivate sociability and conversation. Over time, the salon became a new kind of public space, spawning others hosted by the marquise de Sévigné (author of the aphorism "The more I see of men, the more I admire dogs"), Ninon de l'Enclos, Marie-Thérèse Rodet Geoffrin, Julie de Lespinasse, and, not least, the powerful and talented Madame de Staël, whose own writings helped to spawn the Romantic movement in Europe.[7] (More on her shortly.) The salon, without hyperbole, became one of the most powerful forces in French aristocratic society over the next two centuries, comprising what Cambridge classicist Mary Beard has called "the feminine institution of civility . . . the greatest single influence in developing civilized social behavior." For some philosophers, such as Jürgen Habermas, the salon represents the birth of the bourgeois public sphere, a new formation in society where information could be exchanged and political associations could be made freely.

However different they may have been, both salon and courtly conduct were drawn from a common source: the sixteenth-century tradition of the courtier, made popular by Castiglione. Castiglione's writings were based on what he experienced at the court of Urbino, the most important center of social life in Renaissance Italy. His *Book of the Courtier* painted the gentleman as a model of self-possession and winning confidence. The perfect courtier should have a voice that was "sonorous, clear, sweet, and well-sounding," that was neither too effeminate nor too rough, and "tempered by a calm face and with a play of the eyes that shall give an effect of grace." He matched his "proper bearing" with elegant gestures, and cultivated an attitude that was at once refined, detached, and understated. He should also be athletic, exhibit a warrior spirit, and have a commanding knowledge of the humanities, architecture, classical literature, and the fine arts. The courtier should be, as fitting the time that produced him, a Renaissance man. Above all, he must excel at all of these things with seeming effortlessness, a quality known as *sprezzatura*, a high-minded nonchalance that today we'd simply describe as being cool. This poised gentleman should give the impression of being a natural nobleman and demonstrate the highest moral character—including, through his cultivation and sense of timing, the ability to speak openly and honestly to his superiors.

The Book of the Courtier was tremendously influential. Editions of Castiglione's work appeared in six languages in twenty cities, and the English translation, by Thomas Hoby, in 1561, had lasting sway on the behavior of the English aristocracy. The book had such reach because so many people were looking for guidance. This growth in demand for social instruction during the seventeenth century was due, in part, to the influx of trade-based wealth in northern Europe, which led to an expanded bourgeoisie and hungry individuals climbing the social ranks.* Commercial capitalism and the notion of investment—two activities gaining increased traction throughout Europe—led people to think of their lives increasingly in terms of future payoff. Max Weber's *The Protestant Ethic and the Spirit of Capitalism*, published in 1905, famously argued that this "economic dynamism" of the seventeenth century had much to do with the influence of Protestantism.† Whereas Catholicism had long associated holiness with the renunciation of worldly things (as in monasteries), Protestant sects took industry and thrift to be expressions of a novel kind of hardworking godliness, recommending "intense worldly activity" and "tireless labor" as ways to achieve salvation. It was this work ethic, Weber argued, that gave birth to "sober, bourgeois capitalism with its rational organization of free labor."

This mode of thinking is part of a process that social historians call rationalization, a mode that privileges thought over emotion, self-mastery over spontaneous action, and a cool head over

* The German aristocracy, however, remained comparatively poor due to the economic devastation of the Thirty Years War (1618–48).

† The mention of Weber's theory has long come with critical caveats: he was curiously silent, for example, about the incredible economic success of Catholic countries in the seventeenth century: France, Spain, Italy, Austria, and parts of Belgium. He characterized Christian monastic asceticism as irrational, but contended that it led to the ultra-rational organization, specifically through Puritanism, which, contradictorily, had no monasteries. Weber takes a swipe at Jews for being "pariahs" of capitalism, seemingly because Jews had become economically successful in Europe but did not fit his theory. The towns of Flanders and Lombardy were fervently capitalist far before the Reformation, and many reformers were vigilantly against capitalist acquisition. Nevertheless, as historian Niall Ferguson writes in *Civilization*, Weber was "right for the wrong reasons": the economic growth of Protestant countries after 1700 far outstripped all others, as they became richer, more literate, educated, industrially advanced, and scientifically adept than Catholic countries. Lands colonized by traditionally Protestant countries, like Britain, saw, in the postcolonial era, higher "economic performance and political stability." These trends, Ferguson notes, continue to this day.

instinct and violence. This new kind of behavior encourages the cultivation of psychological reservation, egocentric calculation, the show of "good form," and the elimination of plebeian verbal expressions, feelings, or other markers of "low birth." As more people climbed the social ladder, hiding one's origins became a crucial ingredient of success. Economic calculation, strategy, and long-term effect seeped outside the economic realm and into the consideration of human affairs.

Rigorous training in the arts of self-presentation was necessary, as entrance into the higher echelons of power required navigation through a tangled web of unspoken rules and protocol. Antoine de Courtin's manual *Nouveau traité de la civilité* (1671), to take just one example, offered suggestions on how to hide one's feelings and reactions and to keep, at all times, an even, undisturbed keel, always with deference to worldly power in mind. If you were a guest at a dinner table you should "Take care not to put your hand into the dish before those of higher rank have done so." If, upon eating something scorchingly hot, you "burn your mouth, you should endure it patiently if you can, without showing it." If the burn is unbearable, "you should, before the others have noticed, take your plate promptly in one hand, lift it to your mouth and, while covering your mouth with the other hand, return to the plate what you have in your mouth, and quickly pass it to the footman behind you." Two more entries highlight a change from earlier manners. Courtin writes: "Formerly it was allowed to take from one's mouth what one could not eat and drop it onto the floor, provided it was done skillfully. Now that would be very disgusting"; and, "Formerly one was permitted [. . .] to dip one's bread into the sauce, provided only that one had not already bitten it. Nowadays that would be a kind of rusticity."[8]

The victory of politeness, gentleness, discretion, and courtesy meant a stark blow to frank speech and directness—a stark blow, that is, to the ideal of sincerity. Over the slow course of two centuries, this new regime of behavior at the upper end of society set a well-sealed cap on the expression of robust opinions and beliefs, and introducing a broad gap between what one felt and how one behaved.* Appearance and reality had diverged in the realm of human affairs. And while public presentation has always been a component of social life (indeed, is required for social life to exist), during the later seventeenth century appearance was becoming far more important to how one got along in life.

People began lavishly adorning themselves with more decorative, "upmarket" clothes and jewelry. The flamboyant Cavalier style, for example—associated initially with the supporters of King Charles I—became increasingly popular in both England and France, marking a distinct change from more staid Puritan fashions (which, as we recall, were moving to North America), such as more somber colors and the famous ruff, that tall and broad ruffled collar. In England and France, low-gallon hats with wide drooping brims were adorned with a long, jutting feather on the side. Natural satins and flowing silks replaced starched and stiff fabrics. By 1630, sleeves had become billowy, draped gently below the elbow, revealing the wearer's lower arm for the first time in centuries. Men wore doublets—short bolero-style jackets, made of stiff embroidered fabric—or leather jackets called jerkins. Waistlines rose and were decorated with bows trailing along the sides. Men wore flowing, unstarched breeches trimmed with braid and slashed along the leg seam, with softer, wrinkled hose below; later

* In higher circles, the immediacies of life were entirely restructured. The well-bred in Germany, for example, no longer even spoke German to one another; they spoke French or Latin in order to mirror Louis XIV's court. To write or speak in German was considered plebeian. The word *etiquette* actually derives from Louis XIV's use of small placards or "etiquettes" that reminded guests of the rules of court behavior—which is where we get the word "courtesy."

in the period, men wore pants that gathered below the knees and were adorned with lace frills, known as Rhinegraves, met from the bottom by shin-high, slouchy boots.

From around the 1620s on, wigs, once worn by the ancient Phoenicians, Assyrians, Greeks, and Romans, returned to style. Lice played a role, but so did the demands of fashion. The word "wig" enters the English language in 1675, and their long, flowing curls aimed to create an impression of dignity and worldliness. Pioneered by Louis XIV, wigs were *de rigueur* for men of any substantial social rank throughout seventeenth-century France, and the English began wearing them following the restoration of the monarchy in 1660, under Charles II. Women did not wear wigs, but rather extensions. These were combed upward, slathered with talcum powder, and molded into the shapes of fruits, ships, and other whimsical forms. The work-intensive *pouf à sentiment* was a favorite court style, featuring ornamental objects fastened into the hair: tree branches, flowers, stuffed birds, butterflies, paper cupids, and tiny vegetables.[9] Trends like the hoop skirt reshaped bodily contours; face powder, rouge, and patches of red pigment on the nose, forehead, or chin turned male and female faces into curious visages. Masks came back into fashion for both men and women, as did accessories such as fans, stockings, aprons, and carry baskets. The increased theatricality of court and salon life had turned the body into a plaything to be decorated with fineries and observed with delight.

Often people took the opportunity to show off their elaborate clothing and hairdos, as they still do, at dinner parties. Social dining at court was an elaborate and hierarchical affair, stratified by economic and familial background. The court of Louis XIV hosted a variety of dining formats, each with its own distinctive place settings, gustatory rules, and degrees of formality, from the grandiose Royal Feast to five kinds of *grand* *couvert* (large table-setting) and two of *petit couvert* (small table-setting). Table manners were strictly observed at such events, of course, and one false move could be fatal for one's future in high society.*

It was during this era and well into the subsequent one that dance developed as a main vehicle of social interaction, expressing elegance, control, and civil demeanor. The thirst for dance radiated from Versailles outward across Europe. "Good breeding demands that pleasing and easy manner which can only be gained by dancing," wrote dance and etiquette teacher Pierre Rameau in his manual *The Dancing Master* (1725). The ideal dancer, Rameau taught, should animate the ideals of wit, serenity, poise, timing, harmony, courage, and perfect control. Dance and manners are inextricably interwoven. The ballet plié, for example, is based on a woman's bow: keeping her body and head upright, she bent at the knees and lowered her gaze from the person standing before her. Men and women were expected to bow when entering and leaving a room of guests, when presenting a gift, in greeting or in passing an individual, and at the end of a conversation. Bowing revealed a person's social provenance and knowledge of the byzantine rules of social hierarchy.

Affected, performed, and superannuated, social life at the top had become, to many observers, an elaborate lie. For the powerful,

* The father of American etiquette was none other than the father of our country himself, George Washington. In 1744, at age sixteen, he compiled a list of "Rules of Civility and Decent Behaviour In Company and Conversation," based on books of etiquette popular in both France and England, including Courtin's *Nouveau traité de la civilité*. There are quite a few rules regarding table manners, such as number 107, "If others talk at Table be attentive but talk not with Meat in your Mouth," and, the big no-no, number 92: "Take no Salt or cut Bread with your Knife Greasy," and, of course, number 37, "In Speaking to men of Quality do not lean nor Look them full in the Face, nor approach too near them at lest Keep a full Pace from them."

gone were the days of vulgar expression of immediate urges. The practices of public affectation and private discretion had come to dominate an entire continent and class, fusing Enlightenment self-confidence with a pleasing face. As the titles of Molière's plays *The Affected Young Ladies* (1659) and *The Bourgeois Gentleman* (1670) attest, the poses of aristocratic court life and affectations of the French salons dominated the mental and cultural worlds of the mid-seventeenth century, and would continue well into the next. "Courts are unquestionably the seats of politeness and good-breeding," wrote the calculating and contemptuous Lord Chesterfield to his son in 1749, "were they not so, they would be seats of slaughter and desolation. Those who now smile upon and embrace, would affront and stab each other if manners did not interpose."[10] The marquis de Sade called the entire era an "age of complete corruption," while the German philosopher Johann Fichte criticized its "completed sinfulness." Hegel's *Lectures on the Philosophy of History* (1837) damned "the whole state of seventeenth-century France" as "the highest depravity of morals and spirit—an empire of injustice with the growing consciousness of that state."

Something in the ability of humans to bear pretentiousness had hit a wall, and observations like those of La Rochefoucauld and Molière were becoming more widespread. The satirical impulse to the rescue: it began more prominently to uncover and unmask class pretensions—inspired now, paradoxically enough, by Protestantism's insistence that everyone follow the same moral rules, and that sincerity was a moral ideal. English, Irish, and Scottish broadsheets, pamphlets, and periodicals like *Scots Magazine, Courant, Tatler,* and *The Spectator* unmasked hypocrisy without remorse. In 1709, Irish wit Richard Steele's morally charged *Tatler* aimed "to expose the false arts of life, to pull off the disguises of cunning vanity, and affectation, and recommend a general simplicity in our dress, our discourse, and our behaviour."

Tatler was the most influential magazine of the English-speaking educated classes at he beginning of the eighteenth century.* In enlightened spirit, it aimed to remove mystery from religion, poke fun at social mores, and enliven public debate by lampooning the political and cultural elite. Reporters for *Tatler* were placed in popular coffeehouses to collect hearsay and gossip: manners were written about from White's; the literary world from Will's; news items from St. James's; and antiquarian issues from the Grecian Coffee House. (They left actual news to the newspapers.)

Jonathan Swift and Daniel Defoe prominently parodied political and aristocratic figures in *Tatler* and its daughter publication, *The Spectator*, which Steele founded with Joseph Addison. Swift's own *A Modest Proposal* (1729) famously suggested to Parliament that the poverty-stricken Irish should simply sell their children to the English to stave off famine. "A young healthy child well nursed is at a year old a most delicious, nourishing, and wholesome food, whether stewed, roasted, baked, or boiled," Swift wrote, "and I make no doubt that it will equally serve in a fricassee or ragout." In the long tradition of satire as moral criticism, Swift unleashed a medley of logical clarity, compassion, and fake naïveté in the spirit of charity to highlight

* *Tatler* still exists. After folding in 1711, it was reborn in spirit that same year as *The Spectator*, the goal of which was "to enliven morality with wit, and to temper wit with morality . . . To bring philosophy out of the closets and libraries, schools and colleges, to dwell in clubs and assemblies, at tea-tables and coffeehouses." *Tatler* reappeared in 1901, survived the twentieth century, and is currently published by Condé Nast. Yet whereas the original *Tatler* was dedicated to the stripping of superfluities and royal pomposity from public life, its modern reincarnation is focused on reinstating all of them with panache: high society balls, charity events, horse races, royal outings, shooting parties, fashion, and society gossip. The opening feature piece of a recent issue reads: "Charlene Wittstock tells Natalie Livingstone about her swellegant life with Prince Albert of Monaco." So much for enlightenment.

the hypocrisy of Christian leaders. Sincerity itself takes a hit: "I Profess, in the Sincerity of my Heart," Swift wrote in the introduction to the *Proposal*, "that I have . . . no other motive than the publick Good of my Country, by advancing our Trade, providing for Infants, relieving the Poor, and giving some Pleasure to the Rich."[11]

Chapter IV : NATURAL MAN REDEEMED

The plain and noble effusions of an honest soul speak a language far different from the insincere demonstrations of politeness (and the false appearances) which the customs of the great world demand.

- Jean-Jacques Rousseau, "Letter to M. d'Alembert on the Theater" (1758)

ON A WARM AFTERNOON in October 1749, as the music copyist, failed priest, and aspiring writer Jean-Jacques Rousseau sauntered along a sunny path with his nose buried in a copy of a literary journal called *Mercure de France,* he stumbled across a relatively trite but not uninteresting inquiry posed for an essay competition by the Academy of Dijon: "Has the progress of science and art contributed to the corruption or to the improvement of morals?"[1] Upon reading the question, Rousseau began to sweat and swoon; he felt nauseated and confused. "I was pierced by a thousand rays of light; a multitude of living ideas," he later recalled. "From the moment I read those words I lived in another world and became another man."[2] Taking respite under a tree, he began to cry and sketch out an answer. He would later write that all of "the misfortunes of the remainder of my life were the inevitable result of this moment of madness."

What Rousseau claims to have realized in this epiphany was that, contrary to the prevailing Enlightenment belief in the value of scientific and artistic progress, science and art had not contributed to moral improvement at all. Instead, he wrote in his response, "A Discourse on the Arts and Sciences" (1749), progress in science and art had actually made people more corrupt, miserable, and insincere. Enlightenment and civility were not raising society up; they were quashing the serenity and natural ease of the human soul:

> Before art had molded our behavior, and taught our passions to speak an artificial language, our morals were rude but natural; and the different ways in which we behaved proclaimed at the first glance the difference of our dispositions. . . . Men found their security in the ease with which they could see through one another. . . . In our day, now that more subtle study and a more refined taste has reduced the art of pleasing to a system, there prevails in modern manners a servile and deceptive conformity.[3]

Though he was living in the world of French enlightened affectation, the world satirized by Molière and La Rochefoucauld, Rousseau, who was born and raised in Geneva, was referring not just to his own era but to all eras that have e'er been; his first "Discourse" opens by taking the Dijon jury on a pedantic five-thousand-year romp through human history. Every time a civilization gets involved in making pretty or interesting things or in asking difficult questions—art, music, philosophy, poetry, literature—societies collapse and empires die. So it was with Egypt, Greece, Sparta, Rome, and China. Each had been "corrupted in proportion as the arts and sciences have improved."[4] Art and science were the cause of this decay, because both "owe their birth to our vices." Astronomy, he says, was "born of superstition," rhetoric of "ambition, falsehood, and hatred"; geometry stems from greed, physics from idle curiosity, and moral philosophy—and all the arts—from vanity and pride. All of these disciplines have moved us away from honoring the value of simplicity and natural sincerity. In our quest for attention and money we have lost our patriotism and love of country. The arts are supported by that supreme evil: luxury.

Cities, which promote luxury through commerce, are bastions of corruption, and the world would be better if Paris were wiped from the earth. Capitalism is corrosive of character, and the printing press, too, is a horrible historical faux pas, causing "frightful disorders" (Rousseau doesn't elaborate) and enabling moral uncertainty to "obfuscate God's word."* In a last-ditch plea to rid the world of all its civilized horror, Rousseau suggested in the "Discourse" that if his French contemporaries did not turn back now, away from the iniquity of society and its false institutions, from commerce and industry and education, from all the advances that built up civilization to its current state of spiritual decadence, future generations would throw up their arms in desperation and cry to the heavens, "Almighty God! Thou who holdest in Thy hand the minds of men, deliver us from the fatal arts and sciences of our forefathers; give us back our ignorance, innocence, and poverty, which alone can make us happy and are precious in thy sight."

He won first prize and became instantly famous.

Given Rousseau's suspicion of cultural elites, horror of foreign-language education, dedication to God's law, love of country, and

* In a footnote to the "Discourse," recounting a tale that has been told in several variations, Rousseau reveals a frightening zealotry: "It is related that Caliph Omar, being asked what should be done with the library at Alexandria, answered in these words, 'If the books in the library contain anything contrary to the Alcoran [the Koran], they are evil and ought to be burnt; if they contain only what the Alcoran teaches, they are superfluous.' This reasoning has been cited by our men of letters as the height of absurdity; but if Gregory the Great had been in the place of Omar and the Gospel in place of the Alcoran, the library would still have been burnt, and it would have been perhaps the finest action of his life" (p. 26).

praise of military virtues, we might today place him somewhere on the book-burning religious right. Oddly enough, his body of writings set in motion nearly everything associated with the secular left: socialist Europe, big government, individualism, and the ultimate value of learning to just be yourself.

Whatever its consequences, Rousseau's contrarian argument marked a milestone in the history of Western thought: the process of civilization had molded man into a calculating egotist who no longer responded to the world with immediacy and feeling. Instead, man now calculated his long-term gains and weighed his responses to ensure that the outcome of any given interaction was ultimately to his benefit. Art, science, literature, and learning had helped make man into a kind of machine; they made him selfish and guarded, opaque to his neighbors and hidden to his own true self. It was rather, Rousseau believed, man in his natural state, untouched by social propriety and the affectations demanded by the great world, that pointed the way to freedom and happiness. All of society, its institutions and laws and protocol, Rousseau believed, were nothing but a soul-crushing lie.[5]

The enormous public recognition Rousseau received for an essay extolling the unadorned self enabled him to literally follow suit: he tossed his bourgeois duds and started dressing like a peasant. Renouncing the white stockings and fine shirts of respectable attire, he donned a "good solid coat of broadcloth." He sold his watch, got rid of his sword, swore off "gilt trimmings and powder," and quit his job as a cashier in a tax collection office to go back to being a music copyist, a pursuit he considered more worthy of a "laborer." He transformed outwardly into the man he felt himself to be inwardly. "I pretended nothing," he wrote in his autobiography. "I became really what I seemed":

> I was truly transformed; my friends and acquaintances no longer recognized me. I was no longer the shy, bashful rather than

> modest man. . . . Audacious, proud, undaunted, I carried with me everywhere a confidence, which was firmer in proportion to its simplicity, and had its abode rather in my soul than in my outward demeanor. The contempt for the manners, principles, and prejudices of my age, with which my deep meditations had inspired me, rendered me insensible to the raillery of those who possessed them, and I pulverized their trifling witticisms with my maxims, as I should have crushed an insect between my fingers. What a change![6]

While for anyone else this feeling might mean simply getting a taste of success, for the hyperbolic Rousseau, visiting Geneva in 1754, it meant he was "the only man in France who believes in God." He reconverted to the Calvinism of his youth and would later remind readers that everything he had ever written was "imbued with the same love for the Gospel and the same veneration for Jesus Christ."[7] Rousseau's reconversion to Calvinism enabled him to regain Genevan citizenship—a return, on both accounts, to the fifteen-year-old self who had abandoned both his country and his religion in a fit of rebelliousness.

After the "Discourse," a series of rapidly produced essays and books would follow, in part because Rousseau's doctor had told him, prematurely, that he was dying of kidney disease. Each work would further promote the ideal of sincerity he sought in that first "Discourse." In 1755 he completed "A Discourse on the Origin of Inequality" (the "Second Discourse"), a diatribe against the effects of modern society and money on the natural soul. Society corrupts the individual conscience, Rousseau says, promoting selfishness, greed, and status competition; capitalism is therefore corrosive to liberty. In such a system man is so unfree, in fact, that his insincerity ceases to be a problem: his self-determining autonomy has been so radically destroyed that there is no longer even the agency left within him to choose sincerity over insincerity.

The critique continued in his 1758 "Letter to M. d'Alembert on the Theater," which expresses virulent opposition to a theater in Geneva—the home of Calvin, work, discipline, and good Christian morals. A theater, while appropriate for decadent monarchs, would corrupt a republic like Geneva and drag its humble population into moral decline. (Most Genevan residents agreed with him.) "The plain and noble effusions of an honest soul," Rousseau says of his countrymen, "speak a language far different from the insincere demonstrations of politeness (and the false appearances) which the customs of the great world demand."

Of all the paeans to sincerity penned by Rousseau, it was perhaps his *Confessions* that etch his mark deep into the history of self-revealing literature and go furthest in promoting the ideal of sincerity as the highest moral goal. Essentially the first modern, secular autobiography, the *Confessions,* published posthumously in 1782, offer Rousseau's final attempt to see himself in his entirety, in narrative episodes that reveal all of his moral blemishes—as well as the things for which he holds himself in high esteem. "I am commencing an undertaking, hitherto without precedent, and which will never find an imitator," is how the author of *Confessions* modestly begins. "I desire to set before my fellows the likeness of a man in all the truth of nature, and that man is myself. Myself alone!"[8] The *Confessions* were an attempt to write the most sincere work ever written, so that in the history of humanity at least one person might be seen for who he really is.

The *Confessions* not only bid to make perfect Rousseau's sincerity, they also belittled earlier, comparable efforts—namely, those of Montaigne, whose work Rousseau thought dripped with faux sincerity: "I have always been amused," he writes, "at Montaigne's false ingenuousness and at his pretence of confessing his faults while taking good care to only admit to likeable ones."[9] Rousseau's motive was "entirely different," he would later write in *Reveries of A Solitary Walker,* "For Montaigne wrote his essays only for others to read. I am writing down my reveries for myself alone."[10] The solution to Rousseau's lifelong torment of finding one's true identity and expressing it without affectation is the principle of self-sameness, the joining of inner and outer, of dissolving the distinction between appearance and reality, of "reconciling ourselves with ourselves." To be sincere, to be oneself: that is all.

Against the enormous cultural and intellectual lurch toward scientific progress, Jean-Jacques Rousseau's sincerity had little chance. The medical and industrial advances stemming from Enlightened science and letters were already world-altering: the commercial steam engine, blood pressure measurement, the mercury thermometer, the lightning rod, the sextant, and, important in stench-filled Paris, the valve-type flush toilet, were all invented during the middle of the eighteenth century. The explosion of these inventions and the kind of sophisticated society they engendered would continue unabashed by any accusations of the moral decrepitude they caused. The Enlightenment understanding of the world would entirely dominate the West, relegating Rousseau to that breed of reactionary artistic and political minds who stood against the progress of technology, commerce, and modernization and pined for utopia.

What Rousseau did accomplish, however, was to reinvest human subjectivity with spiritual importance during encroaching skepticism about religion and religious dogma. Rousseau enlarges, as the philosopher Charles Taylor has written, "the scope of the inner voice." He tells his contemporaries to turn away from the views of society, from the coming of mass culture, from consumerism, rationality, and the addictive pathos of capital accumulation. He insists on the solitary inward life as the source of all value and integrity. All that is good in the world originates in the republican tradition of his Calvinist forefathers. In the midst of religion's decay, the intrapersonal unity that God once delivered is now offered by a coherent, authentic, and sincere self.

As is clear, Jean-Jacques Rousseau, champion of unabashed sincerity, was, at root, a Protestant critic of modernity, however much he blasted the established Protestant church for misleading free minds. As the credibility of Christian metaphysics declined in the Enlightenment's push for reason over faith, Rousseau shouted, "Conscience! Conscience! Divine instinct, immortal voice from Heaven . . . infallible judge of good and evil, making man like God!" Indeed, Rousseau would echo Luther and Calvin toward the end of his life when, in a fit of frustration, he uttered, "How many men between God and me!"—rejecting priests and churches and laws in order to be closer to the divine.

Yet despite his profound Calvinist roots and frequent use of the word "reformation" to describe stages in his personal journey, Rousseau was defending a radically subjective idea of religion and reversing the Calvinist principle of original sin. Rousseau insisted that original man, beneath his socialization, was not base, but good. Evidence of this is seen in *Émile* (1762), Rousseau's treatise on education, which argues that a child should do "only what nature asks of him; then he will never do wrong"—this voice of nature within divine nature, nature charged with moral bearing, nature as at once our deepest sense of self and God. "It is by these feelings alone that we perceive fitness and unfitness of things in relation to ourselves," he writes. Rejecting both reason and revelation, the Savoyard vicar in *Émile* insists, "The essential worship is that of the heart. God does not reject its homage, if it is sincere, in whatever form it is offered to him."

Pressure against Rousseau increased with each successive book, each move that encouraged individuals to move further into themselves and away from the Church and state apparatus. The parliament of Paris condemned *Émile* upon its publication in May 1762. On June 11, the States-General of Holland proscribed it and, a week later, the city council of Geneva had the book publicly burned, calling it "destructive of the Christian religion and of all governments." An arrest warrant was issued for Rousseau in Paris, and by the end of the year he was being hunted throughout Europe. He spent time on an island in Lake Bienne, in Switzerland, dressed as an Armenian pauper and living under a false name, Renou. Ordered to leave by the Bern senate, he took up with the Scottish philosopher David Hume in London. But when Rousseau became increasingly paranoid, suspecting Hume of being part of an international conspiracy against him, the Scottish philosopher politely encouraged Rousseau to get the hell out.

In June 1767 Rousseau returned to France, illegally, under the protection and patronage of the prince de Conti (Louis-François I de Bourbon). After yet another period of wandering, he eventually settled in Paris, where he got down to work again as a music copyist and finished the *Confessions* (in 1770). While working on his last book, *Reveries of A Solitary Walker,* in the summer of 1778, he died of a hemorrhage, brought on by the kidney disease he had been warned of over two decades previously. His wife, Thérèse, a Catholic chambermaid, was at his bedside.

Unfortunately, for all of Rousseau's attempts to promulgate a picture of himself as the least hypocritical man who ever lived, the facts of his life simply do not square. He abandoned all five of his children but wrote a book, *Émile,* on how best to raise and educate the young. He wrote operas and comedies but vigorously denounced the theater and the arts. He gladly accepted awards from the French state, using them to fund another diatribe against the French state. His novel *Julie, or The New Heloise* (1761), a bestseller, was a touching story about a passionate love affair between a tutor and his pupil, with the lesson that one should listen to one's inner voice above all others. Rousseau did just that when he abandoned his wife repeatedly to go live on country estates with his wealthy patrons. He wrote book after book condemning the society he desperately hoped would buy his books and agree with their contents.

Because he had justified his impiety, at least, by its sincerity, Rousseau had long been an object of intense comic derision. The French masters of wit and cultivation, the Philosophes, including Voltaire, Diderot, d'Alembert, and Condillac, found Rousseau so ridiculous that they thought he had actually gone insane in his old age—or, if not insane, decked out to the extreme in self-aggrandizement, delusion, paranoia, and moral hypocrisy. Voltaire wrote to Diderot, "The man is artificial from head to foot; his mind and soul are wholly artificial. But it is in vain for him to act the stoic and cynic alternately; he will constantly betray himself and will be suffocated by his own mask."[11] Historian and encyclopedist Jean-François Marmontel wrote that, unlike the model Greek cynic Diogenes (who was reputed to have lived in a barrel out of his contempt for society's fakeness), Rousseau was merely a "pretended cynic" who would "burst with pride and rage in his tub if people stopped paying attention to him."[12] The English essayist Horace Walpole, who met Rousseau through Hume, boasted, "I have a hearty contempt of Rousseau, and I am perfectly indifferent to what the literati of Paris think of the matter."[13] And Samuel Johnson told his biographer James Boswell that Rousseau was among "the worst of men; a rascal who ought to be hunted out of society, as he has been. . . . I should like to have him work in the plantations."[14]

And yet, and yet: Jean-Jacques Rousseau retained an enormous following. After his death, his novels *Julie* and *Émile* mesmerized an even wider readership, particularly among young women, and his political writings made him something of a posthumous darling among burgeoning revolutionary minds. The Jacobin leaders of the French Revolution were attracted to his socialist predilections for the total state regulation of private property, reliance upon individual conscience, a shunting aside of organized religion, a belief in the rights of man and in the corrupting influence of bourgeois society, and his views on the education of the young. They had read *The Social Contract* (1762), the hallmark work of political thought that famously begins, "Man is born free; and everywhere he is in chains." Against the divine right of kings, Rousseau promoted the idea that *all* individuals must surrender to the larger good: "Each of us places his person and authority under the supreme direction of the general will," he writes, "and the group receives each individual as an indivisible part of the whole." The book's refrain, *"Liberté, Égalité, Fraternité,"* became, of course, the slogan of the revolution that would topple the French monarchy and insist on equality, regardless of station. At its core, the revolution was a war on hypocrisy, and this meant, as Hannah Arendt later observed in *On Revolution* (1963):

> a war upon the Court of Versailles as the center of French society. . . . The Revolution offered the opportunity of tearing the mask off of the face of French society, of exposing its rottenness, and, finally, of tearing the façade of corruption down and exposing behind it the unspoiled, honest, face of the people.[15]

The brutal, violent Robespierre, leader of the Reign of Terror, was himself a devotee of Rousseau and had met the sage toward the end of his life; he even crowned Rousseau the revolution's chief theologian in a ceremony following the execution of King Louis XVI. Robespierre even had Rousseau's body exhumed and marched in a grand procession to the Panthéon, the resting place of France's best and brightest—ironically enough, right across from Voltaire, who had always thought Rousseau a pathetic scoundrel.

History, though, has many other tricks, and they are often pushed forward by the vitriol of angry youth. In the years following the Reign of Terror, after the founding of the Directory—the interim governing body that replaced the National Convention—some stability returned to daily life, and people were again hungry for pleasure and entertainment. Young men called Muscadins (because they wore musk) or *Incroyables* ("the incredible"), surfaced in opposition to revolutionary leaders. They and their female counterparts, *Merveilleuses,* ("the marvelous") were royalists, anti-Jacobin and Girondist, *ancien régime*-admiring, moneyed, and bound to the prewar ideology of the nobility. To mock the Revolutionary style populating Parisian streets, the men took to wearing clothes not unlike those of our own hipsters: tight pants, thick glasses, bright green coats with exaggeratedly high collars, and huge, brightly colored ties. Their hair, deliberately disheveled, fell in front of the ears or was cut close.[16] The women wore wigs of assorted colors—blond, black, blue, and green—and elaborate and weird headdresses, and donned semi-transparent tunics made of gauze or linen that displayed both their breasts and buttocks. Attended by these sexy *Merveilleuses,* the *Incroyables* would roam the streets drinking, smoking, mocking, and whacking old Jacobins with wooden clubs—a roving band of drunken dandies. They "were meant to be a parody of fashion," the sociologist Richard Sennett writes. "They expected to be laughed at on the street. . . . Their bodies they and onlookers both treated as a joke."[17]

Across the Atlantic, things were more optimistic in the early 1790s. Though the Bible had long warned against the wiles of "that old serpent, called the Devil, and Satan, which deceiveth the whole world" (Revelation 12:9), American Protestants had just routed that evil from the British policies that had stifled their liberties. Just as the French would later seek transparency in their rulers, deciphering true British motives beneath the friendly bluster had become something of an obsession throughout the colonies in the 1760s and 1770s. Prior to the Revolution, American colonial churches warned of "pernicious schemes" and "hidden intents." As Thomas Jefferson wrote (making the modern reader cringe), the British were bent on "a deliberate, systematical plan of reducing us to slavery."[18] Though they claimed to have the interests of the colonies at heart, their actions—heavy taxation and increasing levels of military dictatorship—spoke something altogether different. The Sugar and Currency Acts of 1764 and the Stamp Act of 1765 raised taxes and prohibited the American colonies from creating an independent economy. The Quartering Act of 1765 insisted that all colonists were obligated to house and feed British soldiers without notice or compensation. Many colonists believed, as the South Carolina merchant Henry Laurens observed, that there was "a malicious Villain acting behind the Curtain."[19] Mercy Otis Warren, a prolific anticolonial essayist and the first woman to publish a history of the American Revolution, in 1805, wrote that it was "necessary to guard at every point against the intrigues of artful or ambitious men." They were, she said, engaged in a "game of deception . . . played over and over."[20]

In this environment, republicanism in America encouraged something like a politics of sincerity: the best society would contain people who communicated openly with one another about their motives, and who agreed to disagree. Benjamin Franklin ranked sincerity second in his "Thirteen Virtues" (1730), writing that one should "Use no hurtful deceit; think innocently and justly, and, if you speak, speak accordingly." In 1756 John Adams celebrated "honesty, sincerity, and openness," characteristics he held as "essential marks of a good mind," that ought to lead men "to avow their opinions and defend them with boldness." Colonial criminal courts agreed: crimes that involved cheating and deception were treated more harshly than those involving acts of violence. And further, as seen in the constitution of Massachusetts (1780), university education should be funded by the state not just for learning about history and religion, but because it would inculcate "sincerity, good humor and all social affections and generous sentiments among the people."

And yet while Leo Strauss's statement that the United States of America is "the only country in the world which was founded in explicit opposition to Machiavellian principles" may be true, John Adams emphasized that the American Revolution had been successful not just because it admired sincerity and the general will, but also because its leaders could employ the opposite: cunning statesmanship. He called the overly earnest French revolutionaries "monks" who "know very little of the world," and stressed "dissimulation" as "the first Maxim of worldly wisdom." In *A Defence of the Constitutions of Government of the United States of America,* Adams actually praises Machiavelli (along with Montesquieu, Plato, and Aristotle) for restoring empirical thinking to politics. He shared with Machiavelli the opinion that human nature was fixed and ruled by passions rather than by adherence to philosophical abstractions. The only thing Machiavelli lacked, Adams thought, was a clear understanding of how important institutions and trust were for the proper functioning of a healthy republic. Revolutionary leaders, he wrote, had "trust in one another, and in the common people."

But this confidence grew not from a belief in man's naturally good origins, as the French revolutionists would hold, but rather from an English sense of mutual promises freely upheld and the ideal of "a perpetual union," as sown in the *Articles of Confederation and Perpetual Union* (1774). Instead of becoming embroiled in internal conspiracies like the French, American revolutionaries were able to create, in that famed phrase, "a more perfect union," a more cohesive society. Echoing this sentiment and its Calvinist origins, Yale University president Timothy Dwight said at a commencement speech in 1798, "If each man conducts himself aright, the community cannot be conducted wrong."

But as hard as the French and Americans may have tried to merge inner motives with public policy—indeed, to create "sincere states"—a disconnect between the inner and the outer persisted. Sincerity was something that may function domestically, among your countrymen, but not among international conspirators. This distinction countered the old Protestant demand that sincerity pierce the whole of one's being or it was worthless. And so emerged Rousseau's followers, the Romantic artists—champions of the religion of the pure self against a cruel, conniving outer world they believed was corrupt and depleted and from which they sought escape.

Chapter V : ROMANTIC ESCAPES

It is not enough to say of sincerity that it is an honorable character of man. It is rather that quality without which he can have nothing honorable.

- George Walker, *Sermons on Various Subjects*, 1808

LIKE ALL "-ISMS," EUROPEAN romanticism is a broad cultural category whose character has long been contested and complicated. Lasting from about 1780 to 1830, its practitioners were many and unruly. Even when looking at the movement from the not-incredibly-distant year of 1836, the Danish philosopher Søren Kierkegaard noted in his *Journals*, "I must first protest against the notion that romanticism can be enclosed within a concept; for romantic precisely means that it oversteps all bounds." The nineteenth-century French literary critic Émile Faguet summed up the Romantic outlook when he said that it expressed "horror at reality . . . and a desire to escape from it . . . a desire to liberate oneself from the real by means of the imagination, to liberate oneself again through solitude and by retiring into the sanctuary of personal feeling."[1] And more recently, the literary scholar Henri Peyre advised that it was "inadvisable to imprison the multifarious features of the romantics of several countries within the walls of a foursquare structure." Nevertheless, he said, Romantics were "athirst for infiniteness, or for unbridled freedom" and they "unfurled their wings to break away from their cells."[2]

Romantics, Peyre means, descended in part from Rousseau's liberation fantasies, harbored a desire to escape forward-moving, rational civilization by worshipping nature, emotion, love, the nostalgic past, the bucolic idyll, violence, the grotesque, the mystical, the outcast, and, failing these, suicide. Indeed, following in the footsteps of Rousseau and English figures like Joseph Warton and William Cowper (both fervent proto-Romantic evangelicals), the Romantics wished to recapture what they imagined to be man's natural innocence, to appear unsoiled and virgin in a depleted society they thought had sacrificed the old, better way of life for technology, rationality, and capital gain. Given its impetus to move inward and away from the world, Romanticism, one might say, is a cultural evolution whereby an originally Protestant concern for locating the sincere self, once undertaken for reasons of salvation, wanders outside the walls of religion and into the sanctity of nature and the self that resists what is new and saccharine and profane in modern society.

Indeed, the push for a revivified religious life among Romantic artists was strong. Many thought the mystery of existence had been stomped out by the steel-toed boot of Enlightenment rationality. Man's spiritual quests and the point of his existence were refashioned by patently non-emotional developments in chemistry, physics, botany, and biology, particularly in early nineteenth-century Scotland, England, Germany, and France. Science had been reframing religious concepts in terms of material science (the soul, death, natural rights, the origin of man) and, in the process, de-"romanticizing" earlier stories.

Part of this "renaissance of wonder" was a very literal revival of the Christian faith, which had always esteemed man as the Son of God, thus making him somehow special and apart from the rest of the natural world. Writers such as Lucile de Chateaubriand, Abbé Félicité de Lamennais, and Friedrich von Hardenberg, better known as Novalis, were explicit in their wishes for a revival of Christianity, though they themselves were by no means standard churchgoers. Importantly, like for Rousseau, Romantic desires were frequently couched in individualist terms, and sometimes spoke vehemently against the dominant Protestantism of Western Europe. That arch-Romantic Johann Wolfgang von Goethe believed that the German Protestants had "too few sacraments," and thought that "Protestantism has given the individual too much to carry." Heaving the responsibility of the world onto each person's shoulders, the Protestants had "robbed the individual of oral confession." Chateaubriand called the Protestant Reformation "a mistake" that "cuts a mean and shameful figure," in contrast to the glory and impressiveness of the late medieval Catholic cathedral, with its pomp of "celebrations, chants, pictures, ornaments, silk veils, draperies, laces, gold, silver, lamps, flowers, and incense of the altars." Though Protestantism may have arduously pushed the argument that it had returned to sincere and "Primitive Christianity," the "Christians who were the architects of the Ulm Cathedral," Chateaubriand wrote, "were other than the children of Luther and Calvin."[3]

Nondenominational mysticism was also an outlet for the Romantic artist-seeker. Novalis, trained as a lawyer but who emerged as a poet and aphorist of remarkable depth, had lost both his fiancée, Sophie von Kühn, and his favorite brother, Erasmus, within the span of a month. He turned increasingly inward, becoming despondent and hungry for, as he wrote, "vocations for the invisible world." When he was twenty-five, Novalis became ever more obsessed with the figure of Christ and the Holy

Spirit—all in the longing to reunite with his beloved fiancée in death. He died four years later not of love-loss, but of the Romantic's now stereotypical demise: tuberculosis.

While the brawny push for a new and emotional religious experience was present in Romantic thought, its object was not always or even primarily old-school Christianity or the light of mystical revelation. The search was rather for something—anything—against the world as it was. When August Wilhelm Schlegel (brother of Friedrich, to be discussed later) explained to the British writer and politician Benjamin Constant that a person could lament the passing of the religious age without being religious himself, Constant, himself a liberal Protestant, observed, "A. W. Schlegel laments the passing of a religion in which he does not believe."[4] Religious belief was interesting to many Romantics for its emotive power and conviction, its ability to fashion the belief in an increasingly factual world interpreted by science and controlled by reason.

Importantly, the artist-poet personality that begins to emerge during the early Romantic period searches not only for pure nature and irrationality but also, in so doing, for a kind of "self-determining freedom," as the philosopher Charles Taylor has written. Self-determining freedom is also a way to describe the trait we call authenticity—a quality of things or people that appeal solely to their own authority. The flight toward authenticity would lead, for example, to a revolt against artistic conventions and literary rules, as they were limitations imposed upon the artist or writer from without, and as such did not mirror his inner life, did not freely "express" who that self was. Authenticity would replace some traditional moral ideals, too, as the age progressed: duty, honor, and country, for example (later Romanticism would, however, give rise to fervent nationalism).

The word "authenticity" stems from the Greek word *authenteo* (αὐθεντέω), which comes from the word *autos*, or "self." *Authenteo* meant to have full power or authority over something; to usurp power; even to be so powerful as to murder someone, or to kill oneself. From this comes the word *authentes,* which meant a master, someone with total authority; or even a murderer. Stemming from this is the mid-fourteenth-century Old French word *autentique,* which meant "authoritative" or "canonical." At least since the eighteenth century, the English word "authentic" (in German *authentische*) has denoted an object or text that corresponds to the facts about it, such as the provenance of a work of art, sacred text, or a coin. Is it authentic? Meaning, is it really what it looks like it is? Do the physical attributes of this specific thing or sacred text correspond to what we know to be its history? These are all questions that help experts decide whether something is real or a forgery. But what could "authentic" possibly mean in relation to people? Aren't all real people not fictitious? Isn't one personality just as authentic as another?

A hallmark work that showed how many people lived fictitious lives was committed to paper by the very man that Rousseau was on his way to visit when he read of the Dijon competition: Denis Diderot, the luminary author of *Philosophical Thoughts* (1746), *Letter on the Blind* (1749), and later, the *Encyclopedia* (1751-52). Diderot's play *Rameau's Nephew,* written between 1761 and 1772, is a satire of morals. Its protagonist is an upright and stoic man (*Moi,* or "Myself")—whom some critics have said is modeled on Diderot himself—who duels it out in a series of conversations with a spineless supplicant (*Lui,* or "He), a talented musician who fancies his own genius, wit, and cultivation but who, to win favor with his patrons, must "crawl on the earth, look about me, and take my positions. . . . I am good at pantomime." (Some critics have identified him as Rousseau.) Ranging across the topics of duty, marriage, genius, art, books, morality, education, and culture, Myself and He meet in the Regency Café, the chess capital of eighteenth-century Paris, excited to discuss the news of the day and the works and lives of their contemporaries (Diderot's own real-life peers included). They contradict each other and themselves, giving rise to the play's often acknowledged density of ironies and undercurrents.

The nephew (He) dedicates much of his ranting to how he is forced to prostitute himself and falsely flatter his patrons in order to find work. He apes the moves of aristocrats, mouthing their words and pleasantries, but always from a disdainful, sometimes ironic remove. "Pay court, know the right people, flatter their tastes and fall in with their whims, serve their vices and second their misdeeds—there's the secret," he says.[5] He knows this behavior is ultimately injurious to his integrity, and that it corrupts his ability to be genuinely engaged with others. He laments it, but the route he has chosen "is surely the easiest." He consequently views the world cynically and thinks nothing of patriotism, duty, helping friends, or educating his children. These bourgeois values are for him "all vanity."

Diderot's Myself character, who speaks little, smilingly condemns the nephew for his obsequious self-abasement. He suggests that the nephew rise above his fate and make himself "independent of misfortune" by being decent, frank, and sensible. "You are people to be pitied," Myself says, to which He poses the following predicament:

> How in the name of sense can one feel, think, rise to heights, and speak with vigor while frequenting people such as those I must frequent to live—in the midst of gossip and the meaningless words one says and hears? [*He then gives a rolling list of gossip about the weather, what so-and-so was wearing, how Madame X does her hair, etc.*] Do you suppose that things like these, repeated over and over every day, kindle the mind and lead to great ideas?

Myself responds:

> No, of course not. It would be better to shut oneself up in a garret, eat a dry crust, drink plain water, and try to find oneself.[6]

Following a monologue in which it is unclear whether the nephew is being ironic or not (it is not clear if even he knows whether he is being ironic or not) in his quasi-praise of Christianity, Truth, the Beautiful, and the "good souls," he has a hysterical fit. He hums arias and lieder, gesticulates wildly, speaks in multiple tongues and voices and volumes, pitches and tones—"I am but a poor wretch . . . My Lord, my Lord, I beg you to let me go . . . O Earth, receive my gold . . . There is my little friend . . . *Aspettare e non venire . . . A cerbina penserete . . .*"—and then starts mimicking orchestral instruments—horns, bassoons, violins—with cheeks bloated, forehead sweating, and hands flailing; he goes on "waving about like a madman, being in himself dancer and ballerina," acting out the parts of an entire opera, diving into twenty different theatrical roles, running around the room of chess players, his powdered face now smeared. At last he stops, out of breath, "like one possessed, frothing at the mouth," and, gathering himself together, he delivers a rationale for the need for new and powerful music and art amidst the crushing bore of everyday life, an escape from the confines of oppressive, fickle society. *Rameau's Nephew* then spells out what would be adopted as the root operating system of Romanticism:

> Our passions have to be strong. The tenderness of the musician and the poet must be extreme . . . the aria must be the peroration of the scene. We need exclamations, interjections, suspensions, interruptions, affirmations, and negations. We call out, invoke, clamor, groan, weep, and laugh openly. No more witticisms, epigrams, neat thoughts—they are too unlike nature.[7] [ellipses in original]

When it was finally published, first in German, in a translation by Goethe, in May 1805, *Rameau's Nephew* was met with enthusiasm by the literati, including the philosopher Hegel, who saw in the play a summary of the spiritual conflict of his age—inward consciousness against the onslaught of a world that had long imprisoned the human soul. He pointed to *Rameau's Nephew* in the *Phenomenology of Spirit* (1807) for its illustration of the "self-estranged consciousness": a person who was distanced from his own inwardness yet still longed for its companionship. But the somber Hegel curiously praised the He character for his ability to transcend—like the hidden Spirit that Hegel believed animated history—the strict confines of society and tradition and to assert his own individual consciousness, however torn (*zerissen*). This rambunctious Spirit inverts, Hegel writes, "all concepts and realities, the universal deception of itself and others; and the shamelessness which gives utterance to this deception is just for that reason the greatest truth."[8]

Other writers swooned equally, but, alas, the wider German public was not interested in reading *Rameau's Nephew,* and the German publisher gave up the effort to broaden its appeal. The work did not appear in its native French until 1821, that edition merely a fraudulent translation of Goethe's version back into French. Two years later, in 1823, *Rameau's Nephew* appeared in French again, but this edition, too, was of dubious provenance. It was not until 1890 that a librarian named George Monval discovered the original in a state archive, allowing the first true version of Diderot's masterpiece to be published in its original language. But by that time *Rameau's Nephew,* in various inauthentic re-translations, had already become a celebrated masterpiece of French Enlightenment satire, spelling out the moral conundrums that were nestling in the minds of young Romantics and offering an alternative to the direction in which the world was headed.

—

***Rameau's Nephew*'s emphasis on the** spontaneous imagination countered the planning and diligence of science by burrowing more deeply into the private realms of dreams and artistic creation. Trying to distance itself from rational, ordered society, this burgeoning Romantic mind sought refuge from a modern world that threatened its sovereignty and purity. This ebbing occurs not just because modern industry and society were seen to encroach upon the sacred self, but because Romantics believed that the gulf between the world out there and the world inside was insurmountable. The Romantic self both feared and longed for direct contact with the world.

This split view was derived, in part, from German idealist philosopher Immanuel Kant's *Critique of Pure Reason* (1781), which argued that "discoveries" about reality said more about how the human mind was set up to organize experience than they said about reality itself. Kant posited categories that were built into the mind prior to all experience (*a priori*), most notably the categories of space and time, substance, causality, and various "synthetic" judgments that could not have been learned by experience (for example, mathematics: you do not need to experience adding two elephants to seven elephants to know that you will have nine elephants; you can deduce this without experiencing it). The mind, Kant believed, thus interpreted the raw data of the world through its existing web of categories. And because the mind had these categories, it experienced the world as orderly, even though the real data of raw experience was chaotic. This chasm between what was inside the mind and what was outside it meant that we could never know nature itself; we could know only what we know of nature. The human mind was forever locked up within itself.

For Kant, whose influence on modern philosophy was Copernican in its immensity, only by experiencing something the mind could not immediately categorize—an aesthetic or religious experience—could we catch a glimpse of nature naked and experience her profundity, an experience Kant called the Sublime.

Among other things, the search for the Sublime engendered an artistic movement that ostensibly reflected nature but, like Romantic poetry, just as equally reflected its makers' inner turmoil, pacific expanse, and restless endeavor: thunderstorms and lighting bolts; gathering cloud formations over rough seas; enormous snow-peaked mountains; vast vistas of shocking color; misty beaches at night tinted with moonlight. Artists like Théodore Géricault, Jean-Baptiste-Camille Corot, Caspar David Friedrich, J. M. W. Turner, Albert Bierstadt, Thomas Cole, and John Constable ("Nature is Spirit Invisible," he said) rendered turbulent, mysterious nature as a sublime force that dwarfed human affairs. Humans were playthings of tender flesh and brittle bone confronting wild and untamed nature, sacrificing their desire for the rational orderliness of civilized life in the face of the Sublime. Caspar David Friedrich's *Wanderer Above the Mist* (1818; seemingly the default cover art for any book about Romanticism), celebrated the lone, wispy-haired, coattailed young rebel standing atop a mountain looking into the distance through an icy blue fog. "Feeling can never be contrary to nature," Friedrich wrote. "It is always consistent with nature."[9]

The Romantic focus on keeping separate the inward self from its outward roles—a view inherited from Protestants—represented a challenge to how people had conceived of themselves since the days of ancient Greece. The traditional model also held that people were comprised of two parts: the real self and the social self, the inner and the outer. But it also held that joining the two together provided an ethical direction: "Give me beauty in the inward soul," Socrates said of this ideal, "and may the outward and the inward be at one." Integrity of personality was achieved by fusing the inner and outer. The whole person was created through his social and political engagement. The social mask was not a burden to be worn with irony or disdain (as with Rameau's nephew) but rather was necessary to a sense of wholeness; without it, one was merely, as Romans deemed, *privatus*, a private person. By bringing ethical concerns into the public sphere but shielding the private life from the public, one could have a public personality and a private life with no sense of betrayal to either. The matching of these internal and external parts—in morality, knowledge, and art—was the Greek and Roman model of spiritual perfection, a model that would be handed down through generations of Western moral thought.

Socially constructed identity had long been embedded in ideas of kinship, tradition, duty, the nation, and even, for some believers, a world of "spirits" that related to man. Older forms of identity inspired a sense of being part of a greater "Chain of Being," as the intellectual historian Arthur Lovejoy called it. This invisible, unbreakable bond stretched from God to man, often in ways that unsurprisingly mirrored the hierarchical status quo of the world: God-Pope-Bishop-Clergy-Nobleman-Landholder-Vassal-Serf-Peasant, and so on. In such an order, one knew one's place, felt a sense of certainty and predictability about one's life. Religious wars had cast established churches into disrepute, smashed the legitimacy of the divine right of kings, overthrown the landed gentry and later—because of the murderous purges of the French Revolution and the violence surrounding liberation—cast doubt upon a benevolent and caring God and the notion of human moral "progress."

The stable world order that had been credible for at least the previous thousand years was beginning to vanish.[10] And so at the beginning of the nineteenth century the old world was once again being dismantled and made anew; modernity was happening. The Romantic personality, living amidst this social and cultural confusion, tried to make his way by going further into himself. Instead of trying to cultivate this "outer self" through social interaction, as the Romans and Greeks had done, as the entire medieval order promoted, he came to see roles as disingenuous. Social identity was a farce, and social conventions were morally base because they involved, at root, deception. The social role was inherited from tradition, circumstance, profession, or class; it was not freely chosen. Beneath your identity as a father, mother, sister, brother, boss, or laborer was an identity more fundamental. The inward self, on the other hand, bound to nature (or God or Spirit) at its base, was free from the sullied world of commerce, industry, and false bourgeois masks; it was a sacred interiority. Such a view reaches back to the one Luther had promoted of the true Christian soul as absolutely free and available to everyone sincere enough to locate it.

Rousseau and his Romantic followers escaped the corrupt modern world through nature—the place where one could tranquilly locate the divine core of one's being—but it was not just nature (or imagined nature) that obsessed the rising Romantic sensibility. Some found escape from the "corrupted present" by making a deliberate leap into the past. The proto-Romantic poet and teenager Thomas Chatterton would often lock himself in his attic, where he stored dusty books, quill pens, and some old medieval parchments he'd found in a chest at a local church in Bristol. There, isolated with his thoughts, Chatterton lived in a dreamy nostalgia for the fifteenth century, writing poems in Middle English (on that medieval parchment) under the assumed character of Thomas Rowley, a monk who composed dark odes like this "Mynstrelles Songe":

Black hys cryne as the wyntere nyghte,
Whyte hys rode as the sommer snowe,
Rodde hys face as the mornynge lyghte,
Cale he lyes ynne the grave belowe;
Mie love ys dedde,
Gon to hys deathe-bedde,
Al under the wyllowe tree.

For years this "Rowlian" poetry was circulated in compendiums of medieval verse, and Thomas Rowley even became known as a rediscovered luminary of English literature. Not until the end of the nineteenth century was there consensus on the true origin of the poems.

But it was not just for his nostalgic escapism that Chatterton had become a Romantic idol; he had killed himself by drinking arsenic in 1770, at the age of seventeen, robbed of youth and innocence after sharing so much beauty. Percy Bysshe Shelley wrote in *Adonais* that Chatterton could "gaze upon nature's naked loveliness." William Wordsworth and Samuel Taylor Coleridge celebrated him in their poems, as did the artist Henry Wallis, in his iconic painting *The Death of Chatterton*. John Keats inscribed his poem "Endymion" "to the memory of Thomas Chatterton," and that rock star of Romanticism himself, Lord Byron, more temperately called him "mad" yet "never vulgar."

Even though Chatterton hid beneath the veil of an invented fourteenth-century monk, he was giving sincere expression to personal longings from behind the pseudonym. When he was forty, William Wordsworth gave voice to this yearning for personal expression in an essay called "Upon Epitaphs" (1810), where he makes clear that sincerity of intention and personal artistic vision should be the new standards of poetry, set against the more formalized, less personal poetic modes of the recent neoclassical past. Sincerity had become a new literary standard by which a writer might be judged:

> When a man is treating an interesting subject, and one which he ought not to treat at all unless he be interested, no faults have such a killing power as those which prove he is not in earnest. . . . Indeed, when the internal evidence proves that the writer was moved . . . where the charm of sincerity lurks in the language . . .

there are no errors in style or manner for which it will not be a recompense.

For the first time, sincerity of expression was becoming the high-water mark of poetic quality, beyond considerations of stylistic excellence.

Lord Byron, of course, would come to occupy the popular imagination as the quintessential English Romantic poet whose sensitive, unpredictable, and heroic suffering doomed him to an early death. Byron believed himself to be "a strange mélange of good and evil"—so much so, he wrote, "that it would be difficult to describe me."[11] The unique inner self was for the Romantic sensibility a thing ineffable, formless, and possessed of untamable passions. As he wrote in the 1817 confessional poem "Manfred":

I could not tame my nature down; for he
Must serve who fain and would sway—and soothe—and sue—
And watch all time—and pry into all place—
And be a living lie—who would become
A mighty thing amongst the mean—and such
The mass are; I disdained to mingle with
A herd, though to be leader—and of wolves.
The lion is alone, and so am I.

The "Byronic hero" came to encapsulate a certain kind of idealized Romantic personality: a noble yet flawed character who possessed great talent, deep passion, and unsullied ideals. He was awash in contradictions and inconsistencies. He disliked social institutions and held no respect for the ways of the world, or rank and privilege—though he almost always possessed both. The Byronic hero's tragedy comes from his fearless confrontation with his imperfect self, from his inability to achieve true love and lasting relationships due to social impediments, exile, or some other outward imposition. He is a wanderer and wonderer, his true self thwarted by society; only in nature can he find refuge. The dejected hero ultimately self-destructs or is felled early by tragedy (as Byron was at thirty-six, while playing at war in Greece).

The Romantic figure aimed to experience reality in a wholly new way and by himself, without mediation, as a solitary hero, Byron's "lion alone." He would ingest the world not by the bone-dry reasoning of the foregone Enlightenment, but through feeling, sentiment, imagination, instinct, passion, dream, and unquenchable nostalgic longing—the latter encapsulated in a singularly perfect German word: *Sehnsucht*. These modes of experience were spontaneous, unsystematic, and unique to each individual, unintelligible to physics, chemistry, mechanics, and geography. As the natural sciences were expanding their reach and learning more about nature's truths, Romantics were unconcerned: their expansive inner selves were more important than truth. To be Romantic was to insist on the continued importance of unrestrained human feeling and even violence in the face of cold, pragmatic rationality.

But this burst of creativity meant something new for the quality of sincerity: increasingly, it was moving out of the realm of religion, where it had been forged from Protestant theology, and into the secular (though spiritual) world of art. People no longer tried to be sincere only in order to please God; rather, sincerity was becoming a way to earnestly express feelings, to trumpet the truth of oneself, and therefore to make art that was more pure and self-expressive than what had come before. This does not mean that God was not still a part of this search for sincerity; vestiges of traditional religion were resurgent, to be sure, and Protestant churches still promoted sincerity in their congregations. In some instances, Romanticism and Protestantism—and Romanticism and Catholicism—were nearly the same.[12]

Tellingly, the big names associated with German Romanticism and the Sturm und Drang movement (named after Friedrich Maximilian Klinger's play about the American Revolution and the importance of passionate feeling) who aimed to counter the Enlightenment movement towards rationality—Novalis, Goethe, and Schiller, along with Herder, Fichte, Friedrich, Kleist, Tieck, Hölderlin, the Schlegel brothers, Schleiermacher, and Solger—were all raised Pietist, Calvinist, or otherwise Reformed Protestant.* In their Romantic expressions they dragged along with them the vestiges of Protestantism's stress on sincerity, of living according to the inner voice, of the importance of immediacy and experience—they transformed that call into art, literature, poetry, and philosophy. German Romanticism, while certainly containing elements of Catholic longing for image, emotion, and ritual, appears more so to be a secularized version of Protestantism. "It is essential to assert this above everything," wrote Madam de Staël in 1813, "if northern Germany is the country where theological issues were the most stirred up, it is at the same time the one where religious feelings are the most universal. . . . Their artistic and literary genius draws all their inspiration from them."[13]

De Staël's view relied heavily on the philosopher Friedrich Schlegel, the only Romantic philosopher to, ironically enough, convert to Catholicism. Friedrich was a classicist by training and endowed with an equally brilliant sibling, August. In a smattering of writings, the Schlegel brothers articulated the theory of German

* Even the poet Heinrich Heine, who was born Jewish, converted to Protestantism, on June 28, 1825. But Heine did not convert because of his innate attraction to Protestantism's theology. Rather, the Prussian government had begun to legally reinstate anti-Semitism. Jews in Germany at the beginning of the nineteenth century were prohibited from teaching in universities, and Heine had academic aspirations. He famously wrote that his conversion was his "ticket of admission into European culture."

Romanticism as it progressed, particularly in Friedrich's *Athenaeumsfragmente of 1798–1800, Lyceumfragmente (1797), and Lectures on Transcendental Philosophy (1801).* "Romantic," in fact, derives from Friedrich's use of the German noun *Roman*, or "novel," to suggest that the art of literature was the "Socratic dialogue of our age," or, as in his famous review of Goethe's hallmark Romantic work *Wilhelm Meister's Apprenticeship* (1796), that the novel, as a mark of authentic mastery, "not only judges itself but describes itself." The task of the literary work, Schlegel held, was to unveil the possibility of infinite perspectives, to display the relativity of views, and convey a new kind of "feeling for the universe."

Within this grand new feeling he was referring to irony, "the clear consciousness of eternal agility, of an infinitely teeming chaos." Though Schlegel was impressed by the Socratic notion of irony because it was "playful and serious, frank and deeply hidden" and thereby "the freest of all licenses, since through it one rises above one's own self," his use of irony has more to do with how it suspends immediate understanding and reveals hidden meaning. Schlegel first celebrated the playful mood in 1797, in his *Lyceumfragmente*, for its ability to "rise infinitely above all limitations, even above its own art, virtue, or genius; externally, in its execution: the mimic style of a moderately gifted Italian *buffo*."[14]

This is the same stance for which Hegel had praised Rameau's nephew—an ability to transcend all given inhibitions and roles through a loud and satirical, half-crazed laughter, a deliberate mental remove from unserious things. This clown character not only stepped out of his own individual role, he stepped out of all roles, refused the extant order of things. Romantic irony was in this way a new kind of worldview, a quiet understanding of the unfathomableness and absurdity of existence, history, and the universe. "Irony in the *new sense* is self-criticism surmounted," Schlegel wrote. "It is never-ending satire."[15]

In German Romanticism the accepted meaning of irony shifts

from being solely a rhetorical strategy where words convey the opposite of what they mean—its traditional definition since the ancient Roman rhetorician Quintilian—to a strategy of being. Irony became the only true and, most importantly, authentic style of existence. To be ironic was, paradoxically, to be sincere and to stand for the value of real human connectedness in the face of encroaching industrialization, commercialism, and science upon the deepest mysteries of human existence. "As in actual life and in the love which centers in an earthly object," Schlegel wrote in *Philosophy of Life and Philosophy of Language* (1828),

> a good-humored raillery, which amuses itself with some little defect of character, either apparent or real, is not inconsistent with sincerity—not, at least, when both parties have no doubt of each other's affection, and its ardor admits of no increase—but, on the contrary, lends to it an agreeable charm, even so is this true of that other and highest love.[16]

The ironic perspective as a total worldview has in common with a religious sensibility its unifying aspect, its urging human connection that evades the rote confines of the everyday world. This was a way to forge a spiritual life in the midst of a modernity that many Romantics believed was devaluing the mystery of human depth. As the Scottish sociologist Harvie Ferguson has written, the play of irony and sincerity during the Romantic era "is essentially and inherently a spiritual phenomenon."[17] And as Schlegel wrote of his lifelong spiritual search (and eventual conversion to Catholicism, after marrying the gifted novelist Dorothea Veit, herself a convert from Judaism):

> All my life and my years of philosophical discipleship have been filled with the ceaseless quest for the eternal unity of knowledge and love, for a link to an external, historical reality or an ideal

> reality, at first the idea of a school and a new religion of ideas, then a link to the Orient, to Germany, to the liberty of poetry, finally to the Church, because without that the search for freedom and unity would be in vain. Was that need for such a link not a need for protection, for a firm foundation?[18]

When Ralph Waldo Emerson was a junior in college, in 1819, a full set of the works of Johann Wolfgang von Goethe, the pages edged in gilt, arrived at the university library—a gift to Harvard from the author. Goethe's *Sorrows of Young Werther* (1774) and *Wilhelm Meister's Apprenticeship* had been the founding novels of German Romanticism, each relaying the story of a young man who sets out to find love, passion, and his true self against the backdrop of the Enlightenment bourgeois establishment. Goethe became one of the world's first international literary stars, and in the years following the War of 1812, when British culture was scorned, fascination with and translations of his work, as well as that of German thinkers such as Fichte, Schiller, Kant, Schelling, and Jacobi, were to be found in many educated American households and universities from Washington to Boston.

By 1832, Emerson was a graduate of Harvard Divinity School and new minister of the Second Unitarian Church of Boston. He, too, had fallen under the spell of German Romanticism's pathos. He had become tired of the Unitarianism he was preaching—calling it "corpse-cold." Following the emotional appeals of the Second Great Awakening—a Christian revival movement out to remedy modern society and reawaken religious emotions—Unitarianism seemed overly rational, dry, and devoid of heated spiritual passion. More concretely, Emerson thought his calling to preach every afternoon had become routine. So after delivering his "Last Supper" sermon, on October 28, 1832, he quit.

Two months later, on Christmas Day, at age twenty-nine, he

set sail for his first visit to Europe. Touring around Italy, France, England, and Scotland, Emerson met with the big guns of English Romanticism—Wordsworth, Coleridge—and with the Scottish writer Thomas Carlyle, whose American agent he would become. Emerson never did get to Germany—perhaps because he thought he already knew it—but if Goethe had been alive, he wrote, "I would have visited." While on this Continental romp, Emerson gathered most of the ideas that appear in the founding work of American Transcendentalism, *Nature,* which was published, anonymously, in 1836 and took six years to sell out its print run of 500 copies.

Nature was new. America was a blank page ready to be written, Emerson argued, outside the confinement of calcified European forms—the ideal state for which Romantics had been searching. Nature supplied the American with all he needed for happiness: commodity, beauty, language, discipline, idealism, spirit, and prospects. In the follow-up to this rapturous paean to natural individualism, "Self-Reliance," Emerson sang the virtues of the individual who harnessed the power of natural instruction and forged his own trail. He famously wrote in 1841:

> Whoso would be a man must be a nonconformist. He who would gather immortal palms must not be hindered in the name of goodness, but must explore if it be goodness. Nothing is at last sacred but the integrity of your own mind. Absolve you to yourself and you shall have the suffrage of the world. . . . What have I to do with the sacredness of traditions if I live wholly from within?[19]

Generalized, internalized social resistance, the unshackling of oneself from "foolish consistency," he believed, was crucial to the health of the soul. The freedom of this new authentic man was paramount, for "everywhere society conspires against him." Emerson's philosophical peer across the Atlantic, John Stuart Mill, would argue equally strongly for individual self-determination, writing, "Where not the person's own character, but the traditions and customs of other people are the rule of conduct, there is wanting one of the principal ingredients of human happiness and quite the chief ingredient of individual and social progress."[20]

During the American Romantic glory years of 1850–55, German and English influence led to the flowering of masterpieces concentrated mostly in New England: Emerson's *Representative Men,* Nathaniel Hawthorne's *The Scarlet Letter* and *The House of the Seven Gables,* Herman Melville's *Moby-Dick* and *Pierre,* Henry David Thoreau's *Walden.* These and other works were touched by the poetic encounter with nature seen in Wordsworth; by Byron's romantic posturing and wild personality; by the lush imagery of Keats; by the lyricism of Shelley; and, as seen in Edgar Allan Poe, by the Gothicism of Mary Shelley.

But the American style of Romanticism, backlit by the Puritan language of salvation, guilt, and providence, developed its own character. It was forged on a continent of total wilderness amidst the inspired political rhetoric of freedom and equality for all—unsullied, as Emerson wrote in *Nature,* by the epochs of human history that had transpired on European soil. Unlike the genteel Bostonian Henry Wadsworth Longfellow, Emerson departed from a heavily affected British style and instead urged Americans, in its opening lines, to fashion an "original relation to the universe." American Romantics strived in their own work, self-consciously, to be new and original. So much so that in hindsight some American Romantics—Hawthorne, Melville, Poe—appear to be more different than alike in their views of the human condition, use of literary forms, and projections for the future. But American Romantics were unified—whether in literature, philosophy, or painting—by a fascination with the darker recesses of the mind that hid behind the ideology of American progress.

The eighteenth-century Enlightenment had deposited a wealth

of optimism about man's possibilities and perfectibility—through public education, democratic institutions, and belief in man's own inner capacities. The ideals of this youngest, most vibrant democracy asserted the value of individuals, regardless of where they were raised or how educated they were. But these values, in the 1850s, applied only to white males. The clash of American ideals and realities led writers and painters and poets to champion the morality of individualism while keeping an eye on the darker side of what many saw as a fragmenting society in a Romanticism all their own. Social critique was couched in the art of peeking behind the optimistic claims of politics and "progress."

Contributing to a sense of loss and splintering, many saw a rising American materialism and focus on business costing the mind and spirit dearly. By the middle of the nineteenth century, over 150 intentional religious communities—the Shakers, Oneida, and Brook Farm—had been founded by spiritual settlers totally disillusioned with America's increasing focus on material acquisition and its resulting social inequality. Thousands of Romantic-inspired seekers were saying no to that society and opting for simplicity and self-reliance.

The popular façade of hardscrabble individualist virtue was erected on the national stage in 1840, when the Whigs pitted William Henry Harrison against Martin Van Buren for the presidency. The university-educated son of a wealthy Virginia plantation owner, Harrison was featured on campaign posters as a log-cabin-owning roughneck, sitting in the door jamb nursing a keg of hard cider—a poor but sincere everyman. Incumbent Van Buren (the first US president to be born an American citizen) was pitched by the Whigs as a ruffle-shirted elite Easterner desperately out of touch with the common folk. Political kitsch, which always comes down on the side of "the people," began with the Harrison-Van Buren race: when Harrison was swept into office in a landslide win, the wave of corny objects did not disappoint: libations flowed from bottles of Old Cabin-brand whiskey and hard cider bottles shaped like little log cabins to celebrate the winner. Then, on March 4, 1841, a cold and rainy day, Harrison, keeping up his manly image and foregoing a coat, delivered a two-hour inaugural address, the longest in American history. He caught pneumonia and died a month later.

The election entertained Emerson. He lamented the pretentious "electioneering placards" defacing the woods near his home, "suspended on the oaks or bulrushes," and he called Harrison the "Indignation President" who belonged to a "puny generation." Emerson was not surprised when Harrison "could not stand the excitement of seventeen millions [sic] of people but died of the Presidency within a month." Emerson saw defiant individualism better exemplified in his bearded friend, and former student, Henry David Thoreau, who camped out for two years in the Concord woods and refused to pay taxes. Thoreau had gone to the woods because he "wanted to live deliberately, to front only the essential facts of life." His quasi-exit from society in 1854 (he returned to his nearby parents' house to do laundry) was a plunge into lived, sensual experience. Emerson called Thoreau's life "sincerity itself"—a life, in hindsight, that exemplifies all the Romantic tropes: nostalgia for lost innocence, escape from industrialization, worship of nature, the value of direct experience, and heeding the unique march of one's inner drummer. Solitude in nature practically guaranteed the quality of personal sincerity, as it had for proto-Romantic figures like Joseph Warton or for Rousseau. For Emerson the formula was very simple: "Every man alone is sincere. At the entrance of another person, hypocrisy begins."[21]

Emerson saw Thoreau as the man who, in the midst of rapid commercialization, might "fortify the convictions of prophets in the ethical laws by his holy living." He hoped that his example of spartan existence and material efficiency might help mold a more spiritualized American future. But Thoreau's move to the woods was not a move to reform the world, not an example he wished others to live by. It was rather a model, he hoped, by which "each one [might] be very careful to find out and pursue his own way, and not his father's or mother's or neighbor's instead."[22] Worse was to copy people—even those whose lives appeared to be more simple and pure—in order to appear to live a life that was truly yours. Blaze your own trail.

By virtue of their contradictions and laments, Emerson and Thoreau acknowledged sincerity as a paradoxical goal—the more one strives for it, the less likely it is to appear at all. An insincere person who feigns sincerity wears a dangerous, deceptive mask. In addition to these pitfalls, there is the fact that if one decides to be absolutely true to oneself, sincerity with others becomes secondary. One can now easily justify the strategy and manipulation that sincerity had set out to combat. In other words, as long as one is being true to one's own longings, desires, vision, sense of who one is, then why should one care whether one lies, cheats or steals? These are simply outward perceptions imposed by tradition and law. What matters is one's adherence to one's inner self and calling. Absent a sense of shared ethics, the original Reformation directive to heed one's individual conscience was leading the impulse to be sincere further from its spiritual roots. As individualism in America became more solipsistic and the Civil War ravaged the population, "The men believe not the women, nor the women the men," Walt Whitman despondently wrote in 1871. "And the aim of all the littérateurs is to find something to make fun of. . . . Genuine belief has left us."

Chapter VI : CASCADING CYNICISM

The truly sincere person ends up understanding that he is always lying.

- Friedrich Nietzsche, *The Will to Power,* 1901

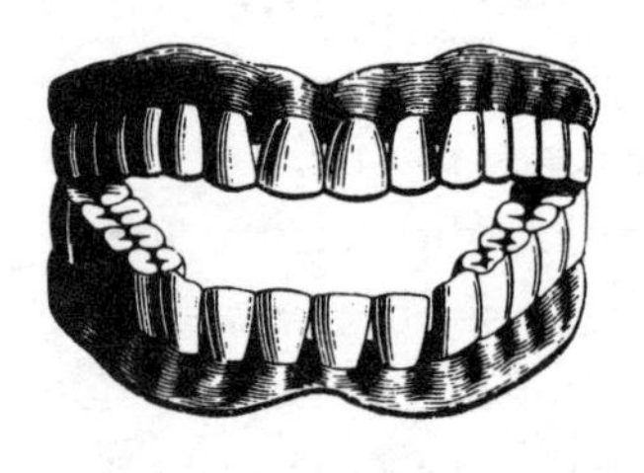

THE WORD "ARTIST," DESIGNATING someone engaged professionally in the fine arts, first appeared in the English language during the Romantic era, in 1823.[1] Stemming from the French *artiste,* derived from the Latin *ars* (meaning "skill"), the word had earlier referred to someone who was a craftsman, a person with a specific technical ability. But being an artist in this new sense particular to modernism meant not only possessing an artistic skill, it meant being dedicated entirely to a life of aesthetic creation, whether in painting, sculpture, poetry, music, or on the stage. Because of the freedom granted to the artist by virtue of his imagination, he appeared as a figure in opposition to the normal restrictions of bourgeois life. He was the bohemian who ventured into the marginal realms of society—and the mind—where the bourgeois man did not allow himself to go.

Art at the fin de siècle, partly still pickled in robust Romanticism and partly patted dry of its creeping sentimentality, thus achieved its particular significance not just from what it did or looked like, but from the figure of the avant-garde artist who made it. Amidst the confusion and alienation of industrialized life, the artist offered salvation to society by being someone who lived in a manner more in touch with the elemental forms of life that were vanishing from view: the old bucolic existence, the pleasures of the local, the immediacy of emotions, the embeddedness of social existence.

"All that is solid, melts into air, all that is holy is profaned," Marx and Engels observed of the arrival of the new industrial system that wiped away social ties and cast perpetual uncertainty into the economy. In such a world, the modern artist is a lone soul cast into a sea of brutishness, his sensitivity neither appreciated nor understood, whose work, incomprehensible to his contemporaries, was made for generations of future seers. The "genius myth," as it has come to be called, was born in this era, and it ushered in a cult of the artist personality with a host of names now represented on countless posters, calendars, and mugs: Vincent van Gogh gave up his efforts toward the Protestant ministry in order to evolve into its secular equivalent: an artist who would idealize peasants in a field, the swirling accent of God in nature's sky, the harder side of life evidenced in a pair of broken shoes and labor-bitten hands, or the vast expanse of a field that calls for reaping. Van Gogh's alcoholism, poverty, ineptness, and insanity confirm him as a visionary who cared nothing for petty comforts and values, a dreamer who lived only for his art. Trailblazing image-makers Pablo Picasso and Georges Braque violently destroyed the traditional picture space; and Picasso filled it with

Romantic themes: prostitutes, criminals, violence, sexuality, bestiality, myth, children, and the West's obsession with its colonial subjects' primitivism: African masks and sculptures. (Their images reflected a fractured reality: "The world today does not make sense," Picasso said, "so why should I make pictures that do?") Likewise against the grain, Henri de Toulouse-Lautrec, who was short and unattractive and had congenital deformities stemming from family inbreeding, ventured out into the Parisian night with a drawing pad in search of drink, dance, and debauchery; Edvard Munch found society to be an alienating nightmare to run away from;* Paul Gauguin left the Western world entirely, bolting from the crushing obligations of French family life to Tahiti, where he would paint the fifteen-year-old girls he slept with, standing in front of an unsullied paradise of green palms, white sand, and the blue South Pacific; Otto Modersohn and Paula Modersohn-Becker, both close to the arch-Romantic Rainer Maria Rilke, escaped into the sprawling northern German moor, much like their French forerunners of the Barbizon school, who moved into the Fontainebleau forest to paint nature up close, far from the corrupting influence of Parisian life with its machines, railroads, mills, and forges that were giving birth to a modern economy. In

* Munch's *The Scream*, of 1893, has become the quintessential image of modern despair and alienation. Luckily for the modern consumer, the work has been pressed into service in a swath of pop-culture pastiches and parodies. The ad campaign for *Home Alone* (1990) recapitulates *The Scream* in Macaulay Culkin's unforgettable face-grabbing. Horror-film director Wes Craven's *Scream* series (now on its fourth installment) stars a mysterious killer who dons the iconic mask modeled after the Munch painting. Munch's *Scream* has long adorned t-shirts and mugs announcing "horror" at Monday mornings, on a life-size inflatable punching-bag doll, and in tattoo form on marathon runner Andrea Bowman's leg to symbolize her "agonizing" workouts. But Munch's screamer's biggest gig has been as the TV pitchman for the 1997 Pontiac Sunfire. An image of the real car drives through a poorly animated spatial rendering of the Munch landscape as the Screamer's hands rise Culkinesquely to his cheeks. The voiceover says, "If you ever take your Pontiac Sunfire driving through some famous expressionist painting, it'll fit right in, because it looks like a work of art." The Screamer then checks out the car and gets in, driving off into the ochre landscape decked out in Ray-Ban sunglasses. The Pontiac Sunfire "drives like a real scream, starting at just $13,500." Modern life, it turns out, is much less alienating if you have a cool car.

Paris, Arthur Rimbaud and Paul Verlaine drank heavily, went to prison, ushered in a Symbolist revolution, and fought each other with a radical love that resulted in various *Illuminations*; later, Henri Matisse returned decisively to childhood innocence, play, *joie de vivre*, as well as to the Japanese and Asian otherness then in vogue; Maurice de Vlaminck and Fauvism radically offset the natural world's visual spectrum; Emil Nolde, Ernst Ludwig Kirchner, Wassily Kandinsky, Franz Marc, and Der Blaue Reiter in Germany celebrated the primeval vitality of children, fresh ways of seeing and making color, the beginning of truly nonrepresentational painting, and a grotesque expression of modern life and its sounds boiled down to the most rudimentary forms.

The reason for this tedious wealth of examples—and there are so many more—is to hear the echo of Jean-Jacques Rousseau and the subsequent Romantic impulse: go forward and leap toward vigilant, violent self-expression; stress your own experience over the alienating commercial and social developments surrounding your unique life. March inward and downward into yourself and then be that self in the world, regardless of what the world says about it. Look toward the outer margins of society for all that is real and irreducible, all that has yet to be contaminated by modernity. The ideal of sincerity—the raising up of the individual's truly felt, directly lived experience of the world, the state of consciousness pre-affect—courses through the veins of all of these modernist sensibilities, insisting artists, poets, philosophers, musicians, and writers flee the world and find themselves.

The modern artist was a new figure who was culturally permitted to say things prohibited to others, things that were dangerous and wild and true: "I can only advise you to consider whether all professions are not . . . full of demands, full of enmity against the individual," wrote Rilke in his touchstone *Letters to a Young Poet* (1908). The young recipient of these letters, Franz Xaver Kappus, had been uncertain about entering business and military service and had sent Rilke some of his own poems. Rilke, whose own Romantic lines abound with angels, roses, hearts, darkened landscapes, and Greek myth, responded in what would become a trope of authenticity: the true individual stands against a society filled with working stiffs who fulfilled their "mute and sullen humdrum duty."[2] But one need not be resentful, Rilke pleads, for "the world is not against us." Instead of fighting, the artist should "be solitary the way one was solitary as a child, when the grown-ups were around involved with things that seemed important" and look to the professional world "from out of the depth of one's own world," as "something unfamiliar," and to maintain a "wise incomprehension." Cultivating inwardness, innocence, wonder, and a gentle alienation was the way to remain truly human.

Not all Romantic cheerleaders of radical individualism at the end of the nineteenth century found refuge in this kind of soft sentiment. Friedrich Nietzsche, most notably, gave modern man a new commandment: "Be hard." Nietzsche's new hero was the *Übermensch,* the superman (or overman), that bygone Roman or Greek or barbarian of ruthless self-interest who had preceded the Christian categories of good and evil, the figure who followed the brutal rules of earth instead of cowing to the dictates of a fantastical afterlife. This superman, introduced in *The Joyful Wisdom* (1882), moved beyond the traditional world-picture of Christian morality and its childish stories, its dissatisfaction and resentment, its nagging sense of "conscience."

The Christian virtues of self-sacrifice, humility, honesty, sincerity, forbearance, and equality stemmed, Nietzsche believed, from a morality of slaves and the disenfranchised among whom Christianity had got its start: beggar women in the slums of Jerusalem. For Nietzsche, Christianity hangs on to its poverty-stricken origins and brings man down, destroying his strong native urges. Over a millennium of religiously inspired inner and outer punishment—guilt, beheading, war, burning, torture, confinement, all in the name of God's "higher order"—had domesticated Western man away from his deepest instincts and into a pathological passivity and deference. "[Christianity] has turned the world into a hospital in which everyone is sick," he wrote in the *The Joyful Wisdom*. Man had been neutered, and now the biological values of the past—self-triumph, winning, *survival*—had been made shameful. The resentful "Christian resolution to find the world ugly and bad," he wrote, "has made the world ugly and bad."[3]

Nietzsche's view of sincerity was obviously not the heartwarming kind that resulted in the unifying of human sentiment once the façades of society were stripped away, as Rousseau and his Romantic followers had believed. His unmasking of the hardened self revealed a dominating soul that would use any amoral trick or mask to take what it wanted. "I teach you the superman," he writes in *Thus Spoke Zarathustra* (1885). "Man is something to be overcome."[4] Success, strategy, brute power, warrior virtues, no holds barred: *that* is sincerity, *that* is saying what you really mean. All the rest is mewling and disingenuous self-deception. "The great man fights the elements in his time that hinder his own greatness," he wrote in *The Will to Power* (1901), "in other words: his own freedom and sincerity."[5] It was advice to be followed if Western man was to escape from the decadence of late nineteenth-century bourgeois culture. In *Untimely Meditations* (1876) he writes, "Everything that makes for sincerity is a further step toward true culture," and "the heroism of sincerity . . . [is that it] ceases to turn us into playthings of time."

Nietzsche also suggested the correlate to this new timbre of sincerity: the slave morality of the "dull Protestant mind" had created a society comprised of insincere Christianized shells.*

* While the young Nietzsche, a philologist and Greek scholar, thought highly of Luther, even saw himself as a quasi-inheritor of the rebellious German Protestant tradition set against the intellectual bondage of Catholicism—even as late as 1876—the older

The Christians' "will to illusion"—willing belief in the untrue—had in turn produced the vile falseness that permeated modern bourgeois society and its stinking aura of untruthfulness. It was this very falseness from which Romantics, starting with Rousseau, had long tried to escape with the internal aid of their hard-won sincerity. But, curiously, by denying all external sources of moral authority over one's own conscience, Protestant Christianity's logic eventually bites its own tail, such that "sincerity finally turns against morality itself." Nietzsche's analysis of this world-changing reversal was best paraphrased by the Frankfurt School philosopher Max Horkheimer, in 1947:

> By the very negation of the will to self-preservation on earth in favor of the preservation of the eternal soul, Christianity asserted the infinite value of each man. . . . The price was the repression of vital instincts, and since such repression is never successful, an insincerity pervades our culture.[6]

Western society is at root insincere because it has fully purchased the fantastic lie of Christian metaphysics: that God is beyond science; that he still somehow cares for and watches over you; that power does not actually rule; that loving your enemy will matter; that the meek shall inherit the earth; and that all of this belief will be rewarded in an afterlife. "Slow self-annihilation!" Nietzsche writes. The only way back to sincere, real life, to brutal truth, was to renounce this whole fetid illusion and learn to be an adult about things. "Let us consider this idea in its most terrifying form:

Nietzsche made jokes at the expense of that same tradition. "How much beer there is in Protestant Christianity!" he wrote in *The Will to Power.* "Can one even imagine a spiritually staler, lazier, more comfortably relaxed form of the Christian faith than that of the average Protestant in Germany?" (Number 89; March-June 1888). Elsewhere, in *Beyond Good and Evil* (1886), Nietzsche calls Protestantism that "sincere, austere slave-faith" that gave the world a "Luther [and] Cromwell, or some other northern barbarian of the spirit remained attached to his God and Christianity. . ."

Existence, as it is, without meaning or goal, but inescapable, recurrent, without a finale into nothingness. Those who cannot bear the sentence, 'There is no salvation,' *ought* to perish."[7]

For all his brilliant frothing, Nietzsche, who died insane in 1900, was reacting against a contemporary European social order, legal code, foreign policy, and regimes of punishment that were based on well-meaning Christian ideas. European nations still loudly proclaimed their Christian faith, indeed cited their Christian goals as a motivation for war or for expanding into colonial lands on darker-skinned continents that desperately needed Christ and even more desperately begged to be relieved of their natural resources. Wars that slaughtered tens of thousands were waged by leaders proclaiming to have God in their hearts. That iron-fisted Prussian Otto von Bismarck, a devout pietistic Protestant who hot-forged the German Empire, famously remarked, "A statesman . . . must wait until he hears the steps of God sounding through events, then leap up and grasp the hem of His garment," and, "No civilization other than that which is Christian is worth seeking or possessing." Western European leaders, ostensibly devout, had long fostered the frosty reality of national interest above all, particularly during the long and violent nineteenth century, which saw, in addition to the Napoleonic, Crimean, Italian, and Franco-Prussian wars, over three dozen other conflicts erupt from the Caucasus to Spain.

The ruling male personality type of the time was a well-tailored, bearded or mustachioed fellow of polished manners and military rank—think Austrian emperor Franz Joseph I, whose personal motto was "My trust in ancient virtue"—who perfectly fused two antagonistic personalities: the realist who had left behind good and evil, and the idealist whose hypermoralism was trotted out to guide society toward the higher national good. Even in declarations of war the rules of Christian politeness were to be observed. When they were, echoes of Ben Jonson's Tribulation

Wholesome could be heard: "Good brother, we must bend to all means to give furtherance to the holy cause." These men of the mid-nineteenth century were realist Christian Machiavellian nationalists who believed themselves to serve an authority higher than personal morality and who had learned to get their hands dirty: the open-eyed statecraft of Bismarck, Clausewitz, Metternich, and Talleyrand; the enormous reach of military and political empires German, Austrian, and British. They and the statesmen who followed in their footsteps harbored a worldly cynicism and an unemotional investment in universal "Christianization" by all means necessary.

While Christianity provided a nice mouthpiece for political leaders, by the end of the nineteenth century religion was actually in steep decline as a regulating force on the behavior of individuals. Despite the opposition to Darwin's "atheistic" theories and the multiple revival movements sweeping across United States (the Third Great Awakening, Jehovah's Witnesses, Mormonism, Nazarene, and Christian Science),[8] secularism, realism, and reason born of the Enlightenment had taken hold for good: praise be science, medicine, money, industrialization, war, and better weaponry. The material benefits and comforts of modern society were bringing people out of poverty and oppression, as well as creating, through industry, new global markets. All these factors led to the decline in religion as the dominant organizing force in Western culture, and they led Nietzsche to claim not only that God was dead but that, unlike God's earlier performance, he was never coming back to life.

But there actually was a way back to the spiritual sense in human life—not through God, but through art. "It is much more common for a person to appear to have character because he always acts in accord with his temperament," Nietzsche wrote in *Human, All Too Human* (1878), "rather than because he always acts in accord with his principles."[9] The British poet and critic

Matthew Arnold concurred, writing in his influential 1880 essay "The Study of Poetry" that "most of what now passes with us for religion and philosophy will be replaced by poetry." The Romantic temperament had led consistently to an obsession with all things not Christian and not bourgeois: the outcast and asocial; the insane; the childish; the wild, raw, and the untamed—all those who either cannot rightly understand God or who revolt against God's preordained order. Romanticism had been hollowed of its Christian core, but it retained some of its Christian values, and increasingly it is the figure of the artist who brings a new hope of escape from the corrupted present and into the realm of aesthetics, a kind of new religion.

The overtly religious impulse, however, did carry on into some later nineteenth-century art. Neo-romanticism, a movement appearing amidst the grave sincerity and moral dramas of Victorian era, was tinged with sentimentality and escapism. The Arts and Crafts movement, John Ruskin, Dante Gabriel Rossetti and the Pre-Raphaelites, William Morris, and Edward Burne-Jones all were backward-looking: fascinated by medieval revivalism, neo-Gothic architecture, a local sense of place and hominess, Renaissance tales, utopian landscapes and ruins, romantic love, the beauty of history, and the half-naked female figure. "If you want a golden rule that will fit everything, this is it," wrote William Morris. "Have nothing in your houses that you do not know to be useful or believe to be beautiful." Neo-romanticism, as such, represents the dying throes of the "man's core nature is good" argument. It fostered self-conscious innocence, a determined escape from the "ugliness" of modern society through an absolutely idealized return to the figures, practices, and forms of the past.

You did not necessarily have to make things in order to embrace this new kind of aesthetic living. Of primary importance was that you were dedicated to living a beautiful and original life. During the nineteenth century a new figure arose to provide a smiling antagonism to religion's stress on moral earnestness: the dandy. Originally seen in the Parisian *muscadins* and during the English Regency period in figures such as "Beau" Brummell (1778-1840), the dandy cultivated a kind of nostalgia for leisurely aristocratic life amidst the social leveling of the Industrial Revolution. Not really religious and certainly allergic to true belief, he was out instead to unleash a bemused elitism as a point of social protest against all things ugly that were transpiring in the world, be it industrialization or democracy. Mostly, he was against bad form.

More so, the dandy mocked what he saw as the empty lives of the bourgeois through his eccentric dress and behavior—or by acting just like them. Brummell, to use the example, was an immaculately shaved and tidy Oxford graduate with no particular interests who wore perfectly fitted coats over crisply starched linen shirts, set off by an elaborately knotted and tasteful cravat. He dressed like this as a statement against the wildly colorful velvets, lace, and breeches then fashionable. The dandy expressed himself through how he dressed. "A Dandy is a clothes-wearing Man," wrote Thomas Carlyle in *Sartor Resartus* (1838), his quasi-treatise on the meaning of clothes, "a Man whose trade, office, and existence consists in the wearing of Clothes." Every faculty of the dandy's "soul, spirit, purse, and person is heroically consecrated to this one object," he wrote: "The wearing of Clothes wisely and well: so that the others dress to live, he lives to dress." While taking infinite pains to appear in perfect form, he affected utter indifference to how he looked.

With impeccable manners and equipoise, the dandy harked back to Castiglione's sixteenth-century courtly gentleman. Yet in this deliberate aping of aristocratic manners, the dandy undercut the earnestness of the mores of the present, suggesting instead that it was all a farce. The French poet Charles Baudelaire said the dandy replaced the earnestness of religion by elevating "aesthetics into a living religion." This detachment, fostered by aesthetic cosmopolitans, gave rise to the figure of the *flâneur,* "a person who walks the city in order to experience it," as Baudelaire wrote. He was a stroller, a walker, an anonymous city-goer. Gustave Flaubert further cultivated the idea that this kind of distance was required to lead an aesthetic life. "The less [the artist] feels a thing, the better equipped he is to express it," he wrote in an 1871 letter. "But he must possess the ability to make himself feel it."[10] Pure, unbridled emotion, Flaubert thought, was not the hallmark of great genius; it was self-indulgent. Like science, literature and art must strive for impersonality in order to reach generality and truth.

As the century progressed and this distancing maneuver became a subculture unto itself, sincerity as the direct expression of one's truly felt feelings became gauche, plebian, and cliché, all of which Flaubert spent his life avoiding. His contemporary across the Channel, Oscar Wilde, would soon unleash acerbic maxims that further drove a wedge between personal appearance and intrapersonal reality. The old formula of having the inner match the outer was for the dandy bad and philistine form. "Man is least himself when he talks in his own person," Wilde blithely wrote. "Give him a mask and he will tell you the truth." Art was that mask that allowed for the expression of true things.

During the second half of the nineteenth century, the English working class had largely deserted the church. The upper classes had largely deserted it, too, and their ostensible Victorian piousness was essentially a social propriety. Wilde sensed the increasing hollowness of his countrymen's religious belief, and by becoming a virtuoso of social performance, by out-gentlemanning the gentleman, he mocked their manners and mores in near-perfect camouflage. "The first duty in life is to be as artificial as possible," he wrote in *Phrases and Philosophies for the Use of the Young* (1894).

True sincerity of belief worn by the middling classes as a mark of uprightness had become for Wilde and other professional dandies not only hollow but a mark of small-minded narcissism that, if not lorded over properly, could escape and wreak havoc. "A little sincerity is a dangerous thing," he famously observed in his 1888 essay "The Critic as Artist." "And a great deal of it is absolutely fatal."

Wilde thought that the urge to express one's true feelings in the manner of Rameau's nephew, or poets who spilled their souls onto the page, or musicians who scribbled overwrought compositions, had wilted into "all bad poetry." He saw interesting truths arising not from shedding the social mask and trying to get to the turbulent "real self" underneath, but from deliberately wearing an exaggerated mask—playfully, forcefully, scornfully—and unjoining genuine feeling from its direct expression in an act of engaged social antagonism. His antagonism toward respectable bourgeois values—duty, honor, religious faith, heterosexuality—caused him to be despised by many. His death in a Left Bank hotel in Paris at age forty-six, of meningitis, was met with particular relish, not least because his own forbidden sexuality had branded him a criminal in straitlaced Victorian England, from which he was ultimately exiled after serving time in Reading jail. The London *Times* obituary noted that the exiled playwright died "broken in health as well as bankrupt in fame and fortune. Death has soon ended what must have been a life of wretchedness and unavailing regret."[11] And the *New York Times,* enraptured by the notion that the artist should say what he really feels, opined that "as a dramatist, Wilde was hampered by his utter lack of sincerity and his inability to master the technical side of playwriting. But . . . his droll view of life made some of his plays rather effective with a limited audience."[12]

—

In the early 1900s, Walter Morgenthaler and Hans Prinzhorn—two psychiatrists, Swiss and German respectively—began taking an increased interest in their schizophrenic patients' drawings. Although there had been studies of the "art of the insane" since the end of the previous century, those were concerned solely with seeking a connection between aesthetic style and the symptoms of mental disease. Did schizoids paint differently from the maniacal? Did depressives scribble differently from the neurotic? Doctors ventured normative criteria for how patients employed perspective, proportion, scale, and color choice. Descriptors included "strange," "obscene," "erotic," and "incoherent."

Walter Morgenthaler did something different. He studied the work of a single patient, Adolf Wölfli, a violent, child-molesting psychotic with a balding pate and deep-set eyes who was often locked in solitary confinement. Morgenthaler had come to see his patient not just as a troubled person but as an artist of profound intensity: "Every Monday morning Wölfli is given a new pencil and two large sheets of unprinted newsprint. The pencil is used up in two days." Given this limited dispensation, Wölfli "often writes with pieces only five to seven millimeters long, and even with the broken-off points of lead, which he handles deftly, holding them between his fingernails."[13]

Permitted more art supplies—and the chewing tobacco he said helped him work better—Wölfli began to draw phantasmagorical scenes of nonexistent places—vast, sprawling, obsessively detailed fields of seemingly tiled or plated ground; rich vertical fields of color that reached to the very edges of the paper. Morgenthaler closely studied Wölfli's aesthetic style, located his iconographic motifs and recurring symbols, and explored the connections he made between word and image, color and emotion. Morgenthaler's unwearied study, begun in 1908, resulted in a groundbreaking book, *Ein Geisteskranker als Kunstler,* published in 1921. (It was published in English as *Madness and Art: The Life and Works of Adolf Wölfli.*) For the first time, the drawings of an insane person had been reclassified as art.*

In the following year, 1922, Hans Prinzhorn, a dashing young doctor who had been trained as an art historian and was working at a hospital in Heidelberg, completed a study called *Bildnerei der Geisteskranken* (*Artistry of the Mentally Ill*). In it he surveyed over five thousand artworks by 450 mentally ill patients throughout Europe: chewed bread and wooden sculptures by Karl Brendel in Germany; watercolors of violent biblical scenes by Peter Moog in the Netherlands; obsessive graphs, swirling skies, and scenes of knights battling the forces of evil. Prinzhorn's familiarity with the Munich avant-garde and their novel experiments with color and form—specifically in the new abstract works of Kandinsky and the haunted drawings of Alfred Kubin—led Prinzhorn to conclude that, when it came to looking at their works, there was little difference between the madman and the normal creative artist. One could only judge the aesthetic merits of the works themselves, not their origins. His exhaustive catalogue, like Morgenthaler's, raised the art of the insane to be on par with that of classically trained artists. Both books made an enormous impression on the European aesthetic vanguard, and soon artists such as Paul Klee were backhandedly praising their own work by saying, "The doctors are of the opinion that my paintings are basically the work of a sick person."[14]

Shortly after seeing Prinzhorn's book, the French artist Jean

* Attention to Wölfli has spiked in our postmodern-exhausted search for real and raw human artistic expression over the last decade. Aside from the American Folk Art Museum show, in New York, in 2003, there have been numerous retrospectives in the US and Europe, and at the Adolf Wölfli Foundation in Bern, Switzerland, the city where Wölfli was institutionalized and which houses the man's 25,000-page imaginary life story, which includes 1,600 illustrations and 1,500 collages, as well as other works by the mentally ill in the Morgenthaler Collection.

Dubuffet became obsessed with the "drawings, paintings, and all works of art emanating from obscure personalities, maniacs." While serving in the military in 1923 at the Eiffel Tower's meteorological center, he came across the notebooks of a "demented visionary" named Clémentine Ripoche, a woman who drew comical-looking clouds made of tanks and military processions and then interpreted what they meant. Her explanations were pure paranoid gibberish, but Dubuffet saw in her sketches and explanations—as well as in other works by mentally disturbed people he had begun to collect—a trove of "spontaneous impulses, animated by fantasy, even delirium." He corresponded with Ripoche for over a year, transcribed every letter she ever wrote to him, and watched as she slipped further away into dementia. Dubuffet eventually characterized her work, and all work born of the untrained eye and naïve emotional intensity, as *art brut*, or raw art. It was as if he had been reborn: after searching long for raw subjective expression, he had finally found it in "strangers to the beaten track of catalogued art," people who made art that stemmed from "pure and authentic creative impulses—where the worries of competition, acclaim, and social promotion do not interfere."[15] Dubuffet would fashion his own visual aesthetic to suggest someone who had lost his mind.*

Klee, Kandinsky, Dubuffet, and their comrades pounced on what they saw as a fresh way out of deadened aesthetic forms following the unbelievable horror of the First World War, which had destroyed the notion of innate human goodness and the idea that scientific progress was leading mankind out of darkness.[16] Klee kept a copy of Prinzhorn's book in his studio, and the art theory courses he taught at the Bauhaus, alongside other giants of

* While once stunning in its difference, outsider art has now been converted into a successful art-marketing category: the Outsider Art Fair has taken place in New York since 1992. The Museum of Bad Art, which exhibits art made far outside the halls of art schools and the gallery system, opened in Boston in 1994 and now resides in the cushy commuter suburb of Needham.

modernism in the 1920s, emphasized the importance of spontaneity and regaining a childlike perception of the world. Kandinsky, in his own writings, stressed not only the importance of looking at the world anew, but of cultivating a trove of new emotions that "only art can divine, which only art can express by the means of expression which are hers alone."

Because the sensitive artist was "a seer of the decadence of the spiritual atmosphere" and "a reformer," it was only the artist who would lead humanity out of the "terrible atmosphere of empty desolation" and into the "spiritual in art."[17] Children and the insane—and the artist as reformer and seer—were innocent of the mustard gas, biological warfare, mass executions, and limb-severing shrapnel that had destroyed the ideals of the civilized West. The sincere ideal that had once found a home in religious affections was relocated in the spontaneous visual expression of those untouched by sanctioned aesthetic styles and academic training. To have studied to become an artist, to have learned how to draw and paint, were limitations on the inherently free creative mind. To have skill was to have participated in the falsified institutionalization of human creativity. As the surrealist leader André Breton would observe, only insanity guaranteed "total authenticity."[18]

Klee, Kandinsky, and Dubuffet were joined in their celebration by Jean Arp, Marc Chagall, Emil Nolde, Oscar Kokoschka, Joan Miró, Max Ernst, Pablo Picasso, Henri Matisse, Gabriele Münter, Ernst Ludwig Kirchner, and Lyonel Feininger, just to name a few. Not surprisingly, these same artists would later be included in the Nazis' *Entartete Kunst* (Degenerate Art) exhibition in 1937. Alongside their works, Nazi officials included drawings and paintings by none other than the mentally ill themselves. Whereas the artists' motivation for looking to the insane was to escape depleted aesthetic forms and find new ways of expression, the Nazis' comparison was made in order to show the "Jewish infiltration" of German culture and the utterly unsalvageable decadence of modernism.

The exhibition, which opened in Munich on July 19, 1937, contained some 650 paintings, sculptures, prints, and books "borrowed" from the collections of thirty-two German museums. The exhibition remained on view until November 30, and then traveled to eleven other cities in Germany and Austria, accompanied by propaganda that explained how modernism was a Jewish-Bolshevik conspiracy hell-bent on destroying the purity of German culture. Of the 112 artists in the show, six were Jewish.

The timbre of sincerity at the beginning of the twentieth century relied upon the peculiar combination of Nietzsche's reframing of sincerity as the brutal, dominating instinct repressed by sham Christianity, Wilde's mocking of sugary emotion, and the curious fascination with insanity as artistically authentic. Rather than suggesting that the goodness of humanity would rise up if the shackles of civilization were cast off, this new Nietzsche-dandy-insanity continuum insisted that the selfish and cunning soul, given its choice, would finally come and take what it wanted without excuse or apology. Stripped of the niceties of life, or simply laughing them out of their own home, this conflation of forces had an influence on none other than Sigmund Freud, who ultimately reframed human behavior as motivated by darkly tumultuous forces. The "unconscious" was unavailable to the conscious mind. The sincerity-seeking Rousseau had feared as much in his later years, noting that as hard as we may look, there would always be something "hidden about ourselves."

Freud's ideas radically reconfigured the Protestant notion of a place inside that was more "primary" than other conscious parts. The traditional "holy space" reserved for the reception and discovery of God was supplanted by the very un-Christian drives for sex, violence, death, and pleasure. Thanks to the ego, according to Freud, the expression of these drives on the social level is mediated and dulled through art, language, and other psycho-strategic formulations. Freud's theory of society recapitulates, at its core, the Rousseauian model of the freedom-desiring individual versus oppressive civilization. His 1930 essay *Civilization and Its Discontents* admits, "Our civilization is largely responsible for our misery."[19] But where Rousseau insisted that unsocialized man was good, innocent, and happy, Freud shows him to be a homicidal little beast who wants to have sex with his mother and murder his father. But, unlike for Rousseau, for Freud civilization is not "bad"; rather, it is necessary to keep man's brutality in check. Culture is what results from the sublimation of all our repressed desires and frustrations, which is why we are attracted to art; in it, we recognize the things we otherwise cannot say or do. In art we may recognize our sincerest selves.

At the same time, this creates some problems for the notion of sincerity. Freud insists that whenever we go deep enough inside (for example, through psychoanalysis), we will always find the same antisocial desires for sex and violence. And though they will manifest themselves in person-specific narratives and symbolism, these drives are the same in everyone. Our projection of a warm, kind, Christian goodness into the world is thus a necessarily insincere act, a promotion of how we would like to be but not how we deep-down actually are. The ego constructs this proper, social self—a superego—for us and keeps the darker, libidinal forces at bay. In Freud, the only part of the self that is not aware of itself, that acts without our control or conscious oversight—the id—is truly sincere.[20] Given this model, sincerity is impossible unless you are a sociopath.

From afar, the surrealist poet and theorist André Breton thought that Freud was a liberator of dreams and of the unconscious powers of the mind, the "greatest psychologist of our time," a genius madman. Though Breton had yet to read any of Freud's books (though several had recently been translated into French), he'd read a summary of Freud's ideas found in two compendiums, *Précis de Psychiatrie* and *La Psychanalyse*. Bedazzled, a few months later, in October 1921, he arrived at Freud's apartment in Vienna.

First lament: Freud's plain bourgeois quarters were located in a boring part of the city. Second: he came to the door dressed in a three-piece tweed suit, his beard perfectly groomed and his manners impeccable. He was, in all affect, the perfect gentleman. Breton was deeply disappointed. He later described Freud as "an old man without elegance who receives [patients] in the poor consulting room one would expect from a local doctor." Even worse, Freud was not sympathetic to Breton's novel experiments in "automatic writing." These neurotic scribblings by returning World War I soldiers wracked by shell shock had obsessed Breton when he was a medical psychiatry student in Nantes. He believed the writings bubbled up from a more fundamental and therefore truer place than the conscious mind could access. Regardless of his enthusiasm, Breton was unable to engage the professorial Freud in any significant way, and Freud ducked behind polite generalities. Legend has it that when Breton pressed Freud about how he could go on so much about the wild and liberated unconscious but be such a boring bourgeois stiff, Freud, ever the well-bred European, simply said, "My dear man, just because we know now that the unconscious exerts a power over us, does not mean we have to live by it."[21]

Despite Freud's indifference, Breton remained full of enthusiasm for automatic writing and the meaning of dreams—the images that arose out of the depths when the conscious mind went on break. Here, at last, was an infinite trove of new meanings to be discovered and interpreted, a veritable Pandora's box of explosively anti-rational forces. But dreams without their dreamers meant nothing to Freud, a point he made clear every time Breton unsuccessfully solicited him to write something about the surrealists' interest in the "meaning of dreams."* A collection of random dreams "without the connected association, without knowledge of the circumstances under which it has been dreamt," Freud wrote, "does not have any meaning to me, and I can barely imagine what it would mean to others."[22]

André Breton and the surrealists—inheritors of the great Romantic celebration of the untamed, uncensored, spontaneous, superego-skirting mind—obviously disagreed. Dreams not only meant symbolic sorts of things, they also meant, more generally, spontaneity, free association, escape from the burden of oppressive rationality and order. Surrealists championed the unleashing of irrationality and surprise upon the world, setting out to shock the bourgeois public and disturb the orderliness of daily life—and of the aesthetic dominance of other European movements then underway: the Bauhaus and constructivism; the domestic ornament of Art Deco; the anti-subjectivity of de Stijl. To be surrealist meant to rebel against artistic propriety and authority, against training and skill, to assert the irrational self; it meant making things that were deliberately ugly or aesthetically painful: Hugo Ball's torturously deformed dolls, Buñuel's famed sliced eyeball; Max Ernst's monsters; Dalí's sexualized landscapes; Giorgio de Chirico's eerie non-places; Méret Oppenheim's fur-covered teacup (wildness reclaiming civilized dining).

Decorum and protocol were supplanted by transgression and symbolic violence. "We are still living under the reign of logic, but the logical processes of our time apply only to the solution of problems of secondary interest," reads the first line of the *First Surrealist*

* It was not until Freud met Salvador Dalí that he became interested in anything the surrealists were doing. "Until now," Freud wrote to a friend, "I have been inclined to regard the surrealists . . . as complete fools. That young Spaniard, with his candid, fanatical eyes and his undeniable technical mastery has changed my estimate." But Freud, like future critics, saw through the surrealists' perfectly contrived, orderly irrationality: "In classical paintings, I look for the unconscious. In a surrealist painting, for the conscious." (Both quotes from Gamwell, *Dreams*.)

Manifesto, published in 1924. The finer European sensibility was to be razed—religion, politics, sexual mores, authority, rationality, control, the law. "Perhaps the imagination is on the verge of recovering its rights," the *Manifesto* offers. The rebellion against established order was, in a way, retaliation for Europeans having thrown their entire continent into an insane and horrific war by the most rational means of science and strategy. It was only by upsetting the bourgeois world order that something more real and true, some fundamental part of human nature, could come bubbling to the surface.

The allure of this kind of subjective, "authentic" expression at the heart of European modernism was positively magnetic. It had become increasingly so after the 1913 Armory Show in New York City, which brought the European avant-garde to an American audience in order to "lead the public taste in art, rather than follow it." The works of Paul Cézanne, Marcel Duchamp, Matisse, Francis Picabia, and Picasso were exhibited alongside those of Americans including George Bellows, Joseph Stella, Mary Cassatt, and Marsden Hartley. The juxtaposition was extreme. The art from Europe looked nothing like its American counterpart, which somehow no longer seemed new or modern. American figurative art was immediately pushed back on its heels, its practitioners issuing pamphlets and essays in defense of their tradition. "I have no fear that our kind of art will prevail or even that it can long endure," nervously wrote the artist Kenyon Cox. He was sure that abstraction and intentional ugliness were nothing but fads—against which he promptly argued in a book-length polemic. In *Concerning Painting* (1917), Cox reasoned:

> For at least fourteen thousand years, from the time of the cavemen to our own day, painting has been an imitative art, and it seems likely that it will continue to be so. That it should, within

> a few years, entirely reverse its current, and should flow in the opposite direction for thousands of years to come seems highly improbable, not to say incredible.[23]

Cox's side, of course, would not triumph. Nonrepresentational work had something to say about the oddness of the contemporary world, something that straightforward image-making could not harness. That same year, over 2,500 works by 1,300 artists were exhibited at the Grand Central Palace in New York City at the Society of Independent Artists show. Among the works was one sculpture that would change the notion of art (and the importance of sincere artistic intention) forever: Marcel Duchamp's *Fountain*, exhibited under the pseudonym Richard Mutt.

The work was nothing more than an industrially-produced urinal placed upon a pedestal. The Society initially rejected it, but the decision only set off a discursive furor in American art criticism about the meaning of art, the role of the artist, and the very definition of art itself. At stake in the debate among the Society of Independent Artists' board members (one of which was Duchamp before he resigned when the work was rejected) was the artists' "sincerity" in exhibiting *Fountain*. Most of the board of directors did not know whether Richard Mutt was a real person, so a few of them proposed inviting him to give a lecture about the importance of art and to explain his intentions. Were they "sincere or done out of bravado?", as one director, Katherine Sophie Dreier, asked. Alas, Richard Mutt never accepted the offer.

Publicity about the "sculpture" intensified, however, and when it was exhibited and subsequently photographed at Alfred Stieglitz's 291 gallery (shortly before its mysterious disappearance), some forward-looking minds began to question the distinction between art and the most common aspects of human life. What is it that actually makes an art object more valuable than some ordinary thing? In an issue of the art journal *The Blind Man*, critic Beatrice Wood suggested:

> Whether Mr. Mutt made the fountain with his own hands or not has no importance. He CHOSE it. He took an article of life, placed it so that its useful significance disappeared under the new title and point of view—created a new thought for that object. To raise something up for aesthetic value was simply an act of doing so.[24]

Sincerity of intention—the idea that one earnestly wished to have an object from the world reconsidered as art—came to trump hundreds of years of academic practice and training in the arts, a practice that found itself now relegated to the category of craft. One hears echoes of Wordsworth and his insistence that sincerity in art is more important than skill. Technique and mastery were learnable, yes; but making art came from lacerating old concepts and unveiling new ones, from really meaning the idea. Hello, conceptual art.

That *Fountain* was "ready-made" was not just some half-assed trick; it stemmed also in part from Duchamp's true awe of modern industry. In 1912, as he walked along the rows of new motors at the Salon de la Locomotion Aerienne with fellow artists Fernand Léger and Constantin Brancusi, he turned to Brancusi, Léger later recalled, and said outright, "Painting is finished. Who can do better than a propeller? Tell me, can you do that?"[25] By the end of the year, Duchamp had virtually stopped painting.

The shift from an artist making to an artist choosing was an expression of the growing modernist cult of the artist as magical Midas, as alchemist, as a seer and reformer of worlds. To reach into everyday objects and simply touch them was to elevate the commonplace and, as some critics noted, to devalue the realm of fine art. Moreover, it showed just how much power the artist-as-authentic-being had garnered since the word had come into existence in 1823. The artist, as the German sculptor and aesthetic revolutionary Joseph Beuys would later epitomize, was a kind of shaman, a seer of worlds otherwise invisible in everyday life—and he offered a way back to a charmed existence. With the Society of Independent Artists' show in 1917, the radical aesthetic impulse that had begun in Paris and Berlin had come to American artists and critics—and to the commercial world they lived in.

In 1917, American advertising was on the upswing of power and influence as a generation helped to keep the national economy productive in order to supply the fighting forces in Europe with food, clothes, and materiel. President Woodrow Wilson addressed advertisers specifically in a proclamation of April 15, 1917: "All advertising agencies . . . would perhaps render a very substantial and timely service to the country if they would give [this proclamation] widespread repetition." With a booming economy in the war and immediate postwar years, increasing numbers of people could afford to go shopping, and modern art provided a template for hungry advertisers. "I believe in the next few years we shall see a much finer type of art used in advertising," said Nathaniel Pousette-Dart, a Minnesota-born art director, artist, and critic. "The artist will be able to express himself *sincerely*," he continued, "[and] not be forced, as he is today, to work within the scope of a bag of tricks."[26]

Art directors from across the United States saw that their staid profession could benefit from some of the raw life provided by imported European modern art, as well as homegrown bohemian culture, jazz and swing, and their liberation from Victorian emotional heaviness. Representing products as new and enlivened would appeal to consumers who wanted to feel the same way. Women were smoking (and, thanks to the Nineteenth Amendment, voting), fashion was moving markets, and regimes of taste were giving increased sway to how individuals wanted to be seen.

The Romantic ideal of expressing one's unique self would fuse with the commercial world to better charm consumers with an irresistible aura of uniqueness.

The advertising-as-art debate came to a head during the 1920s and 1930s as art directors considered whether advertisements should display the illustrator's signature. The signature reflected a Romantic ideology of individual authenticity, yet an artist who signed his work asserted an authorship that was at odds with the basic purpose of mass advertising of uniformly made products. Nevertheless, illustrators were increasingly encouraged to "let loose" and to express themselves more freely, even though some felt that commercial art was a bad influence on their more serious work. Pousette-Dart told an art appreciation class he taught that this view was wrong: "Commercial Art, properly approached," he said, "can improve, rather than injure, the ability to create pure art." A distinctive illustrative style would lead to a "hallmark of individuality." The commercial artist was to be celebrated for expressing his "unique inner self," which is why his artistic creations "must be sincere."[27]

The Rousseauian-Romantic trope of pre-civilized man also began appearing in advertisements in the 1920s. It appealed to consumers' libidinal core while simultaneously offering new products that lamented the decadence of the modern life that made those products possible. Ipana toothpaste, for example, suggested the ill effects of modern luxury by showing a restaurant peopled with ladies languishing at the foreground table and a Rubenesque couple in the background, attended to by a portly waiter. "Eating today is a *lazy* pleasure," the ad read; modern eating habits were bad for your teeth. Another Ipana ad shows a dainty blonde gnawing on an entire beef shank. The copy: "Terrible! - Say the Books of Etiquette" but "Excellent! - Says Dental Authority." Grape Nuts famously went back to "Nature's plan" by making your jaw and innards "do hard work—and plenty of it." An advertisement for

E. Squibb pharmaceuticals deplored how "Man, in his struggle to be civilized, became his own arch-enemy," and accusingly asserted that "Civilization has *cheated* you . . . Your intestines have gone lazy." Dentyne gum offered a way back to mandibular vigor by introducing a "natural new health habit"—chewing an admixture of polyethylene and polyvinyl acetate flavored to taste like spearmint leaf—in order to "correct the mistakes of civilization." On the other end of the alimentary canal, Fleischmann's yeast announced that constipation was "civilization's greatest curse" and offered civilized shoppers the cure. Likewise, Post Bran Flakes and Whole Bran both aimed to restore consumers to regularity with a pre-civilization diet, encouraging modern ladies to get plenty of roughage and to "get slim, radiant—and eat like a cave woman."[28]

It was still rare for photography to be used in advertising in the 1920s. Only around 6 percent of national ads in newspapers featured them, and magazines used them just as infrequently. But by the end of the decade, as prices dropped during the Depression, photography made enormous inroads in the advertising world. Advertisers eventually discovered that photographs permitted a greater degree of "reality." "Buyers do not question photographic evidence of merit," wrote the Photographers' Association of America to its advertising clients. "They believe what the camera tells them because they know that nothing tells the truth so well."[29] Though photography employed distortion, lighting, scale, and abstraction, art directors never tired of emphasizing its "sincerity" to potential clients. Inspired by the Romantic artist who dared to express his particular vision, and by new European ideas of what art was actually for, American advertising photographers were inspired by admen to gaze at their subjects "unconventionally," to try out new ways of seeing. Under this hazy artistic aspiration the difference between artifice and realism became so blurred that a columnist at the advertising industry journal *Printer's Ink* could write, in April 1930, "Moods are not easily manufactured. If they are to appeal to the reader as genuine and unposed, they should be based on absolute sincerity. Thus the special staging."[30]

When the anti-artifice impulse of the avant-garde is encroached upon by the advertising world, the avant-garde must seek newer paths to originality—or at least, for the time being, try not to look so much like advertising. The literary urban dweller of the 1920s viewed commercialism as the nefarious nexus of society and money, the two prime perpetrators of insincerity and inauthenticity. Early twentieth-century "hep" subcultures assumed the old Romantic position: reminding the white middle class of their spiritually blind trade-offs.

Greenwich Village in the 1920s was, of course, the locus of American bohemia. Writers, actors, artists, and idealists alike shoved in alongside one another to experience the burgeoning cultural force of Gotham following the 1913 Armory Show. Critics and writers such as Randolph Bourne, Mabel Dodge, Floyd Dell, Eugene O'Neill, and Edna St. Vincent Millay (who wrote that her time in New York was "very, very poor, and very, very merry") forged a life of chic urban poverty and self-assured creativity. They read and published in small literary magazines like *The Seven Arts*, *The Masses*, and *The Dial* (whose first editor was writer and women's advocate Margaret Fuller, the first female permitted to use Harvard College's library). Central to their sense of living bohemian was that it kept one closer to the hard realities of life—and in so doing kept one young and sincere. Randolph Bourne praised the virtue in his essay "Youth and Life," writing, in 1913, that sincerity was that ability "to keep one's reactions warm and true . . . the secret of perpetual youth [and] salvation." It might be said that an intellectual and literary enclave formed itself around this sentiment and in resistance to the commercialism that was raising American standards of living to unprecedented levels.

While the Harlem Renaissance showed white bohemians that authentic living was to be found in black otherness, the movement's own artists, writers, and intellectuals—Jacob Lawrence, Langston Hughes, Countee Cullen, Mary White Ovington, Alain Locke, W. E. B. Du Bois—developed original critical and poetic voices that had previously been entirely silenced in America; they now leaped into the world like fire. Hughes's 1926 essay "The Negro Artist and the Racial Mountain" offered a curt yet proud sentiment that would become something of a banner:

> The younger Negro artists who create now intend to express our individual dark-skinned selves without fear or shame. If white people are pleased we are glad. If they are not, it doesn't matter. We know we are beautiful. And ugly, too.

Harlem was also the portal through which jazz, blues, and ragtime were pumped into Manhattan from Chicago, New Orleans, and Birmingham. A whole generation of sympathetic white newcomers was awed and moved as dances such as the foxtrot, bunny hop, black bottom, and Charleston (derived from an Ashanti ancestor dance) brought black and white steppers together swaying and swinging to the hybrid sounds of the New York night. On August 10, 1920, Mamie Smith recorded "Crazy Blues," sliding music out on a shellacked plate and selling 75,000 copies in the first month, one million within the year.[31] The combination of technology, advertising, and the yearning for new aesthetic experiences was going to mean big money for a lot of people. This "birth of the cool," the marriage of cultural black and white, is the creation of perhaps the first truly authentic American culture, a marriage that would come to dominate the entire Western cultural world—and beyond—by the end of the century.[32]

While the artists and writers of the Harlem Renaissance were reacting to generations of oppression and disenfranchisement, their white urban counterparts were reacting in part to the Gilded Age success ethic and the posthumous popularity of Horatio Alger's ideal of the self-made man. The notion of success in America was tied to active moral character rather than passive inheritance of wealth. At its core, this ethic insisted that God chooses to bestow plenty on those he deems morally worthy. Upward mobility, devotion to material success, and conspicuous consumption were promoted in part by Christian self-help books, many of which stressed a new morality of acquisitiveness and the piety of getting ahead. Books like Frank Haddock's *Power for Success through Culture of Vibrant Magnetism, Business Power, Practical Psychology,* and *Power of Will* outlined psychological and emotional disciplines that would help one to convey an air of achievement and naturalness. Exercise No. 10 in *Power of Will* reads: "Stand erect. Summon a sense of resolution. Absorbed in self, think calmly but with power these words, 'I am standing erect. All is well! I am conscious of nothing but good!' Attaining the Mood indicated, walk slowly and deliberately about the room."[33]

In 1925, a hymn to the God of American business called "A Man's Thanksgiving" appeared in the advertising publication *The Jaqua Way*:

God of businessmen, I thank thee for
the fellowship of red-blooded men
with songs in their hearts and
handclasps that are sincere;
I thank thee for the telephones and
telegrams that link me with home
and office, no matter where I am.
I thank Thee for children, friendships,
books, fishing, the game of golf,
my pipe, and the open fire on a
chilly evening. Amen.

In the context of Calvin Coolidge's comment that "the chief business of the American people is business," figures like the feverishly Christianity-and-business proselytizer Bruce Barton pointed his paeans to sincere salesmanship directly at the readers of *Jaqua Way,* who took them to heart. "Jesus would be a national advertiser," Barton wrote in his bestselling book *The Man Nobody Knows* (1925), urging admen and salesmen to take pride in the ultimate piety of their endeavor. "Sincerity glistened like sunshine through every sentence [Jesus] uttered," he wrote. Likewise, "the advertisements which persuade people to act are written by men with . . . a deep sincerity regarding the merits of the goods they have to sell."[34] Copywriters, too, had to really mean what they were writing—and to mean it with panache! After all, Barton writes, "Jesus hated prosy dullness."

In part as a reaction to what bohemian types saw as an ersatz ethos of happiness and the bizarre marriage of religious faith with consumerism, the 1910s and 1920s witnessed the birth of modern American cynicism. The novels of Theodore Dreiser, Jack London, and Frank Norris showed the darker side of achievement: anxiety, status obsession, chronic and inexplicable unhappiness. "Our civilization is still in a middle stage," Dreiser wrote, "scarcely beast, in that it is no longer wholly guided by instinct; scarcely human, in that it is not yet wholly guided by reason." Cynicism toward success, which William James had called, in a 1906 letter to H. G. Wells, America's "bitch-goddess" and "our national disease," was a way to get at the real effects of an ethic that consumed American life at the expense of, as some saw, actual happiness, wisdom, and sincerity. Cynical mind-sets in art and literature provided a counterweight to the romantic escapes of advertising, the false reality of the camera, the profit-mongering of management executives, and the moral blindness of Americans who struggled for success at all costs.

In critic Harold Stearns's *Civilization in the United States, An*

Inquiry by Thirty-six Americans (1922), a sample of Village bohemians delivered a verdict on the state of mainstream America: the country lacked emotion; Americans were hypocritical and shallow and cared nothing for culture; American values were misplaced in purely commercial activity. Sure, communism and socialism were alluring counter-ideologies, but the only way for the individual to truly maintain sanity in such a world was to move to Europe, which Stearns and others did, settling in Paris in the past and future footsteps of their countrymen Ernest Hemingway, F. Scott Fitzgerald, Archibald MacLeish, James Baldwin, Ezra Pound, Gertrude Stein, and T. S. Eliot (who himself, like Flaubert, wrote *against* sincere expression: "Poetry is not a turning loose of emotion, but an escape from emotion; it is not the expression of personality, but an escape from personality."[35]) As the ideological battles of the twentieth century were getting underway, not everyone was partisan. The Lost Generation was on the side only of themselves and their art. "The events of 1919 left us cynical rather than revolutionary," Fitzgerald wrote about the end of the First World War and the Russian Revolution. "It was characteristic of the Jazz Age that it had no interest in politics at all."[36]

Well, some people of the Jazz Age. H. L. Mencken, the first American to translate Nietzsche and the first person to write a book about him in English, in 1908, was emblematic of the growing cynical stance, albeit of the more journalistically and politically engaged kind. A wealthy bachelor and columnist at the *Baltimore Sun*, Mencken castigated his contemporaries in publishing and politics for a spectrum of idiocies, including their rampant religious fanaticism: "A church is a place in which gentlemen who have never been to heaven brag about it to persons who will never get there." He unleashed columns, magazines, and book upon book that set out to take down all species of American stupidity and fawningly fake Christianity. Cynical criticism was a way to keep the country honest. The fittingly anti-sincere subtitle of the literary magazine he edited with the writer George Jean Nathan, *The Smart Set,* announced it as "A Magazine of Cleverness." (It folded in 1930 just shortly after the return to national seriousness, the Great Crash.) Upon discovering the work of Mencken, the young Richard Wright gushed, "I pictured the man as a raging demon . . . laughing at the weaknesses of people, mocking God, authority. . . . He was using words as a weapon, using them as one would use a club."[37] Reading Mencken made Wright want to become a writer against the society that he felt had rejected him.

Dorothy Parker sang a curmudgeonly, esteem-razing solo, too, observing, "If you want to know what God thinks of money, just look at the people he gave it to." The perpetually sozzled W. C. Fields blasted middle-class values with barbs like "Anyone who hates children and animals can't be all bad," and "I am free of all prejudices. I hate everyone equally." And Ambrose Bierce offered the entire world seen through the cynic's eye in *The Devil's Dictionary* (1911), originally published as *The Cynic's Word Book* in 1906. The paper trail back to original Protestantism is difficult to miss: "Rite: A religious or semi-religious ceremony fixed by law, precept, or custom with the essential oil of sincerity carefully squeezed out of it." (Bierce, by the way, in the entry for "Seal," also makes note of the apocryphal Roman origins of the word "sincere," *sine cera,* for "without wax.")

Subsequent to its Nietzschean lashings, sincerity had for some become a suspicious moral demand. Just three years after Nietzsche's death, the Irish dramatist George Bernard Shaw had in 1903 staged his four-act play *Man and Superman,* which announced sincerity's tarnished charm: "It is dangerous to be sincere, unless you are also stupid." The death knell of a Romanticism that yearned for soft, understanding sincerity was sounded by Jacques Rivière (whose own journals bespeak an intense devotion to the sincere ideal), who wrote in the mid-1920s, "Romanticism is not only an art that is out of style. It is in truth an inferior art, a sort of monster in the history of literature. . . . We have nothing but a façade before us."[38] By 1930, even that silver-haired model of proper British intellectualism, Bertrand Russell, would rejoice in an attitude that had felled the propped-up abstractions of Religion, Nation, Progress, Beauty, and Truth in his "On Youthful Cynicism." "Any person who visits the Universities of the Western world is liable to be struck by the fact that the intelligent young of the present day are cynical to a far greater extent than was the case formerly," Russell wrote. "In the old days it was possible to worship truth," he snarkily remarks. (Wait for it . . .) "Indeed the sincerity of the worship was demonstrated by the practice of human sacrifice."

Following the moral catastrophe and horror of the Second World War, European cynicism toward public and political statements became all the more rampant. And even as Americans rejoiced in their victory over fascism in Europe, they were anxious at home about how they appeared to others. True, businesses were hiring and the postwar economy was booming. But this also meant that neighbors were watching and, regardless of your woes, it was time to put on a happy face. The continuing popularity of Dale Carnegie's 1936 *How to Win Friends and Influence People* was evidence of the instrumentalization of friendliness in the service of personal gain. One of the book's "fundamental techniques of handling people" was, "Give honest and sincere appreciation."

Literary cynicism in America, despite the whirling economy and increased standard of living for millions, continued to condemn the culture of fakeness. Its most quotable zenith is Holden Caulfield's indignant declaration, "I hate phonies," which his creator J. D. Salinger aimed straight at the blight of the success-personality and the spontaneity-crushing adult he saw sweeping postwar America. The six-foot-two, gray-haired teenager hero—alienated, angry, alternately cynical and hopeful—yearns only to protect authentic, un*adult*erated life; to be a "catcher in the rye" standing at the ready to clutch children fallen from the cliff at the end of a rye field, saving their metaphorical youth from obliteration. The only person Caulfield can talk to is his younger sister, Phoebe. But when Holden realizes that he cannot save even her from growing up, he lands temporarily in an institution. At the end of the book, his cynical guardedness recommends a stance of a-sincerity to the coming generations of high-school English students: "Do not tell anybody anything," he warns; "if you do, you start missing everybody."

The most blistering critique of the 1940s' and 1950s' American success culture came, of course, from the Beats: Allen Ginsberg, Jack Kerouac, William S. Burroughs, Neal Cassady. All were influenced to some degree by the depressed postwar European existentialist philosophy then being furiously translated into English: Nietzsche, Kierkegaard, Heidegger, Jaspers, Sartre, Fromm, and Camus. The existentialists themselves echoed the moral imperatives of their own French tradition: Rousseau and the salvation offered by authenticity. They advocated confronting the darker side of life head-on and having the "courage to be," as the title of a 1952 book by the American existentialist theologian Paul Tillich declared. The inauthentic person, the Beats believed, was cowardly in facing up to the hard facts of his own identity, of living up to who he actually was. This inauthentic person did not live the life that had been determined for him from inside, by its own inner logic, but rather from the dictates hurled upon him by advertising, religion, tradition, and the demands of the labor market. This was the situation of the "mass man," the Beats and existentialists railed, and he was condemned as an unfree being, as a person living under the sugary illusion of freedom. This is the existentialist critique of the modern personality, who exemplified what the German exile philosopher Herbert Marcuse would call "one-dimensional man."

Jean-Paul Sartre's *Being and Nothingness*, published in 1943, had a strong—albeit cryptic and prolix—influence on Beat ways of thinking and living. "What *are we* then if we have the constant obligation to make ourselves what *we are* if our mode of being is having the obligation to be what we are?," Sartre asked. "Being is consciousness of being," he replied. This abstract observation had a striking consequence for sincerity: to be conscious of one's sincerity necessarily makes one insincere. To deny this basic and insurmountable insincerity constituted what he famously called *mauvaise foi*, bad faith, "a lie to oneself in the unity of a single consciousness." Bad faith is the uncritical acceptance of the guise one wears as a social character, of the social categorization of one's formal identity. This is the inauthentic man; man defined by what he does, where he lives, where he is from; man who willingly wears a mask and is convinced it is himself; man who does not see himself as a subjective agent ultimately alone and unique—free—but rather as determined purely by his conditions. A person who lives in bad faith cannot or will not transcend the role he has been given in order to see his life in the broader context of human existence, which, in the end, is meaningless.

The sincere man, however, as writers stretching back to Montaigne had discerned, is engaged in a ceaseless search for his own motives, his own true desires. But since, in Sartre's psychology, a person is always more than what he imagines himself to be, even his belief that he can be sincere in discovering his motives is illusory: "The essential structure of sincerity does not differ from that of bad faith," Sartre writes, because "constant sincerity" is a "constant effort to adhere to oneself." And this, he concludes, results in "a constant effort to dissociate oneself from oneself," or to take oneself as both object and subject at the same time. Sincerity for Sartre is an unachievable state. The fundamental nature of man is that he is insincere in all things.

What mattered most to the Beats was less the achievement of

sincerity than the authenticity of personal experience—the radical opposite of what they saw transpiring in American life. Consequently, they embraced everything and anything opposite. Ken Kesey's *One Flew Over the Cuckoo's Nest* (1962) relocates authentic life, as André Breton and the surrealists had done, to the inside of a mental asylum—and identifies true freedom with the figure of the Native American, Chief Bromden, the only person in the story to actually escape (alive). Beats too sought escape, in roaming movement—as in *On the Road* and the Merry Pranksters' bus—instead of immovable sobriety and uprightness; they sought poverty instead of money, decadence and intoxication over "getting ahead," and, above all, the freedom found in the sacrilege of immediate pleasure and in saying real things to a culture they thought was thoroughly "bullshit." Beat poet Amiri Baraka saw his comrades as living in the wreckage of a civilization. These new Romantics both were and sought the cultural outsider because "Burroughs's addicts, Kerouac's mobile young voyeurs, and my own Negroes are literally not included in the mainstream of American life."[39] Neither was Richard Wright, the Mencken-inspired expatriate author of *Native Son* (1940) who befriended Sartre and Camus in Paris before turning to his second novel, straightforwardly titled *The Outsider* (1953). Norman Mailer's essay "The White Negro" (1957)—a work that untangled the Beats' relation to blackness and the attitude of hip—spoke to their attraction to the marginal, to the kicked aside, to "the inner life and the violent life, the orgy and the dream of love, the desire to murder and the desire to create."[40]

Meanwhile, Miles Davis, Thelonious Monk, and Charlie Parker were bringing the outsider image of cool remove to its apogee. In opposition to the heavily produced and jittery rock and roll of Elvis Presley, they were moved by some deeper inner musical force, resulting in near-mystical, spontaneous, free-form jazz, all the while intravenously suffused by a drug that stripped away any concern for exteriors. All told, the Beat generation was done with the American misalignment of what it said and what it did—the very structure of insincerity. Writing a letter to his father in 1957, Allen Ginsberg lamented:

> Whitman long ago complained that unless the material power of America were leavened by some kind of spiritual infusion we would wind up among the "fabled damned." It seems we are approaching that state as far as I can see. Only way out is individuals taking responsibility and saying what they actually feel—which is an enormous human achievement in any society.[41]

Tennessee Williams had likewise conveyed this desperate mid-century grasp at a fading sincerity in a short, phantasmagorical play called *Camino Real* (1953). The Camino Real (the Royal Road) is a claustrophobic, dead-end, authoritarian-feeling place in a vaguely Latin American country surrounded by desert. The town's central plaza is a metaphor for the depraved city, peopled by beggars, prostitutes, thieves, vendors, and street cleaners who laugh as they cart off the dead. Starvation, greed, and apathy have immobilized the Camino Real population, among whom reside some crowd-pleasing characters from Romantic literary history—Don Quixote, Casanova, Lord Byron. Getting out of Camino Real is difficult, as public transportation comes along only seldom.

Enter Kilroy—an innocent, all-American sailor with "a heart as big as the head of a baby." (The name Kilroy was a reference to the omnipresent World War II graffito of a bald man with his nose hanging over a wall, accompanied by the text "Kilroy was here." A national joke well into the 1950s, Kilroy's origins remain mysterious, though he was the symbol of the American everyman.)*

* The graffito "Kilroy was here" has a confounding and curious history worthy of an epic movie by Steven Spielberg (rights and royalties departments, please take note). Kilroy graffiti surfaced around Europe wherever American servicemen were stationed. In Britain, the image of the man was called Chad, and at some point the words

Despite the charming pluck of *Camino Real*'s Kilroy, he, too, is robbed, conned, and nearly wrecked by the town's overwhelming baseness—until he encounters Esmeralda, the daughter of a Gypsy.

Kilroy tries to woo Esmeralda after she tells him that her virginity is restored at a fiesta each month and that this is the "wonderful thing about Gypsies' daughters." Kilroy responds, "You can say that again!"

> *Esmeralda:* I don't like you like that.
> *Kilroy*: Like what?
> *Esmeralda*: Cynical and sarcastic.
> *Kilroy*: I am sincere.
> *Esmeralda*: Lots of boys aren't sincere.
> *Kilroy*: Maybe they aren't but I am.
> *Esmeralda*: Everyone says he's sincere, but everyone isn't sincere. If everyone was sincere who says he's sincere there wouldn't be half so many insincere ones in the world and there would be lots, lots, lots more really sincere ones!

The last line could easily have been written by Diderot, Voltaire, Emerson, Nietzsche, or Mencken. If people would simply admit that they were often not sincere—that they often acted from ulterior motives—a whole new crop of sincere people would emerge. Nevertheless, Kilroy tries to convince Esmeralda of his real, artless sincerity. "I am sincere," he offers again. His advances are met in kind:

"Kilroy was here" merged with Chad, becoming a hybrid Anglo-American tag. Urban legend has it that a Quincy, MA, shipyard inspector named J. J. Kilroy may have been the inspiration. Another story has German intelligence officers finding the phrase on captured American equipment, which led Hitler to deduce that Kilroy was a code name for a high-level Allied spy. After the war, at the Potsdam Conference in 1945, Stalin supposedly found Kilroy graffiti in the VIP bathroom and ordered his aides to find out who Kilroy was. "Kilroy was here" lived on in literature—in Joseph Heller's *Catch-22* and Thomas Pynchon's *V*—and in popular culture, such as when he appeared with Bugs Bunny and on Styx's eleventh album (1983).

Esmeralda: I am sincere.
Kilroy: I am sincere.
Esmeralda: I am sincere.
Kilroy: I am sincere.
Esmeralda: I am sincere.
Kilroy: I am sincere.
Esmeralda: I am sincere.[42]

Hardly any technique could be more effective than this dizzying and desperate repetition in emphasizing the extreme, modern difficulty of convincing another person that one really is who one says one is and that one really means what one says.

When Williams's experimental drama opened on Broadway in 1953, it baffled critics. Its existentialist surreality did not square with what people thought of the successful playwright of *A Streetcar Named Desire, Summer and Smoke,* and *The Glass Menagerie*. One *New York Times* critic called it "a dark mirror of Mr. Williams's concept of life."[43] The longer view has positioned *Camino Real* as Williams's most profound play, a work whose insider and forward-looking irony, disdain for daft dead-end towns, and respect for the artistic courage it takes to resist them ultimately offer the salvation of love and human warmth in a cold, bleak world. In it, sincerity, while complicated to express, plays the part of a nostalgic, emotional tether. All was not lost.

Artists and writers were not the only ones taking swipes at the social conditions they imagined to be eroding individuals at midcentury. A vocal handful of now familiar social scientists were hobbling the rising middle classes with tracts against life-deadening conformity. David Riesman's *The Lonely Crowd* (1950), C. Wright Mills's *White Collar* (1951), Sloan Wilson's *The Man in the Gray Flannel Suit* (1955), Erving Goffman's *The Presentation of Self in Everyday Life* (1959), William H. Whyte, Jr.'s *The Organization Man* (1956), and

John Kenneth Galbraith's *The Affluent Society* (1958) all promoted the idea that a new and worrisome social class had arisen in America. It was comprised of well-off, indolent, consumerist, suburban, and politically conservative selves concerned with keeping up with, among other families, the Joneses. A society of this kind, the authors argued, gave easy rise to large corporations and bureaucracies, where individuals were molded into functioning cogs. People were losing the capacity to critique power and authority openly, they thought, instead preferring to "get along" with others in order to get ahead.

David Riesman's *The Lonely Crowd* dissected American society into three distinct social types: the "tradition-directed," who looked to the past as a model of how to live in the present; the "inner-directed," who found direction by looking to their own sense of right and wrong; and the "other-directed," who looked to the norms and standards of peers to determine how to live, what to buy, and how to look. This last type had a weak sense of self, Riesman wrote; they wanted "to be loved rather than esteemed," and had a smothering need for the "assurance that they were emotionally in tune with others." By the late 1940s this other-directed personality, he believed, had come to dominate the social landscape. This shift away from the inner-directed character was having negative effects throughout the culture, Riesman thought, evidenced in a loss of local leadership and a cowed deference to political or bureaucratic authority.

In a section entitled "Tolerance and the Cult of Sincerity," he observed how the yearning for sincerity was a key component of outer-directed morality. Citing examples from popular music, he quotes people saying, "I like Dinah Shore because she's so sincere," or "You can just feel how sincere [Frank Sinatra] is." Something new was happening, a radical separation of the artist and the art, something Wordsworth may not have seen coming: sincerity as a standard of aesthetic judgment had shifted attention from the actual music to the way the performer behaved or related to the audience. In putting themselves at the mercy of listeners, performers were judged for how much they actually meant what they performed. And because performers knew that sincerity had become the new standard of judgment, they tried ever harder to seem like "the sincere artist," Riesman writes—"the artist who tries hard." Sincerity as a standard for judgment was also evidence of "how little listeners can trust themselves or others in daily life."[44] Riesman attributed admiration for sincerity in pop singers to the performer's "apparent freedom . . . to express emotions that others cannot or dare not express," their seeming willingness to "make themselves vulnerable" to the judgment of fans. The sincere performer offers emotional openness and, in exchange, demands emotional tolerance or critical leniency. The outer-directed person thus seeks "sincerity" in order to replace his own shaky independent judgment with the sense that he is emotionally close to the performer.

Presidential politics, Riesman believed, was no different. At the time he was writing, suburbanites were expressing increasingly conservative opinions. Dwight Eisenhower, himself a moderate conservative (and perhaps the last president to be devoid of all irony or cynicism), oversaw an era of optimism and patriotic growth, even as capitalism was locking horns across the globe, rebuilding Europe, and competing for spheres of influence. Eisenhower's administration was effective at home, building new dams for electricity and agricultural irrigation, adding the Department of Health, Education, and Welfare to the cabinet, and expanding Roosevelt's New Deal programs, in particular Social Security. The interstate highway system, inspired by the German autobahn, was built not only to facilitate commuting but to allow the military easy access to major cities in case of nuclear attack. The Sputnik launch, in 1957, triggered Eisenhower's 1958 National Defense Education Act, which poured hundreds of millions of dollars into math and science education and college scholarships. As a committed integrationist, Eisenhower signed into law the first significant civil rights legislation since 1875 and sent the Arkansas National Guard into Little Rock to enforce *Brown vs. Board of Education*.

Despite all this, Riesman was not convinced that a president need be sincere in what he says. In fact, Riesman writes, "The desire for a sincere Presidential candidate, such as Eisenhower, is a desire to escape from cynicism and apathy into commitment and enthusiasm—an excuse for the return of repressed qualities."[45] Though the other-directed personality considers sincerity in politics important, an audience bent on detecting sincerity may only be detecting its rehearsed appearance: "Just because such a premium is put on sincerity, a premium is put on faking it."[46] Secondly, the electorate, in demanding sincerity, abdicates its democratic and critical duty of evaluating leadership qualities more important than sincerity, such as intelligence, geopolitical knowledge, honesty, decisiveness, and political effectiveness. If the concern for sincerity overrides the evaluation of these qualities, Riesman warns, "The concern for sincerity in political personalities becomes a vice."

C. Wright Mills's pioneering 1951 study *White Collar: The American Middle Classes* is an equally blistering sociological polemic about the rise of the managerial class in America. The "internally split, fragmented" self of the white-collar creature exhibited the same outward-directed qualities that worried Riesman, being "externally . . . dependent on larger forces."[47] Mills saw the American character in the midst of a dramatic shift: away from the independent spirit of farmers and small businesses and toward a rising corporate America, where groupthink crushed the expression of individual opinions. Not that all was perfect in our agricultural age, but the larger trend, Mills thought, spelled "the decline of the independent individual and the rise of the little man in the American mind."[48]

Mills's interviews and social surveys of American managers and salesmen uncovered what he called a new "personality market," where the individual "instrumentalizes" himself as a tool for selling. Professionalized insincerity permitted "kindness and friendliness [to] become aspects of personalized service or of public relations of big firms." With rote insincerity, Mills wrote, "the Successful Person thus makes an instrument of his own appearance and personality."[49] He felt that this Successful Person was overtaking the American business landscape, and that the business landscape itself was taking over ever larger portions of the American economy. Ergo, America was beginning to adopt the characteristics of a corporation: habitually insincere, and increasingly unable to drop its insincerity outside the workplace. Insincerity, Mills believed, was thus becoming "the characteristic of twentieth-century existence"; American life was transforming into "society as a great salesroom," an "enormous file," and an "incorporated brain," all of which was leading to "a new universe of management and manipulation."[50]

White Collar has often been characterized as a diatribe rather than a sociologically impartial study. Curiously enough, this might have something not insignificantly to do with Mills's own identity as the permanently engaged dissident: "I am an outlander," he would later reflect, "deep down and for good."[51] Even "impartial" sociology in America had fallen under the romantic spell of the unique and genuine outsider position.

The concern over rising trends of insincerity and pressures to conform was also analyzed in Erving Goffman's *The Presentation of Self in Everyday Life*, published in 1956. Our social performances are like theater, Goffman suggested: self-presentation takes place on a "stage" with other "actors" who follow cues to how to behave in nearly every situation. How to deliver the best performance as ourselves would come to be known in social science (and more welcomingly by political strategists) as "impression management."* Some are better at it than others.

Like Riesman and Mills, Goffman saw two personality types becoming increasingly prevalent in American society at mid-century: the sincere believer and the cynic. These two types often inhered in the same person—indeed, they were filling up the American social landscape. The self-splitting referred to by Rousseau, Diderot, Freud, and Sartre is echoed in Goffman's view of the modern-day performer—which we all are, he says, regardless of any conviction to the contrary. This social actor "can be fully taken in by his own act; . . . be sincerely convinced that the impression of reality which he stages is the real reality," and then, later, no longer buy into his own false performance.[52] "When the individual has no belief in his own act and no ultimate concern with the beliefs of his audience," Goffman writes, "we may call him cynical, reserving the term 'sincere' for individuals who believe in the impression fostered by their own performance."[53]

Crucially, in Goffman's view, it was becoming increasingly *necessary* for people to buy into their own performance in order to survive in a modern economy dependent on selling false impressions to others. The class of people most dedicated to the adoption of false impressions was the middle class of managers and salesmen, a population that occupied influential sectors of the American economy and the newly sprouted suburbs of the 1950s.

By 1960, in fact, the middle class and its representative managerial class constituted two-thirds of the American population—and some 60 million of them had packed up and headed for the suburbs, the great green between. Middle-class suburban culture

* The American sociologist Arlie Russell Hochschild, of the University of California, Berkeley, introduced the concept "emotional labor" to address how forced sincerity has been managed and required of workers in modern service industries. More darkly, she also notes how the personality that is managed and presented to the public can overtake the actual personality of the worker away from the job. See her pioneering study *The Managed Heart*.

was increasingly American culture: not urban and not rural, enjoying postwar prosperity, domestic harmony, television, the good life, steady jobs, church, and, above all, consumption. The June 20, 1960, issue of *Time* magazine ran a cover story on this new geographical shift, noting that suburbia now

> weaves through the hills beyond the cities, marches across flatlands that once were farms and pastures, dips into gullies and woodlands, straddles the rocky hillocks and surrounds the lonesome crossroads. Oftener than not it has a lilting polyphony that sings of trees (Streamwood, Elmwood, Lakewood. Kirkwood), the rolling country (Cedar Hill, Cockrell Hill, Forest Hills), or the primeval timberlands (Forest Grove, Park Forest, Oak Park, Deer Park). But it has its roots in such venerable names as Salem, Greenwich, Chester, Berkeley, Evanston, Sewickley and Rye.[54]

Suburbia remained connected to nature through the names of the things it had destroyed: forest, grove, oak, deer. It kept the Romantic fascination with nature as restorative space by hollowing out parks and fake lakes in their stead. And while there were millions of genuinely happy people who enjoyed living in suburbia, a counterculture push against it was on the rise. Walker Percy's existentially inspired novel *The Moviegoer* and Richard Yates's *Revolutionary Road,* both of which debuted in 1961 (the National Book Award for Fiction went to the former), bespoke the alienated American soul trapped within the confines of a pleasant looking American dream, desperate to escape (the former into the movies, the latter to Paris).

Conditions across the Atlantic were no different. Writing from London, the art and literary critic Herbert Read, a tearful devotee of the late Romantics and veteran of the First World War, captured the increasingly divergent spirit of the times in a book appropriately called *The Contrary Experience* (1963). In it Read recapitulated the disenchantment felt by increasing numbers of young people alienated from the direction in which modern society was headed: "All modern developments—weed-killers, motor-cars, tractors, mechanization, tourism, the radio, the cinema, urbanization (words as ugly as the things they signify)—have combined to destroy the countryside that was evident to my innocent eye."[55] Read's lament recapitulates all the Romantic allergies to industrialization, commerce, and homogenized society; it spells out a simple formula for all that has gone wrong with the world since the eighteenth century: the quest for capital gain and efficiency has killed all that is beautiful. His long-fingered grasp at the "innocent eye" reanimates for artists the slippery ideal of personal sincerity, which, echoing Wordsworth, he wrote, "is the only thing . . . indispensible for the possession of a good style."[56]

Read's other aptly named and reflective account of sincerity in literature and life, *The Cult of Sincerity* (1968), remorsefully opines that modern life has actually crushed what was left of sincerity, killed a romance with the old world, and enfeebled the idea that self-expression in art offers aesthetic—and spiritual—salvation. "Sincerity! All my life I have been reproved for attempting to use this word." And yet around him many autobiographies (by authors such as Céline, Miller, Genet, and Burroughs) made claims for the open, unaffected self. "Are these writings 'sincere'?" Read asks. "Gone, of course, is any claim to natural innocence; these writers would rather boast of their natural depravity and claim the virtue of courage for their self-exposures."[57] This loss of innocence was evident in the decline of the phrase "Yours sincerely," which had paradoxically become, Read wrote, "the most insincere" thing one could write. A slick coat of falseness was drowning all that was deep and real in Western social life—yet again.

The all-out rebellion against suburban middle-class taste as sick, unnatural, and repressed would find explosive expression throughout the 1960s in literature and film and political activism, but it already had serious detractors in the aggressive canvases of the European-inspired (or -born) avant-garde. The paintings of Arshile Gorky, Adolph Gottlieb, Jane Frank, Jackson Pollock, Hans Hofmann, Helen Frankenthaler, Barnett Newman, Willem and Elaine de Kooning, Clyfford Still, and Franz Kline all in one way or another made an unspoken plea for sincerity and authenticity through the unleashing of violent impulses, unclean lines, and picture spaces devoid of conscious, rational order. If all that was bourgeois made sense and was consumable and pretty, art's job was to stand against it.

As the first native-born American painterly style, abstract expressionism aimed, like the work of the Beats who grew up alongside it, to recover unpleasant feelings, kindle extreme emotional intensity, and enlarge the self beyond the confines of philistine America. Willem de Kooning's violent attack on the canvas resulted in wounded, half-representational men and women; Pollock turned the entire canvas into a violent arena; Helen Frankenthaler's enormous unprepared canvases swam with thinly applied new forms that escaped linear rationality; Philip Guston's mockingly figurative cartoon paintings made life both a joke and more deadly serious; Franz Kline's iron girder-like black bars deny entry. The color-field painter Barnett Newman wrote on April 9, 1955, to his gallerist, the champion of abstract expressionism Sidney Janis, that his whole motivation for becoming an artist was his "struggle against bourgeois society . . . the total rejection of it."[58]

Cultivation of the untamed as a means to get at the authentic self and escape the saccharine quality of popular culture was guided, in part, by the enormously influential (and eventually programmatic) art theory of Clement Greenberg. In the fall of 1939 he had argued in "Avant-Garde and Kitsch," an essay published in *Partisan Review,* that avant-garde art and kitsch products grew up next to each other following the Industrial Revolution. Modern art became avant-garde when it made a moral judgment that the world was corrupt and turned inward, away from the world and into abstraction. Art decided to stand against the cheapening of culture as mass commodity. Kitsch—which likely derived from the German verb *verkitschen*, to cheapen something, and which Greenberg defined in a letter to a friend as "crap"—emerged in its place.

The word "kitsch" was originally used to describe inexpensive, quickly produced pictures or sketches (there is an argument that the German word *kitsch* actually derives from a mispronunciation of the English word "sketch") in 1860s' Munich. These pictures were purchased by the newly moneyed of Munich society in order to display "good taste" at a good price, as they attempted to compete with the standards of Munich's wealthier cultural elite. That elite—and the generations of critics of mass culture that would follow—determined that the particular aesthetics of kitsch revealed more about its owners' desire to display aesthetic taste than about their desire to actually acquire it through, say, reading, studying, or learning about art history. Kitsch, that is, was not only fake art; it also revealed the fakeness of its owners and their yearning to be more than what they were. In today's parlance, kitsch owners attempt to gain the most cultural capital for the least economic capital. This mass-market production of cheap art not only provided easy product for the market, it also, less winningly, Greenberg argued, killed off the authentic folk culture that was popular before kitsch came along.

Modern avant-garde painting over the past century had been yearning to escape its role as pretending to be something else, Greenberg thought; it wanted to be simply what it was: oil paint on woven cotton canvas. Greenberg's philosophical break with the past saw painting as slowly but surely divesting itself of the illusion of three-dimensional picture space, starting with Cézanne in the 1880s. Cézanne's landscape paintings began to show patches of pure flatness that made no attempt to look like real space. Artists such as van Gogh, Braque, Piet Mondrian, and, finally, Picasso were painting canvases that began to confess their own two-dimensionality. Paintings were just paint on canvas, not the objects they portrayed. Canvases were flat surfaces. Sculpture was simply solid material, not the forms it represented. Poems were just words, not the scenes and senses they tried to conjure. Novels, too, were just words, not the virtual worlds they constructed. In order for art to be honest, Greenberg declared, it needed to simply pay attention to what it actually was.

By following this oddly contagious Greenbergian logic—which essentially steered the making of art and the terms of criticism in New York through the mid-twentieth century—art ends up at what are often called the last paintings: *The Black Paintings* by Ad Reinhardt, which he worked on from 1953 until his death, in 1967. He called these large-scale all-black canvases (with barely detectable squares floating in the "background") a "free, unmanipulated, unmanipulatable, useless, unmarketable, irreducible, unphotographable, unreproducible, inexplicable icon." *The Black Paintings* represented nothing. They did not deceive. They were what they were. They were themselves. Akin to Emerson's description of Thoreau in the 1850s, Ad Reinhardt's black paintings achieved what modern art—and the Protestant religion—had for so long wanted to be: sincerity itself.

Chapter VII : LONG LIVE "SINCERITY"

Sincerity is always subject to proof.

- John F. Kennedy, inaugural address, January 20, 1961

"DURING THE 1960S, I think people forgot what emotions were supposed to be," Andy Warhol wrote in 1975. "And I don't think they've ever remembered."[1] This observation runs counter to how we are used to thinking about the Age of Aquarius. After all, the 1960s (as caricatured) welcomed emotional naturalness, communal living, flower power, getting in touch with your feelings, free love, and the final obliteration of bourgeois repressive forces (and clothing), all of which heterosexual, unenthused Christian society had for centuries heaved upon the errant. Rebelling against the conformity of the 1940s and 1950s, hippies were Rousseau's dream come true: freedom to be who you really are, a return to nature unadorned.

Vegetarian and whole-food markets and cafés sprouted like alfalfa in cities across America; homemade garments and jewelry skirted a national economy that spent taxpayer dollars on a war few believed in; the folk music revival stood against all that was hokey in American pop and newly popular R&B. Critics of the New Left and mainstream alike, such as Paul Goodman, author of *Growing Up Absurd* (1960), were hoping for big-picture changes: "We are not going to give up the mass faith in scientific technology that is the religion of modern times," he wrote, "and yet we cannot continue with it, as it has been perverted. So I look for a 'New Reformation.'"[2] While the rebel youth of the 1960s romanticized living and dead icons of total reform—Che Guevara, Fidel Castro, Dietrich Bonhoffer, Jesus—they actually espoused something closer to free-market libertarianism in their uncompromising search for freedom from all rules and authority over the sacred self. Charles Reich lamented in *The Greening of America* (1970) that the country had lost its innocent dream "shared by the colonists and the immigrants, by Jefferson, Emerson, and the Puritan preachers." Young members of the hippie generation aimed to find, as the 1962 Port Huron Statement of the Students for a Democratic Society declared, "unrealized potentiality for self-cultivation, self-direction, self-understanding, and creativity." Men and women alike were seeking "a meaning in life that is personally authentic." The declaration continued:

> Not only did tarnish appear on our image of American virtue, not only did disillusion occur when the hypocrisy of American ideals was discovered, but we began to sense that what we had originally seen as the American Golden Age was actually the decline of an era. The worldwide outbreak of revolution against colonialism and imperialism, the entrenchment of totalitarian states, the menace of war, overpopulation, international disorder, supertechnology—these trends were testing the tenacity of our own commitment to democracy and freedom and our abilities to visualize their application to a world in upheaval.

This bitter lament of a decaying America motivated the decades' protests, sit-ins, and idyllic visions of social revolution. The same sentiments could be found in the underground, taboo-breaking comics of R. Crumb and S. Clay Wilson; their characters rejected tailored suits, well-fitting dresses, uniforms, and slacks, in favor of loose-fitting clothes and unisex denim—the working man's authentic gear with roots in a purer age (remember Rousseau also ditched his fancy duds for the worker's).*

"Hippie" itself derives from the 1950s' term "hip," meaning someone in the know: someone who knew what was cool, how to behave, and what the newest cultural productions were. Drugs were a means not just to explore altered states of mind, but to tune down emotional response and to just be, as in the 1966 San Francisco Human Be-In. Whereas 1950s hipsters like William Burroughs ironically mimicked the button-down styles and ties of the business world, hippies shed their bourgeois garb altogether, preferring denim, beads, and the ethnic duds of Mexican, Indian, and Moroccan cultures. All of inauthentic Western culture was to be discarded in exchange for the authentic other.

But the 1960s were not just this caricature of putt-putting Volkswagen Beetles, pot, and longhairs without jobs. While that complex era summons many ghosts of our expressive Romantic past, it is just as much the decade of an anti-sincerity pose: cool reserve. This other Romantic strain reaches back through Machiavelli, Nietzsche, Wilde, and, further, to Castiglione's *sprezzatura*

* It is important to note that the hippie lifestyle was not met with understanding by the working class themselves, and that hippies generally did not find the working class of the 1960s sympathetic. Rather, "by and large hippies saw working-class manners as conservative, sentimental, and sometimes downright threatening," write Dick Pountain and David Robins in *Cool Rules*. Meanwhile, some sections of the "bourgeois" liberal middle class were quite supportive of the younger generation of rebels, despite the obligatory uproar. The liberal middle classes would eventually adopt the sexy rebel ethos and fuse it with existing pleasures, beginning with *Playboy's* January 1967 interview with revolutionary leader Fidel Castro ("A candid conversation with the bellicose dictator of communist Cuba")—cozied up alongside a recipe for the perfect gin martini.

gentleman: an adorned, aloof, and disenchanted figure who hides inopportune feelings behind a mask of indifference, disdain, or feigned delight. To be unshakable, unflappable, and detached was to distance oneself from the world outside and to be anchored in the inward self. Hippies, in this way, also chose to "drop out"—to remain cool—to reject the rules of square society.

Alongside dropping out, the hippie era also bred a permanently engaged suspicion and insider intelligence, a cynical critique of lying politicians, Cold War deceptions, and general disapproval of where society had gone. And just where was the society of the mid-1960s? Racism was rampant and civil rights leaders were being murdered. The credit card had been introduced a decade earlier, and consumer debt skyrocketed 800 percent. The postwar economic boom seemed to have no end, and yet millions of Americans, despite Johnson's War on Poverty, continued to live in poverty. Still, the standard of living for most of the population was higher than it had ever been.

Consuming these disjointed economic and social realities of race and class, hippies became increasingly estranged from their unjust host society and its ostensibly high-minded American ideals. "Sincerity doesn't mean anything," the playwright Edward Albee wrote in 1962. "A person can be sincere and be more destructive than a person who is insincere." Hippies combined their earnest devotion to political change with ironic disengagement from a society they knew to be doing well but at the cost of the environment, peace, and spiritual wellness. "No one who lived through those times could doubt that beneath the mock orientalism lay total detachment," wrote Dick Pountain and David Robins in their look back on the era and its hip contagion, *Cool Rules* (2000). "You might vigorously contradict someone's opinion only to receive the blissed-out reply, 'That's cool, too, man.'"[3] Tom Wolfe, the supreme chronicler of the era, observed, "The hippies were religious and incontrovertibly hip at the same time."[4]

It is often said that John F. Kennedy was the first cool president; to doubt others' earnestness of intention was part of the cool psyche. He explicitly expressed his skepticism toward sincerity in his inaugural address, on January 20, 1961, setting a clear tone of doubt by saying circuitously to the Soviets, "Let us begin anew—remembering on both sides that civility is not a sign of weakness, and sincerity is always subject to proof." In other words, Mr. Khrushchev, America no longer believes in your sincerity. It may never have, but by the time Kennedy took office, cynicism and skepticism of motive had become such a pervasive cultural force, such a telltale sign of worldliness, that even the authorities were allowed—or were perhaps required—to admit their importance.

The strange hippie elixir of cool, gentleness, and detachment had caught hold of ever larger portions of middle America as the 1970s began, and it showed in popular culture. Bands that had been making hippie headlines—the Rolling Stones, Led Zeppelin, Jefferson Starship—were now flying in private jets, having children, and buying up estates in the English countryside and sprawling split-levels in the Hollywood Hills. Excess and debauchery were married with the image of cool remove, creating an air of loungy aristocratic decadence and counterculture fun that everyone wanted to be part of.

But by 1972, as a popular aging-hippie adage announced, the "fun was over." The 1970s' counterculture leader and socialist Michael Harrington famously signaled the end by observing, "Free love and all-night drinking and art for art's sake were consequences of a single stern imperative: Thou shalt not be bourgeois." Once the bourgeois began consuming the sounds and accoutrements of the anti-establishment, the flame of resistance was extinguished. Warren Hinckle, the editor of the Catholic leftist magazine *Ramparts*, observed in 1967, "If the people looking in from the suburbs want change, clothes, fun, and some lightheadedness from the new gypsies, the hippies are delivering—and some of them are becoming rich hippies because of it."[5] Yippie leader Jerry Rubin declared that the spread of the hippie ideal had "signaled the total end of the Protestant ethic: screw work, we want to know ourselves." Perhaps most absurdly emblematic of this demise was the twelve-inch, black-and-white portable Zenith television set called the Sidekick (model F1343B1) that was "decked out, top and sides, in blue denim." This kitsch melding of lifestyles even came with an earphone for discreet listening to hard rock.

Thomas Frank's hallmark reframing of 1960s' and 1970s' counterculture, *The Conquest of Cool* (1997), ingeniously analyzes the growth and dissemination of its logic in American capitalism into our own time. "According to the standard story," Frank writes, "business was the monolithic bad guy who had caused America to become a place of puritanical conformity and empty consumerism; business was the great symbolic foil against which the young rebels defined themselves." The reality, he explains, was far more cynical: "From its very beginnings down to the present, business dogged the counterculture with a fake counterculture," Frank writes:

> a commercial replica that seemed to ape its every move for the titillation of the TV-watching millions and the nation's corporate sponsors. Every rock band with a substantial following was immediately honored with a host of imitators; the 1967 "summer of love" was as much a product of lascivious television specials and *Life* magazine stories as it was an expression of youthful disaffection; Hearst launched a psychedelic magazine in 1968; and even hostility to co-optation had a desperately "authentic" shadow, documented by a famous 1968 print ad for Columbia Records titled "But The Man Can't Bust Our Music." So oppressive was the climate of national voyeurism that, as early as the fall of 1967, the San Francisco Diggers had held a funeral for "Hippie, devoted son of mass media."[6]

The trend Frank elucidated—foreseen in part by social thinkers such as Vance Packard, Daniel Bell, C. Wright Mills, William H. Whyte, Jr., David Riesman, Christopher Lasch, and the Frankfurt School—shows how "hip capitalism" came to usurp the counterculture message for its own ends. The quaint counterculture dichotomy of "hip" versus "square" was adopted by corporate America to sell, well, almost anything—from Magnavox stereos to Camel cigarettes to Schwinn bicycles. This is the story, Frank writes, of "the bohemian cultural style's trajectory from adversarial to hegemonic; the story of hip's mutation from native language of the alienated to that of advertising." Still brimming with insight, *The Conquest of Cool*'s logic has become a standard piece of knowledge for—as David Riesman might have said—all "inside dopesters."

As the paradoxical economic logic of hip capitalism was getting underway, a number of books and essays—curiously—began investigating the historical notion of sincerity right alongside it: Patricia M. Ball's "Sincerity: The Rise and Fall of a Critical Term" in the *Modern Language Review* (1964); *The Jargon of Authenticity*, by Theodor Adorno (1964; English edition, 1973); *Literature and Sincerity*, by Henri Peyre (1963); *The Cult of Sincerity*, by Herbert Read (1968); *The Politics of Authenticity*, by Marshall Berman (1970); *Sincerity and Authenticity*, by Lionel Trilling (1971); and *The Sincere Ideal: Studies on Sincerity in Eighteenth-Century Literature*, by Leon Guilhamet (1974). Each work in its own way surveyed how sincerity as an aim of literature and literary criticism had played out over the preceding several hundred years. During an era obsessed with liberation and cool, those sharp minds set out to discover what had happened to the moral quality of sincerity.

Critic Henri Peyre professed in 1963 that "the concept of sincerity has become the most potent idée-force in the literature and psychology of our age," but just a decade later Lionel Trilling would counter with this sentence: "To praise a work of literature by calling it *sincere* is now at best a way of saying that although it need be given no aesthetic or intellectual admiration, it was at least conceived in innocence of heart."[7] In an age of increasing irony and political and commercial shiftiness, sincerity as a moral and aesthetic criterion had been dramatically handicapped. At the dawn of the 1970s, many critics seemed to fret that something very real about personal sincerity, some core requirement for its realization, had been irrevocably lost.

On June 14, 1972, there was a break-in at the Watergate complex in Washington, DC, which was home to the Democratic National Committee. The five suspects were convicted of attempted burglary and wiretapping in January 1973, at which time the FBI was already investigating payment to those men originating from the Committee to Re-Elect the President. Some of the burglars, the investigation revealed, had ties to the Nixon administration and to the Central Intelligence Agency. The resulting cover-up fiasco would lead all the way to the president of the United States. Richard M. Nixon, the investigation found, had been involved personally in the obstruction of justice, wiretapping, and in attempts to damage political opponents and the antiwar movement. The Watergate scandal changed the tenor of American politics forever. The highest elected American official looked directly at the American population through their television sets on November 17, 1973, with hundreds of Associated Press journalists in the room, and insisted, "People have got to know whether or not their President is a crook. Well, I am not a crook. I've earned everything I got."

On August 8, 1974, at 9:01 p.m. EST, Nixon did earn everything he got. After two years of political wrestling and national embarrassment, after the *Washington Post* had begun to uncover the byzantine complexities of the scandal, Nixon announced his imminent departure: "I shall resign the office of the Presidency at noon tomorrow." That moment signaled the symbolic end of trust in American politics, and with it, the death of the idea that it was possible to demand sincerity from the nation's highest officials—those who were supposed to represent the very best of American values to the world.

No matter. If you couldn't find the best at the top, you might as well continue to concentrate on yourself. Tom Wolfe's hilarious and brilliant 1976 *New York* magazine essay "The 'Me' Decade and the Third Great Awakening" chronicled the renewed desire to get beyond political falsities and to concentrate instead on the newest god of America: Me. "The new alchemical dream," Wolfe wrote, "is changing one's personality—remaking, remodeling, elevating, and polishing one's very *self* . . . and observing, studying, and doting on it. (Me!)" Riffing off the absurdity of new cults and fraying 1960s' sentiments, Wolfe detailed the explosion of self-help retreats that involved activities such as primal yelling and extended drum circles. The New Age communes of the "back-to-the-land" movements of the 1960s and 1970s (such as Paper Farm in northern California and the Twin Oaks Community in Virginia) offered, along with sustainability, a menu of self-discovery that went, Wolfe writes, something like this:

> I, with the help of my brothers and sisters, must strip away all the shams and excess baggage of society and my upbringing in order to find the Real Me. Scientology uses the word "clear" to identify the state that one must strive for. But just what is that state? And what will the Real Me be like? It is at this point that the new movements tend to take on a religious or spiritual atmosphere. In one form or another they arrive at an axiom first propounded by the Gnostic Christians some 1,800 years ago: namely, that at the apex of every human soul there exists a spark of the light of God. In most mortals that spark is "asleep" (the Gnostics' word),

> all but smothered by the façades and general falseness of society. But those souls who are clear can find that spark within themselves and unite their souls with God's. And with that conviction comes the second assumption: There is an *other order* that actually reigns supreme in the world. Like the light of God itself, this *other order* is invisible to most mortals. But he who has dug himself out from under the junk heap of civilization can discover it.[8]

It was as if Jean-Jacques Rousseau himself were leading the drum circle. Wolfe's essay offers a perfect recounting of the drive to find one's inner self—that magnetic logic of sincerity and authenticity that began with the Reformation, ran through Rousseau, ignited Romanticism and aesthetic modernism, and, thanks to hip consumerism, motivated the development of "counterculture" self-discovery. Christopher Lasch's term for the psychological ethos of the 1970s: *The Culture of Narcissism*.

The "Me Decade" eventually did discover itself, but it was less pretty than the spirituality movements had hoped. Films like *Taxi Driver* envisioned revenge fantasies against rampant urban crime, and Clint Eastwood became the lone Dirty Harry warrior who had had enough of politeness. The critical year of 1969 had been idolized on film in *Easy Rider*, with Peter Fonda, Dennis Hopper, and Jack Nicholson riding around as outlaw bikers in the American Southwest in search of freedom and themselves. Political radicals like the Weathermen turned to terrorism, and the Black Panthers armed themselves for defense and revolution. As the echoes of alternative political ideologies hummed around the nation's universities during the Cold War ("Is Communism really so bad?"), the July 14, 1975, issue of *Time* magazine asked, "Can Capitalism Survive?" The cover of the June 30 issue, "Crime: Why and What to Do," featured a beady-eyed man in a tight black ski mask pointing an enormous semi-automatic pistol at the reader's face. *Apocalypse Now*, which premiered in 1979, reminded the public of the bleaker side of humanity lying behind its civility—and of the recently ended war that had resulted in 58,000 deaths and 150,000 injured, many of the latter left to roam American streets broken and insane. These grim facts jarred with the plucky *Life* magazine cover of September 1977 that announced the arrival of "The New Youth: Tough, Caring, Wary, Practical, Supercool."

Amidst all this depressing news, at least one artist stopped fighting and gave American consumers what they wanted most: money, celebrity, glitz, and the familiar comfort of tomato soup. Andy Warhol's sensibility, in retrospect, seems perfectly suited to the decade of disappointed cynical remove. Unlike some of his more earnest modernist predecessors, he was not out to fix anything. In fact, the tireless art-historical itch to find the social critique in Warhol's work reveals more about our own addiction to the Romantic idea that art must attempt to fix society than about any secret critical impulse in Warhol. This is not to say that Warhol did not push an unspoken ideal of social egalitarianism. But his was not an ideological effort; he simply watched what the great equalizer, consumer capitalism, was doing, and then repeated it deadpan in art.

A 1967 sculpture, *You're In*—a wooden case filled with silver-painted Coke bottles—illustrates the point that with consumer capitalism, everyone could be "in," and at a great discount. Warhol summed up his own view like this:

> What's great about this country is that America started the tradition where the richest consumers buy essentially the same thing as the poorest. You can be watching TV and see Coca-Cola and you know that the President drinks Coke, Liz Taylor drinks Coke, and just think, you can drink Coke, too. A Coke is a Coke and no amount of money can get you a better Coke than the one the bum on the corner is drinking.[9]

Whereas the art of Marcel Duchamp and the Dadaists fought explicitly against what Duchamp called "bloody earnestness," Warhol dropped the clear hints at critical irony altogether, and, in a fresh dandy style, left the audience's expectations of art's social role to do all the work. This emptiness cascaded into disappointment for nervous critics who believed that art should do more than just sit there. After all, the social and political art of the time did precisely the opposite: it continued to offer critique of the status quo—Hans Haacke's outing of New York slumlords and other systems of capitalist power; the Guerrilla Girls' attack on patriarchy; conceptual art's vaporization of the consumer art object; Earth art's implicit critique of the gallery system by moving outside it. Warhol's work, on the other hand, displayed an autistically cool remove, a simple observer's eye. His gadding about at parties and taking pictures of celebrities, and his getting very unsecretly rich while doing it, combined the free-market logic of commercial capitalism with the notion that art need not do a damn thing but make money. Art was, after all, a business.

It need not, as art, even be particularly "original." In 1965 Warhol was offered a solo show at the National Gallery of Canada.* When he stacked up his Brillo boxes in the museum, the Canadian government criticized his work for not being "original sculpture." Asked by a sober journalist from Canadian public television if he agreed, a young Warhol, decked out in dark shades and a smirk, responded, "Uh, yes."

* A pleasing twist that surely made Warhol grin: in 1964 an art dealer in Toronto tried to import eighty of Warhol's Brillo boxes into Canada, each one valued at $250. The customs agents tried to collect 20 percent duty on the entire value of the "merchandise." To resolve the issue of whether the boxes were artworks or products, the duty agents contacted the acting director of the National Gallery of Canada, Charles Comfort. After examining a few photographs of the boxes, he reported back that they were clearly not sculptures. Two directors later, the Radcliffe-educated and first female director of the National Gallery of Canada, Jean Sutherland Boggs, shocked sensibilities by lifting the ban on the purchase of American contemporary art and bought the Brillo boxes for the gallery's permanent collection—and for much more than $250 apiece.

Interviewer: "Why do you agree?"

Warhol: Well, because it's not original.

Interviewer: Why have you bothered to do that, then? Why not create something new?

Warhol: Um, because it's easier to do. . . .

Interviewer: Andy, do you think that Pop Art has reached a point where it is becoming repetitious now?

Warhol: Yes.[10]

In the film clip of this interview (available on YouTube as part of a PBS special), Warhol exchanges knowing glances with a companion at his side and answers with particular cleverness. And yet never have sincerity and irony been so happily married—a practically indiscernible pair—as they were in the personality of Andy Warhol. He means what he says . . . right? His answers are entirely honest and accurate: the Brillo boxes are not original, in fact; they are copies of actual Brillo boxes. This kind of work is easier to do because you don't have to come up with some new form *ex nihilo.* Pop Art had become repetitious because the formula was clear: take detritus from popular culture and, to make it art, as Jasper Johns advised, just "do something to it, and then do something else to it."

Andy's art is exactly what it is. It is not traditionally "original" or "inventive," it does not allude to any Romantic tropes or yearning for escape from the evils of the capitalist present. Rather, in its cool distance it offers an antidote to the more earnestly engaged art of the time and admits its desire for fame and money. In a reaction to the Brillo box show (its first) at Sable Gallery, in 1964, the then-upstart art critic Arthur Danto—for whom Warhol would become an increasingly meaningful figure in all of twentieth-century art—wrote that he had just witnessed "the end of Western art." If you include Ad Reinhardt's *Black Paintings,* art died twice in 1964—once of sincerity, once of irony.

—

The abstract expressionism of the 1940s and 1950s had assumed the Romantic task of brutalizing society and convention through violently painted images. Such expressionist disregard for tradition was supposed to exhibit a new kind of artistic sincerity and to transfer to the artist a quality of the strong, Romantic self that opposed the rules. (In real life, Pollock's drunken pissing in Peggy Guggenheim's fireplace did the trick, as did Clement Greenberg's punching the playwright Lionel Abel in the face at a cocktail party).* Nearly three decades later, the postmodern artist had become conscious of the conventionality and conformity of the subjective response. The expressive self had become a trope of humanism. To "self-express" had become a cliché already by the mid-1970s, unleashing waves of art that had nothing to do with personal subjectivity: photorealism, video art, late minimalism, Earth art, political art, and continuing strands of Pop Art.

Art critic Donald Kuspit's *Signs of Psyche in Modern and Postmodern Art* (1993) argued that art in the 1980s was no longer avant-garde but had rather become instead "avant-gardist"—art that looked avant-garde but was not. Why wasn't it actually avant-garde? Because, as Warhol so happily displayed, art had gotten entirely into bed with the commercial economy, which up until then had been an implicit foe of authentic modern art. Art, that is, no longer offered critical resistance to the status quo of the market system. But this did not, however, stop artists from displaying the old Romantic urge to seem as if they opposed the blanket overtaking of the strong, resistant self. The neo-Expressionist work of Julian Schnabel, for example, rehearses the return of "authentic" subjectivity in what Kuspit believes is appearance alone. "Neo-Expressionism constructs its face-saving façade of sincerity

* The intellectual historian Louis Menand, in a September 5, 2011, *New Yorker* article about the critic Dwight Macdonald, "Browbeaten," writes that Greenberg wrote to the appalled Macdonald that he "only used to punch surrealists" (p. 75).

in response to [the] postmodern disillusionment of modern art's failure to create a more sincere society."[11] Schnabel, he says, provides merely the "illusion of depth of experience," in paintings that deliver all the right traces and indexes of what an "expressive self" should look like (Schnabel himself exhibited a very expressive self, writes Cathleen McGuigan in a 1982 issue of *ARTnews*: "Gregarious and direct, he worked parties like a political candidate at a Fourth of July picnic.") In other words, he had the look of spontaneity made with cunning finesse.

The other direction that art took in the 1980s was a move away from all traces of the subjective self, including its very ability to be creative. Artists who played with this ironic/empty excess included Jeff Koons, Haim Steinbach, Cindy Sherman, and Sherrie Levine, who, all in their own ways—and recalling the impersonal logic of Wilde or T. S. Eliot—promoted the argument that art had nothing to do with personal subjective expression. These 1980s' celebrity artists offered instead perfect, industrially produced objects (Koons's basketballs floating in a tank of water; brand-new vacuum cleaners under plexiglass); or photographs of photographs already famous (Levine's photographs of Walker Evans's Depression-era photographs from his and James Agee's *Let Us Now Praise Famous Men*). Both the Schnabel and Levine directions, Kuspit suggests, represent pure cynicism—a disappointed idealism that mocks the effort at originality and self-expression.

Some European art, particularly in Germany, with its ancient obsession with the "deep self," continued along the model of strong expression, seen particularly in the work of Georg Baselitz, Anselm Kiefer, A.R. Penck, and Jörg Immendorff. Several of these figures, tellingly, had escaped from East Germany—a place dominated by a regime that enforced socialist realism and celebrated the idea that the collective was what mattered, not you, hence art was made for the good of the state; self-expressiveness was irredeemably bourgeois because it celebrated individualism.

Nevertheless, many avant-garde thinkers on the free side of the Iron Curtain suspected the radical individual self to be a cliché. In 1967 the French critic Roland Barthes had published an essay called "The Death of the Author" in the American magazine *Aspen* (it was published in French a year later). *Aspen* (created by former *Women's Wear Daily* and *Advertising Age* editor Phyllis Johnson), was a bit like *McSweeney's*; it came in a customized box filled with lots of fun extras: posters, records, postcards, or super-8 films. It suspended publication in 1971.

The issue in which Barthes' essay appears—a double issue, numbers five and six—included material by the giants of late modernism: Marcel Duchamp, Hans Richter, Robert Rauschenberg, Susan Sontag, Merce Cunningham, William S. Burroughs, and Dan Graham (Andy Warhol had designed issue number three). Barthes' essay argued that the intention and biography of a writer had nothing to do with his or her "text," a word he used to indicate an artwork or any kind of cultural production, but in particular the work of writers. That text, once offered to the public, was open to infinite meanings and should not be limited to its origins. Limiting the meaning to its author's intention was, Barthes argued, simply an arbitrary way of interpreting the work. Why should the multitude of readers, with their myriad backgrounds and ways of reading texts, be limited to what the author of the text wanted to say? Barthes wanted to free up interpretation, and that freeing had everything to do with liberation from the history of what had come to denote sincerity—what the artist or writer "really meant":

> The author is a modern figure, a product of our society insofar as, emerging from the Middle Ages with English empiricism, French rationalism, and the personal faith of the Reformation, it discovered the prestige of the individual, of, as it is more nobly put, the "human person." It is thus logical that in literature it should be

> this positivism, the epitome and culmination of capitalist ideology, which has attached the greatest importance to the "person" of the author.[12]

Barthes' essay and the Marxist literary critical impulse to sideline the creator of the artwork from its interpretation had an enormous influence on art and literary criticism of the 1970s, spawning an entire school of literary criticism, deconstruction, and a way of reading called the Yale School, which included figures such as Jacques Derrida, Paul de Man, Geoffrey Hartman, J. Hillis Miller, and, to a far lesser extent, Harold Bloom, who eventually disengaged.

The effect of the Yale School and the death-of-the-author environment on the nation's art-critical infrastructure was to downplay the notion that an expressive artist had anything worthy or interesting to say that could not be reinterpreted in some other way with just as much validity. Even if the artist did have anything worth saying, the dominant critical impulse divorced the person from the text or artwork in order to allow for the "free range of signifiers." All of this Marxist and poststructural theory had the effect—due to its increasing dominance in American artistic and literary circles—of making the expressive self seem silly and inconsequential. Artists that held onto the idea quickly became "old school" humanists nostalgic for the *modern* idea of the strong self. Ergo, the term "postmodern."

Artists of the 1980s were on the hunt for other interesting aesthetic strategies to get them out of this dead end, and one strategy was to offend the public, as Dada had discovered, worked. The author reinstated undeniable subjective force but without the old way of "showing" this expression. The photographer Andres Serrano made national news when he stuck a plastic crucifix in a jar of his own urine and took a picture of it. *Piss Christ* (1987) received a $15,000 prize from the Southeastern Center for Contemporary

Art, an organization sponsored in part by the National Endowment for the Arts, an organization, in turn, funded by US taxpayers "to support the survival of the best of all forms that reflect the American heritage in its full range of cultural and ethnic diversity and to provide national leadership on behalf of the arts."

Naturally, this did not sit well with conservatives on the Senate Finance Committee, which oversees how much money the NEA receives. Senator Jesse Helms (R-NC), a devout and vocal conservative Christian, along with Alfonse D'Amato, the Republican junior senator from New York, led a hearing on the misappropriation of NEA money. D'Amato delivered a heated argument against funding an organization that would support Serrano's "piece of trash." Helms remarked that the senator from New York was "absolutely correct" in his indignation at the blasphemy of "the so-called artwork." "I do not know Mr. Andres Serrano," Helms said, "and I hope I never meet him. Because he is not an artist, he is a jerk."[13] For the North Carolina senator the case was particularly sensitive: the Southeastern Center for Contemporary Art is located in Winston-Salem.

The public got a second dose of moral outrage in the late 1980s when the gay photographer Robert Mapplethorpe, with funding provided by the NEA, took a photograph of a black man's penis peeking out of a pair of pressed polyester trousers (*Man in Polyester Suit*, 1980) and hung the photo alongside images of pristine white tiger lilies. The public was also offended when the artist Jeff Koons (not funded by the NEA) took to encasing everyday objects in plexiglass, as in his vacuum-cleaner series, *New Hoover Celebrity IV, New Hoover Convertible, New Shelton 5 Gallon Wet/Dry, New Shelton 10 Gallon Wet / Dry, Double-decker* (1981–86). Koons also deftly moved kitsch objects—like sculptures of Michael Jackson with his pet monkey, Bubbles; balloon animals; or a Jack Daniels train-shaped whiskey bottle—into the art gallery. A former Wall Street commodities broker, Koons countered Greenberg's dichotomy of kitsch vs. avant-garde by proving that kitsch forms could be fine art if you simply made them out of different materials (he remade many of his kitsch objects in highly polished stainless steel). Free of requirements to express anything about the human condition or themselves, the postmodern artists of the late 1980s unleashed cleverness to obtain attention and fame. By all accounts, they succeeded.

Thanks to increased global trade and steady deregulation of financial and other markets, an explosion of private wealth in the 1980s spawned an art market that, by and large, has been mostly bullish ever since (since 2008 there have been bearish moments). Art galleries of the late 1980s, to return to Donald Kuspit's critical firsthand view of the decade, "had reconciled themselves to the shock value of avant-garde art." Art and the market were holding hands, the latter admitting that the former did, in fact, "have a point" about inauthentic society. After years of avant-garde art existing on the fringes of society, setting itself in opposition to the market, a truce was made, Kuspit explains, and when artists stopped fighting the supposedly deleterious effects of commercialism, both of them, as Warhol knew before anyone, would get very rich. At this moment, both parties gave up on the modernist project of reforming broken society. For all they cared, it could stay broken and inauthentic and insincere. This giving up, Kuspit writes, exhibits a cynicism that "expresses itself as world-weary disillusionment, as if the world was to blame for one's own insincerity and inauthenticity."[14] After nearly two centuries of urging society to shed its authenticity-killing obsessions—money, commerce, industry, society, technology—artists instead agreed with gallerists to create a new form of cultural entertainment: the art world.

Brought in from the existential cold and into the cold light of the white cube, the official avant-garde was neutered of its ability to be sincere without becoming a joke. Instead, it acquiesced to being ironic about its own failure, and about the very possibility of sincerity in art. Sincere cynicism expressed as irony now pervaded the outlook of the avant-garde. It looked with a kind of self-satisfied remorse at its own fiasco of reform, and with equal disdain at the dumb society that would not let itself be changed by art. Postmodernism was the proverbial nail in the coffin of the strong, morally-infused, inwardly-pointed self that had been built up since the sixteenth century, an entity that held to the ideals of personal sincerity and authenticity. Sincerity, no longer credible as a standard of aesthetic criticism, had become "sincerity."

Old habits die hard. After a generation of living with this sincerity-is-dead attitude—and it still walks among us—young artists came to see the sanctioned world of contemporary art and its international fairs (Frieze, Armory, Basel, Miami, Documenta), along with its self-congratulatory prizes and glamorous celebrity, as no longer offering an escape from the mainstream world. Paradoxically, now the expensive purchase of "rebellious" art suffices to *represent* resistance to the deadening effects of capital accumulation and humdrum bourgeois life. Darius Grant, a collector and Wall Street hedge fund manager who collects Jean-Michel Basquiat's pricy graffiti-esque paintings, told London's *Sunday Times* that he has noticed a growing interest in "urban art" among his peers. "If you work in this world," he said, "you're still part of the Establishment—it's quite conservative. You can't rebel at work, but you can buy rebellious art that's shocking or subversive." Likewise, the originally fringe graffiti artist Banksy, who now (as perhaps his premonitory name foresaw) sells six-figure works to the likes of Brad Pitt and Kate Moss: "Everyone loves a rebel," explained salesman Gareth Williams, a senior specialist in urban art at the auction house Bonham's.

All of this is slightly ridiculous, and younger artists have been compelled to rebel against the erstwhile rebels. *New York* magazine's art critic, Jerry Saltz, noted what he saw as a large-scale reaction to the glitzy art world that had laughed the sincere self out of the gallery two decades ago. In a May 2010 article called "Sincerity and Irony Hug It Out," Saltz observes:

> I'm noticing a new approach to artmaking in recent museum and gallery shows. . . . It's an attitude that says, *I know that the art I'm creating may seem silly, even stupid, or that it might have been done before, but that doesn't mean this isn't serious.* At once knowingly self-conscious about art, unafraid, and unashamed, these young artists not only see the distinction between earnestness and detachment as artificial; they grasp that they can be ironic and sincere at the same time, and they are making art from this compound-complex state of mind—what Emerson called "alienated majesty."[15]

Saltz's observation is an important one. It points to a contemporary fusion of sincerity and irony (to be discussed in full in the next chapter) in the wake of postmodern dismay. This new attitude is the only possible intelligent position to take when confronted with an art world that has become a business like any other, whose disdainful elitism has alienated people who still want to make art that is interesting and accessible to them and their friends, and that might have something real, critical, funny, smart, or new to say about the culture in which they are living. This sensibility, born of the 1990s, knows two conflicting things very intimately: 1) the cheesiness of traditional "self-expression," which revives the dead myth of individual uniqueness, regardless of how clichéd and boring the end result may be ("Everyone is an artist!"), and 2) a desire to make meaningful things without being nagged by the idea that ironists might laugh at them. The former position fights with the mythical weight of sincerity as an aesthetic value, the latter with the desire to say something sincerely without second-guessing.

Though it pains me to write it, Michael Stipe, the amazing musician who led the now-defunct band REM, has become the kind of artist who advertises the very dull sincere-artist aesthetic. You see, he now makes sculptures. One is called *My Favorite Ever Edition of the New York Times,* which is his favorite edition of the *New York Times* encased in a plexiglass box. Stipe talked about the piece with the *Guardian*: "It is what it is. The date of the edition is not as important as the experience I had reading the paper on that day. It was a Thursday. The *Times* is always great on a Thursday. So I decided to commemorate and memorialize this experience by preserving the edition in Plexiglas."

Stipe insists on the work's depth and on its relationship to a specific moment in his life, although it appears, the *Guardian* interviewer says, "a bit Duchamp." Stipe (looking, the reporter observes, "momentarily offended") responds, "Well, I'm not a prankster. There is a sincerity to what I am doing. Always, and sometimes to a fault. In a way, that's all I've got. . . . It's a need to express myself in another form. It's like something I have to get out of me."[16] Here self-expression has become synonymous with art; and art, as long as it is sincere and self-expressive, is valuable *because* it is sincere and only if it is sincere, regardless of how dull, repetitive, pointless, or unconnected to the development of art history and critical discussion. Under this logic, anything that anyone makes, whether it is a ready-made newspaper in a plastic box or a collection of diary entries pasted to a wall, is art because it was made with sincerity. This is the resulting logic of deadbeat Romanticism.

Some paintings by Sean Landers mark the opposite of this easy mentality. They are at once strikingly relevant and emotionally touching and utterly stupid: they feature a moody clown sailing alone in a boat. Though they seem to express some fundamental emotional purity, when asked in a 2009 interview if there was a "pure place" in art, Landers responded:

> I don't know why, but when I read this question I just thought of my perineum [the strip of flesh between the anus and scrotum]—I thought it might be nice to start these questions off with a little free association. Looking for truth or purity in oneself through making art is like peeling an infinite onion. Each layer alternates between irony and sincerity. I feel more comfortable being ironic and the audience seems to dig my sincerity. So I give them what they want—I tell them about my perineum.

A bit on the overly self-aware, snarky side, yes. But the title of a recent review of Landers's show *Around the World Alone,* hat-tippingly called "Taint Sincerity," by critic Talon Gustafson, looks smartly at the strained attempts Landers makes to stay cool by admitting how uncool he is. Admitting his faults à la Montaigne, Landers appears to be sincere without having to actually say the word. About works like *I'm Not Cool and I Know It* (2005), Gustafson writes that Landers's obsession with avoiding the pitfalls

> between irony and sincerity, smart and dumb . . . keep his work moving along and like any clown worth his spots . . . . [he is] a trickster of sorts, admitting something to draw you in, to disarm you, to make you sympathetic, while concealing his ulterior motives. I wouldn't characterize Landers as sincere, a label often attributed to him. Being sincere is different from being an open book. The former is genuine, the latter is easily understood.[17]

Landers and some other young artists working today—many included in the New Museum's Younger Than Jesus show and then at the 2010 Whitney Biennial—are attempting, as others were in the 1990s, to escape the burdensome shadow of perma-irony while retaining its tactical humor and effectiveness. Many see the self-referential, hyper-irony of the 1990s and hipster 2000s—*Pop Up Video,* Quentin Tarantino, Dave Eggers, *Might* and *McSweeney's,* David Foster Wallace, Young British Artists, all of that—as a simultaneous attempt to regain the legitimacy of sincerity by attempting ironize oneself out of the dead end.

Thirty years after the postmodern proclamation of the death of the author, the sincerely expressive self, the artist with the true concern (personal, political, religious, obsessive) is beginning again to have legitimacy; Saltz's observation of young artists in New York was echoed across the ocean in Berlin on the evening of September 15, 2011, when the novelist Adam Haslett, author of the prizewinning *Union Atlantic,* stood before an esteemed audience that included the US ambassador, noted scholars, and fellow writers and observed that "postmodern irony" no longer had purchase as a critical method for dealing with the social problems at hand in America. Irony had instead been pressed into employment for marketing "pop-culture nostalgia." One imagines he means things like singer Katy Perry's throwback 1950s' tongue-in-cheek fashion, campy remakes of *The A-Team,* or nearly any commercial aimed at the under-forty audience.

Haslett's statement would have pleased the late David Foster Wallace, who published an essay in the *Review of Contemporary Fiction* in 1993 called "E Unibus Pluram," where he brilliantly addressed just how underestimated was the "irony-effect" of watching television on our perception of the world and of fellow citizens. Wallace argued that we have become acclimated to watching people look "natural" on television—cool and unperturbed—and this had, he thought, created a new kind of personality:

> In the "heroic act" of being able to withstand the "megagaze" of millions you have to be just abnormally self-conscious and self-controlled to appear unwatched before cameras and lenses and men with clipboards. This self-conscious appearance of unself-consciousness is the real door to TV's mirror-hall of illusions, and for us, the Audience, it is both medicine and poison.[18]

While "watching television is pleasurable," much of the pleasure in television "lies in making fun of it." This ironic-anthropological disdain has had effects on other real life sentiments, too, Wallace writes, such as "sincerity" and "passion," both of which are "out, TV-wise." "Irony and ridicule are entertaining and effective," he wrote, "and at the same time they are agents of a great despair and stasis in U.S. culture." Ironic distance had created yet another kind of personality, one that used irony to express disdain of mainstream culture even when not watching television. He included himself, his fiction-writer peers, and other artist types who spent an inordinate amount of time watching TV and being indoors.

This newly widespread attitude is perhaps why Wallace had become so tired of irony, already in 1993. It had lost its critical power because the overwhelming presence of television required its permanent deployment. "How have irony, irreverence, and rebellion come to be not liberating but enfeebling in the culture today's avant-garde tries to write about?" he wondered. Irony tyrannizes us. Its knee-jerk deployment implies to any interlocutor, "How totally *banal* of you to ask what I really mean."

Wallace, who committed suicide in 2008 at the age of forty-six, hoped for a return to earnestness in a group of anti-rebels who "might be willing to risk the yawn, the rolled eyes, the cool smile, the nudged ribs, the parody of gifted ironists, the 'Oh, how *banal*.'" Seeking the wellspring that fed earlier anti-sophisticates and longers after earnestness, Wallace hoped for a return to unembarrassed sincerity in the midst of an ironic culture, a place where we could all put down the wink for a little while.*

* Wallace's friend the novelist Jonathan Franzen wrote an essay called "Farther Away," in the April 18, 2011, issue of the *New Yorker*. The article confirms that earnestly yearning Romanticism is alive and well in American literary culture. Franzen tells of his self-imposed exile on a windy and uninhabited island in the South Pacific, five hundred miles off the coast of Chile, called Alejandro Selkirk (Juan Fernandez Island). Franzen takes with him a copy of English literature's first travel novel, Daniel Defoe's *Robinson Crusoe* (1719), as well as a tiny tin of Wallace's ashes. On this isolated and hellish rock, pelted with rain and cold, Franzen wants to reconnect with himself, to break out of the funk that has consumed him over the previous months as he promoted his latest novel, *Freedom*. (He realizes halfway through his escapade that he longs for a martini and to sit on the couch watching football with his girlfriend in California.) The revealing parallel is this: in 1782 the proto-Romantic English poet William Cowper wrote a poem called "Verses Supposed to be Written by Alexander Selkirk," about the Scottish sailor who was marooned on Juan Fernandez Island in the South Pacific in 1704, and on whom Defoe based the character of Crusoe. The fantasy of isolation and total separation from humanity was already a resonant cultural trope, for when Selkirk returned, four years and four months later, he was interviewed by none other than the founder of the *Tatler*, Richard Steele, resulting in an enormously popular article in *The Englishman*, in 1715. With Franzen's return to the exact same place, publishing an equally popular article, it's hard not to see the trope of Romantic isolation as entirely reinvigorated as a curative of the Western soul.

Chapter VIII : HIP AFFECTED EARNESTNESS

Sincerity is impossible unless it pervades the whole being, and the pretence of it saps the very foundation of character.

- James Russell Lowell, *Literary Essays,* 1890

DURING THE RAINY afternoon of Saturday, April 11, 2009, nearly two hundred young adults huddled inside a room in the Vera List Center at the New School in Manhattan. They had gathered for a panel discussion pronouncing the long-awaited death of a social character: "What Was the Hipster?" The conference was organized by Mark Greif, an assistant professor at the New School and a cofounder of the magazine *n+1.*[1]

"Let me just enunciate a string of keywords," Greif said to open up. "Trucker hats; the undershirts called 'wife-beaters,' worn as outerwear; the aesthetic of basement rec-room pornography, flash-lit Polaroids, fake-wood paneling; Pabst Blue Ribbon; porno or pedophile mustaches; aviator glasses; Americana T-shirts for church socials; tube socks; the late albums of Johnny Cash, produced by Rick Rubin; and tattoos." The list could go on: skinny jeans and tight-fitting hoodies, enormously framed eyeglasses, knit caps, keffiyeh scarves, members-only jackets, slouchy '80s boots, Reeboks, velour and terrycloth. Enough.*

Greif was accompanied that afternoon by some of hipsterdom's most critical observers: Christian Lorentzen, author of a noted *Time Out New York* article about saving New York cool called "Why the Hipster Must Die," and Jace Clayton, a New York-based DJ and music producer known for his global view of hipsterism. In the audience was Robert Lanham, whose *Hipster Handbook* offers a thorough taxonomy of facial hair, dress, language, and tastes—particularly those indigenous to Williamsburg, that famed Petri-dish-of-hip neighborhood in Brooklyn.

The panelists gave their statements and then the floor was opened up for discussion. Some audience members said that the hipster really was dead. Some said that he/she was more alive than ever. Some argued that the hipster was an apolitical being, some that he/she was fully on the left, and some that he/she was an unwitting agent of postcolonialism. Still others wondered whether the hipster was tied to the advancing wealth of first-world nations, or if he/she was Norman Mailer's new White Negro. After weaving in and out of these travails and concerns—downward mobility, anticapitalism, neo-bohemia, Slavoj Žižek, Debbie Gibson, *Charles in Charge*—the microphone landed on an audience member who observed:

> There's a sense that to be a hipster is to be permanently and obsessively committed to being "for real"—that hipsters are the "real" people and their lives are authentic and that the experiences

* Not enough, actually. Please see the Hipster Semiotic Appendix at the end of this chapter.

> they're having are meaningful, so if you live in Bushwick in the McKibbin lofts you're "for real" because you have bedbugs and it sucks. And I'm wondering if this commitment to protecting the authenticity of experiences from a generation before—like the *Tiger Beat* posters and Scott Baio and all this stuff—isn't useful and productive.[2]

> *[Silence from the panel.]*

One year and eight days later, on April 19, 2011, a review of the book that proceeded from the *n+1* conference, *What Was the Hipster? A Sociological Investigation*, shared the same skepticism of hipster-bashing that the lone audience member had sounded. In "Was the Hipster All That Bad?" art critic Ben Davis asked, "Is hipster culture sometimes nihilistic, consumerist, asinine? Oh my, yes." But he notes that a certain strain of contemporary art actually owes much to the quirky predilections of hipster culture: the "freaked-out bricolage" of Assume Vivid Astro Focus, the cartoony-sincere paintings of Elizabeth Peyton, the weirdo technology morphings of Cory Arcangel. One might add a ton of inventive music, from the Fleet Foxes to Das Racist to 808 State to Wild Nothing, to the television satire of aging hipsters, *Portlandia*. Davis lamented that the bulk of the *n+1* conference never noticed these positive contributions because it was seemingly too busy "ridiculing girls with bangs or guys wearing tight pants."

He then outlined a clear explanation of the omnipresent, not-necessarily-freely-chosen ironic worldview that melds with a longing for sincerity which has taken up residence in the minds of so many people under age forty:

> I graduated from college in 2001 with a degree in Humanities and Cultural Studies. With no idea what the hell to do with that, I went to work in a bookstore. All my co-workers had degrees in

> English or Philosophy, and we all had scorn for the dumb best-seller tastes of our customers—in exact proportion to our keen awareness of the uselessness of our own cultivated tastes, the worth of which apparently topped out at $12.50 an hour. What do you do in that situation except be ironic?[3]

This kind of irony has nothing to do with pop singer Alanis Morissette's "isn't it ironic" kind of irony. This is far more serious and far more compelling. This attitude has to do with how an entire generation—how repeated generations, in fact—has grown up in the shadow of a culture that values economics and consumption over the values of humanism and artistic enterprise. Davis's expression of becoming ironic not exactly on purpose is as sincere a confession as there is. It is where millions of young people exist in relation to their own culture. "Entire strata of the population have been living for a considerable period in an *inner somewhere-else,*" wrote the German philosopher Peter Sloterdijk of his own early 1980s' generation. "They do not feel bound to what are called the fundamental values of society."

Hipster subculture partakes of this sensibility. It burst onto the scene in the late 1990s (some, including Mark Greif, say exactly in 1999, following the World Trade Organization riots in Seattle), and flourished until around 2007. Traditionally, hipsters were college-educated young adults who resisted entering the traditional workforce after their studies and instead adhered to the old Romantic notion that commercialism was bad for the soul. They declined to enter the for-profit rat race and instead fell into non-mainstream modes of living in cities with high degrees of education, technology, and capital: New York, Portland, Chicago, Boston, Los Angeles, San Diego, Austin, Baltimore, San Francisco, Seattle. These cities were open to new influences, racially mixed, morally relaxed, and gay- and lesbian-friendly—the ancient ingredients for any creative mecca. These new urban émigrés—like the bohemians, hippies, and punks of generations past—worked in bars, coffee shops, cafés, and clubs; some fell into the worlds of design, publishing, marketing, and Web development. But they were mostly concerned with authentically living for themselves and their artistic endeavors. By deliberately opting out of economic-based competition, hipsters became sidelined into a race far more subtle: the race to cool. Hipsters chased the ideals of sincerity and authenticity with a wink. While they wished for a more authentic kind of life than the normal suburban one in which they were raised, they were also aware, nursed on the teat of postmodern theory, that their ideals were unnatural constructs, and therefore hokey or embarrassing.

Following the terrorist attacks of September 11, 2001, the conflict between irony and sincerity among the media-savvy and cynical youth came to a head, not least because ideals became serious business again. Not to take freedom or democracy or unquestioning patriotism entirely seriously was akin to treason. Roger Rosenblatt of *Time* magazine threatened on September 20, 2001, "In this new and chastened time there will be no room for ironists." Historian Taylor Branch wrote in the *Los Angeles Times* that the 9/11 attacks had brought the nation "to a turning point against a generation of cynicism." Gerry Howard, editorial director of Broadway Books, told *Entertainment Weekly*, "I think somebody should do a marker that says irony died on 9-11-01." The *Atlanta Journal Constitution* wishfully opined on the demise of a popular culture "drenched in irony and cynicism" that had become "a playground for postmodern hipsters." At *Newsday*, James Pinkerton hailed a victory for "sincerity, patriotism, and earnestness." And Graydon Carter, the editor of *Vanity Fair*, famously marked it as "the end of the age of irony." As political journalists all joined in on the "death of irony" pronouncements, young hipster and non-hipster ironists were confused: irony had been their default trade for decades, and wouldn't it be the best defense against determined religious zealots who took everything far, far, far, far too seriously—who were super-sincere in wanting to kill Americans?

Nevertheless, ever since 9/11, hipsters have been the target of fun, especially by the tongue-in-cheek set: Robert Lanham's *Hipster Handbook* (2003), Josh Aiello's *A Field Guide to the Urban Hipster* (2003),* and comedian Joe Mande's colorful *Look At This F*cking Hipster* (website, 2009; book, 2010). Websites like hipstersareannoying.com, ihatehipsters.com, hipsterrunoff.com, and countless other blogs have waded into the comedy of hipsters' tiresome competition of insider knowingness. The self-proclaimed anti-hipster movement even has a "critical" argument against them: while hipsters believe they are authentic individuals, they all wear the same things and shop in the same stores and listen to the same music. Their radical individuality is a narcissistic illusion, and it has become culturally tedious. This was certainly part of the *n+1* conference, too. Some of the vitriol of the anti-hipster movement seems to be less about its success than anger at its failure.

Given the hipster's multiple valences, the figure has provided fodder for a handful of cultural excursions into the sincerity-irony matrix in our midst. In the small-budget film *The Cult of Sincerity*, by NYU film school grads Adam Browne, Brendan Choisnet, and Daniel Nayeri, tensions between the two sentiments are aired in the context of a hipster outgrowing his irony. Joseph, the main character, steps up to a microphone at a Brooklyn coffeehouse and begins a Ginsbergesque rant about the twentysomethings of his generation, who he sees as bored, unhappy cynics:

* Both these books play on the joke of science's taxonomical mind. In treating the hipster as a naturally occurring kind, the caricatured voice of faux science gains humorous momentum by misplacing its analytic prowess. This giggling understanding between taxonomist-author and in-the-know reader reveals that cynical satire can permeate absolutely everything; even trained, enlightened learnedness, which has labored for centuries to be the mark of seriousness, is turned easily into a joke.

> I can't shake the idea that we're all a bunch of mean, selfish, sarcastic, sad people! A generation of us. I mean, look at this! We sit around. We roll our eyes at our parents' ideas of hard work, so we romanticize dumpster diving and sleeping till noon . . . Anything homegrown is "parochial," unless it's kitschy, then it's hip, because it does not know how "not-hip" it is. I mean, really, what is that? Clove cigarettes. Ironic trucker hats. Seriously? What kind of douchebags have we turned into? All we have is our sarcasm to hide behind. Well, I am not going to do it anymore. I am going to start a cult of sincerity. It's going to stand against everything I've become.

Joseph wants to find something positive to believe in, but also "simple enough to iron onto a T-shirt." He strives to be generous by running around Brooklyn opening doors for people, planting trees, and apologizing to strangers for his sarcasm, emotional detachment, egotism, and a host of other maladies he deems consequences of living an insincere life.

Radio host Jesse Thorn's program *The Sound of Young America* satirically announced that in the post-9/11 world "irony would be replaced by soft, sweet sincerity. Somewhere, an eagle shed a single tear." But Thorn's position went beyond the mere "dry mocke"; he attempted to repackage sincerity with an ironic twist, offering self-consciously innocent slogans such as "Be More Awesome" and "Maximum Fun." His "New Sincerity" movement began not only as a response to 9/11, but as an effort to move beyond the ironic/cynical postmodernism that he (among many others) saw as the prevailing sensibility before the attacks. The New Sincerity tried to invent a shiny new sentiment, one that would encompass both the credibility of irony and the earnest horror of 9/11. Thorn hilariously propounded on his May 21, 2005, broadcast:

> My position is irony is dead . . . but at the same time, just to return to old-fashioned sincerity, and particularly the kind of

> sentimentality that that draws in with it . . . we don't need it. So that's why we've created the New Sincerity. A perfect example of the New Sincerity is Evel Knievel. There's no way to take Evel Knievel literally. It's impossible. The man has a leather jumpsuit and he drives a rocket car. The leather jumpsuit has red, white, and blue stars and stripes on it. It's absolutely preposterous. On the other hand, there's no way to appreciate Evel Knievel ironically. He's too awesome. He has—I don't know if we've mentioned this—a leather jumpsuit with the Stars and Stripes on it and a rocket-powered car. That's why we appreciate Evel Knievel with The New Sincerity.

Some critics went on to suggest the phrase "new sincerity" for works by filmmakers like Wes Anderson (*The Royal Tenenbaums, The Life Aquatic with Steve Zissou*), Sofia Coppola (*Lost in Translation*), Michel Gondry (*Eternal Sunshine of the Spotless Mind*), Spike Jonze (*Being John Malkovich, Adaptation*), Charlie Kaufman (*Synecdoche, New York*), Zach Braff (*Garden State*), Lars von Trier (*Dancer in the Dark, Dogville, Breaking the Waves, Melancholia*), and the unaffected, unrehearsed, no-props-or-lighting-allowed Dogme 95 movement. Even filmmakers on the dulled edge of jock humor were getting bored sick of irony in the mid-2000s. In a blog piece called "Sincerity Is the New Black," Worm Miller, the writer of National Lampoon's *Dorm Daze,* observed, "I've been feeling this way for a while, but the other day when I passed a hipster clothing store in Hollywood that had a humongous replica of a urinal eating up half its floor, what once might've intrigued me or made me laugh just seemed stupid and boring. It reeked of the kind of bland un-creativeness that portends a dying trend. . . . And right before there's a shift, the trend inevitably becomes stale and lame."[4] That was in 2007.

Even the 2008 election of Barack Obama, a watershed moment for those hoping for a return of sincerity to political life, could not fully counter this nervous oscillation between sincerity and irony as it continued to play out in American popular culture. The film director Ari Gold (not the *Entourage* one) enlisted none other than Neil Peart, the drummer from Rush, to appear in his film about air-drumming competitions, *Adventures of Power* (2009). The film conveys a true love of intricate drum solos *and* a tongue-in-cheek mocking of guys who like to air-drum. Jack Black of *School of Rock* fame also melded irony and sincerity in his praise of Rush—a rock band whose comeback tours have been cheered by overflowing stadiums of jubilant fans feeling like they were seventeen again—in the 2010 documentary *Rush: Behind the Lighted Stage*. After falsetto-singing a stanza of the song "The Spirit of the Radio," Black leans back in a sofa with a pillow on his lap and says:

> When you're hearing lyrics like that, that are so earnest and sincere, talking about honesty in art and asking some of the tougher intellectual questions with that great music behind it, man: they really offered something in rock that was in short supply. *[Make sure to comically elongate the "y" in "supply."]*

This same sentiment of earnest yet ironic sentimentality is evidenced in the 2009 hit Broadway musical *Rock of Ages,* which features twenty-eight of the "best rock ballads," such as "Don't Stop Believin'," "We Built This City," and "I Wanna Know What Love Is." The sounds of Journey, Styx, REO Speedwagon, and Air Supply provide the soundtrack to a story of a small-town girl who falls in love with a famous rock star in Los Angeles in 1987. "We walk the line between irony and sincerity," says director Kristin Hanggi. "I want you to feel the way you felt when you were fifteen and young and alive, and could do anything." (The irony-sincerity sentiment is becoming zeitgeisty: New Line Cinema is currently making a motion picture of *Rock of Ages,* staring Alec Baldwin, Tom Cruise, Paul Giamatti, and Catherine Zeta-Jones.)

But film and stage are not the only places where the irony-sincerity matrix has played out in recent years. Lately there has been a return to musical genres that existed well before 9/11: early punk, disco, rap, New Wave—with an emphasis on sparse Casio keyboard sounds, drum machines, and jangly guitars. Bands like Arcade Fire, Scissor Sisters, CSS, Chairlift, and Temper Trap (among many more) all employ heavy nostalgia and a wink to a less self-conscious, DIY time in music. More prominently, a resurgence of American folk music has occurred over the last decade: indie-folk, freak-folk, psych-folk, and New Weird America: singer-songwriters like Will Oldham, Devendra Banhart, Black Mountain, Sufjan Stevens, Iron and Wine, M. Ward, Bright Eyes, Tiny Vipers, My Morning Jacket, Bon Iver, Scout Niblett, Phosphorescent, and Fleet Foxes. Their attractiveness is based, in part, on the desire for music that is stripped down and honest. Their fans desire albums that are not overproduced or fed through the market-demographic algorithms at BMG or Sony to find out first what sells before they are made.

Through quotidian lyrics with wistful winks to the rustic American past, some neo-folk bands revive the nostalgic sounds of the nineteenth-century Scots-Irish Appalachian outback: acoustic guitars, mandolins, banjos, dobros, falsetto voices, and gospel-like harmonizing. Other works recall the bare-bones folk music of the 1960s, like Simon and Garfunkel, Woody Guthrie, Pete Seeger, Bob Dylan, and Joan Baez. All of it, however, expresses this clear equation: pure voice + instrument = sincerity. This traditional equation, made so famous during the 1960s, communicates emotional escape from the spastic commercialism of top-forty radio.

Increasingly, these indie folk bands are bursting out of urban bedrooms and iPods and into magazine articles, NPR features, and

MTV interviews.* Like their dedicated fans, many of these singer-songwriters wear their beards long and thick, sport flanneled fashion, tight pants, and dorky glasses, and marry stunningly earnest music with a fast ironic understanding. A *New Yorker* review of My Morning Jacket's most recent album, *Circuital* (2011), suggests that the band makes kin of "punks and hippies . . . their differences finally outweighed by affinities." Lead singer Jim James's voice can, unlike most singers, pull off "unironic optimism that shades into nondenominational worship."[5]

American mainstream media that like to think they have a finger on the pulse of youth culture pride themselves on making executive-approved nods to this kind of cool authenticity. ABC News interviewed singer-songwriter Justin Vernon, a.k.a. Bon Iver, at Sound Fix Records in Brooklyn. His first album, *For Emma, Forever Ago,* had been named best album in 2008 by the *Guardian* newspaper and the website Pitchfork, among other laurels. It was praised for its honesty and "hushed intimacy" by Sasha Frere-Jones of the *New Yorker,* who called the singer's haunting falsetto vocals "a combination of the secular and the religious in one cloudy mass . . . as exalted as any sound in American popular music today."[6] Vernon's compelling personal narrative is pure mythical Americana, filled with all the signposts of the Romantic spiritual travelogue: a Wisconsin native's journey to North Carolina; a relationship breakup; a return home to isolation in a northern wood; living alone in a family-owned hunting cabin; killing his own game; a renewed sense of peace; the spark of musical

* And in the case of Fleet Foxes, the in-flight soundtrack of Air France, which began playing the song "Ragged Wood" as a welcome-aboard song within a week of its release. More oddly, perhaps, was '80s-clad John Norris, a former MTV host, who just prior to interviewing the Fleet Foxes in Brooklyn in August 2008, said, "They're pastoral; they're rural; they're even at times spiritual, which proves that sometimes all that hype is actually worth it." The cerebrally jarring thing here is that very hype that Norris is in the act of creating is simultaneously looked upon by him with skepticism as something that might not be worth creating.

genius amidst the backdrop of a snowy forest. Healing. Redemption. Recovery. Nature unadorned.

The interview segment on ABC's Web-only show *The Mix* employed a jumpy, handheld camera (helps to convey authenticity) that pans Vernon's hand gestures and flannel shirt and then glides up to the pressed-Oxford, upturned-sleeves reporter, Dan Harris, who asks:

> Did the making of the album actually make you feel better? Was it healing in some way?
>
> *Vernon:* It really was, and I have trouble kinda talking about, like, the depth of that, and sort of, like, the real qualities of the, like, healing process that it had. But I was, like, really hooked up on a lot of stuff, and that's sort of, like, the story of the record, too, is, like, a period of my life, and it was really hard, and it was really, like, dim and mediocre—kinda, like, indifference, you know, like, all over the place. And, for that, that three months, what it did was sort of like a spiritual reconnection for me, to my own music. And it was really, really important. And I still have never really even been able to explain to my family or even my friends how important that was for me, but . . .
>
> *Harris:* And you made this record . . . all by yourself, in a cabin, in the woods.
>
> *Vernon:* Yeah.
>
> *Harris:* It has caught fire in a way that I haven't seen happen in quite a while. It just came out Tuesday, but it was on the Best of the Year list for Pitchfork last year.
>
> *Vernon*: Yeah.
>
> *Harris*: And it's been blogged about. It's the subject of all this buzz.
>
> *Vernon*: Yeah.

Why does this whole scene feel slightly uncomfortable? Because Vernon may perform himself sincerely in private art but he cannot then give away the mysteries of this deep plumbing of the self in public without seeming cheesy. The inability to articulate feeling has become the best evidence for its sincere, overwhelming power. Moreover, Vernon repeatedly calls his record "honest." Both men, teetering on the edge of admitting their own fictitiousness, know deep down that this descriptor, "honest," has been deployed against the dishonest performance in which they are both presently engaged. Vernon mentions Bob Dylan's *New Morning* album, describing it as "really wrong—like, it's not well produced or anything, but, it's like such an honest record for him." The aesthetic recipe is again clear: honesty trumps production and planning. Sincerity is what counts.

This same sentiment is explicit in another episode of *The Mix*, this one featuring the Brooklyn band The Pains of Being Pure at Heart, a jangly, Clash-lite quartet. Dan Harris asks, "The super-obvious question is, the name: The Pains of Being Pure at Heart; it's a very cumbersome name. Where does that come from?" The band members hem and haw a bit, and then lead singer Kip Berman shyly mutters, "It wasn't just, like, some obscure reference, or, like, the cool guys in the tight pants or something. It was like very, um, very emotionally sincere." Harris pulls out his anti-sincerity pliers and begins to snip:

> *Harris:* Earnest on purpose.
> *Berman:* Well, "earnest on purpose" sounds almost like it's calculated. It's more like just speak genuine and sing about what you want to sing about, and express what you want to say. I mean, you only get about three and a half minutes for anyone to care about what you have to say, so, try to think about it and say something that is sincere and good.

Berman knows he has just confronted resistance to his dewy-eyed claim to sincerity. "Earnest on purpose" bespeaks—as Sartre reminded his queasy readers—a consciousness of what one is doing and how one is acting, an inadvertent admission that one is trying to play the role of the sincere artist. But, Berman maintains, these guys actually are sincere, and not on purpose. Not wanting to be convinced, Harris responds to this skittish hymn to sincerity with a closing salvo of the tight-fisted realism the Romantic self had been running from for two centuries: "My friends would have kicked your ass." (There really are pains to being pure at heart.)

Amidst the toggling between sincerity and irony, *SPIN* magazine asked Beck (the musician, not the TV personality) about his own take on the matter in an interview called "Sincerity Is the New Irony": "When you do a song like 'Debra,' and people think you were being funny and kind of ironic, and then you do a song like 'Lost Cause' and they think you're being very sincere and personal, they champion that. Why do you think people still need sincerity over inauthenticity?" Beck's answer articulates this fused sensibility well, echoing independently Jesse Thorn's New Sincerity:

> Somebody can be moved tremendously by a Neil Diamond song, or a John Tesh song, so it depends on who's listening. I've always been a fan of ambiguity, and I like art that elicits a mixed response. I think the songs you're talking about are pretty obvious: one is pretty tongue-in-cheek, and the other one is pretty heartfelt. But, as far as your question: I think it's more of an American thing, a question of authenticity. I usually call it—I guess as you said—sincerity. I think for me and my favorite artists, it was always a mixture. Dylan, or the Stones, and, you know, most of those acts eventually got fairly goofy at points.[7]

As with art, so with life. Over the past few years, it is not just neo-folk music that has made its nod to the countryside; there has also been a resurgence of a desire to return to the actual countryside, to get off the grid, to live from the land alone. This motivation has much to do, without doubt, as it did during the 1960s and 1970s back-to-the-land movement, with environmental consciousness, frustration with politics, and new methods of self-sustaining power generation. In books like Novella Carpenter's *Farm City* (2009), about urban backyard farm subsistence, Barbara Kingsolver's *Animal Vegetable Miracle* (2007), about gentleman farming, and Colin Beaven's 2009 *No Impact Man: The Adventures of a Guilty Liberal Who Attempts to Save the Planet, and the Discoveries He Makes About Himself and Our Way of Life in the Process,* the return to nature is also an escape from urban irony.

Irish photographer Iain McKell's bestselling book *The New Gypsies* (2011) perfectly displays this Romantic obsession through photographs of a group of post-punk anti-Thatcher protesters known as Travellers, who left the city limits of London in 1986 and moved—without new homes—into the English countryside. They have been wandering there ever since, raising families and living without the luxuries of the modern world for over three decades. Travellers exist outside the state apparatus, have no bank accounts, addresses, or uses for energy beyond the wood they burn and the grass they collect for their horses, which is what they use to pull the carts and wagons they live in. Photographer McKell said in a May 2011 interview, "We are part of nature, we come from nature, but we have been cut off from nature. . . . But the Travellers sleep under the stars, they experience nature 24/7: the moon, the weather, plants, animals, the environment. They are part of it."[8]

While Karl Marx thought the city the best place for history's internal tensions to play out in the "open mixing of classes," these and other examples express in part that hip's deepest visions of the good life are increasingly shaped by an imagination of the old agricultural existence, an attempt to return to, as Herbert Read wrote in 1968, a "cult of sincerity." In this yearning sits the most ancient and conservative of Protestant-Romantic sacred preferences: the virgin landscape in contrast to the fallen civilized world.

Emblematic of this escapist sentiment as it relates to hipsters was a March 2008 *New York Times* article by Allen Salkin called "Leaving Behind the Trucker Hat," about a young man named Benjamin Shute. Shute was raised on the Upper East Side and educated at Amherst College; he settled in Williamsburg, Brooklyn, where he drank Pabst Blue Ribbon, wore a trucker hat and aviator sunglasses, and played darts in a league. After a few years, frustrated with the hipster pose, he ditched the city and moved two hours north to start an organic farm with his friend Miriam Latzer. "I never thought I wanted to farm," Shute said. "But it feels like an honest living." The duo's parents, comprised of a professor, a foundation director, a librarian, and a criminologist, were all "shocked" at the career move. "They think it's crazy that I'm a farmer," Latzer told the *Times*, "they wonder what planet I came from."[9] Back in the city, the agricultural-local fetish was the same: buying artisanal cheeses and breads and organic vegetables was the mark of the proper sensibility. "The Billyburg scene has changed," said Annaliese Griffin, a pro-organic blogger. She told Salkin, "Having a cool cheese in your fridge has taken the place of knowing what the cool band is. Our rock stars are ricotta makers."

As a social character, the hipster has tried hard to camouflage or escape humdrum bourgeois life—an ultimately Christian-inspired existence of banalities and pressed Docker slacks and pained smiles that Nietzsche once called a "slow suicide: a petty bore, durable life; gradually quite ordinary, bourgeois, mediocre."[10] For this reason, the uncivilized child, nature, and the antisocial character continue to inspire hipster fashion (childlike sneakers, clothes that are too small, wife-beaters, hillbilly beards, ethnic tattoos). These are the go-to figures because both child and outsider live freely, the Romantics say, unhampered by the pestering superego that hounds the well-to-do. Civilization has not yet dampened their vital and honest instincts. They are sincere in their crassness, authentic in their uncouthness—unpolished, unaffected, unsophisticated innocents. Their lack of sophistication excuses them from blame for society's ills—capitalism, consumerism, mechanization. Dressing or otherwise looking like these outsiders enacts an implied opposition to social evils and thereby attempts to regain the sheen of authenticity these social types are imputed to possess.

But the hipster's aping of lower-class or fringe groups in order to live more sincerely does something quite sneaky: it permits affinity with the working class or criminal (um, hardly parallel!) while resolutely, through irony, ensuring that they're not mistaken for members of it. This incongruity strikes a careful posture between sentimental association and social distancing. Appearance and reality are distinguishable, lest appearance say something too real. A recent billboard advertising campaign for a newspaper in über-cool Berlin reads, "Berlin is where no one really knows whether you are in or out." The accompanying photograph shows a hipster wearing a horridly colored pleather jacket walking past an overweight working-class man watering the porch flowers outside his street-level apartment wearing the exact same jacket. This cheeky juxtaposition bespeaks a strange confluence: the proletariat—a word forbidden in America—and the bourgeois hipster, given these bad economic times, are becoming increasingly indiscernible. The return of acid-wash jeans would close the gap completely.*

* An ongoing 2009 event highlighted the bourgeois character of hipsters in relation to something long anti-bourgeois: petty crime. When the hipster grifter Kari Ferrell—Korean-born, tattooed, pierced, pixie-haircut, sexually aggressive—landed an administrative job at *Vice*, in Willliamsburg, the response to her was anything but outsiderish. A coworker Googled her and "up popped a photo of his flirtatious new coworker on the Salt Lake City Police Department's Most Wanted list," writes the *New York Observer*. Ferrell was wanted on five different warrants, including for $60,000 in bad checks, forgery, and shoplifting. To win friends and sympathy, Farrell lied that she

It saddens hipsters and thrills clothing manufacturers that trends once hip have caught on with frat guys and sorority girls looking to spice up their wardrobes. American "rebel capitalism" that "commodifies your dissent" now helps the American consumer retail economy along at ever-greater speeds, even amidst its current lethargy. Omnipresent advertisements for hip fashions have been smilingly proclaiming their insiderness: "As featured in *Life & Style* magazine this week, your ordinary hoodie has been jazzed up with fun prints. The celebs love them and so do we!" "Every knitter will adore these timeless, fashionable, and extremely wearable hats, all photographed on models in a chic urban setting." Urban Outfitters: "Product Description: Squared plastic Dad-style aviators, finished with a goldtone metal bridge and fitted with clear lenses. Please note, these Readers do not contain magnifying lenses—they improve your look, not your vision." The Gap advertises "Williamsburg" jeans, in skinny black. Even Mastercard is now beyond your idea of hip: "Skinny Jeans: $160. Vintage Band T-Shirt: $45. Hair Wax: $25. Looking like you just rolled out of bed: Priceless." In fact, entire brand identities have long been built on the Romantic trope: "Just Do It" (Nike), "Go Ahead, You're Worth It" (L'Oréal), "Think Different" (Apple), "Have It Your Way" (Burger King), and the more conniption-inducing "Blaze Your Own Trail: Jack Kerouac Had It Right" (*Golf Digest*, May 2006).

---

had lung cancer, that she was estranged from her parents, and that she was pregnant with the baby of whomsoever she happened to be dating. A series of relationships with trusting men resulted in mysterious disappearances of cell phones, ATM cards, and cash. In 2009 the Salt Lake City Police Department ordered Farrell's extradition from New York state. After being shipped back to Utah, Ferrell made such big headlines in New York for her jokey criminality and arrest that she was subsequently interviewed from prison by ABC News. "I'm just outspoken and I say funny things that are ridiculous and I assumed that people would be able to understand that they're jokes," she said. "Apparently they don't." Misinterpreting irony has never met such swift reprisal as having your wallet stolen. The next year, Farrell was out of jail and hosting the Webutante Ball in Brooklyn and blogging at the snarky website Animal New York. In 2011 she hosted the New York Beard and Moustache Championships.

For half a century, marketing executives, trend scouts, and brand managers have convinced consumers that primal, punky, outsiderish, invigorated life can be attained through things you can buy. Coolness was acquired through consumption, through wearing things and acting in a way that resembled the dress and behavior of the actors and music stars we saw on television or in film. We bought that logic entirely, making cool the nuclear core of our consumer paradise that would advance the profits of corporations. That core, of course, completes the illusion that consumers have not actually sacrificed what is existentially important; by conferring cool, the market hides its own blame in destroying what Rousseau would have said was necessary to cultivate in order to be free: authenticity. Businesses want some of what hip has always offered, the story goes, and when they found out how to get it, they devised the famed cultural contradiction of capitalism: marginality from the center.

This is why hipster culture is so nostalgic. Like the modern art from which it originates, it has to continuously plumb the recent past for things not yet incorporated into the marketing machine. This neo-camp brain recalls bits of schlock culture and theme songs of pop shows from the 1970s and 1980s because, being not that old, it still can. These fuzzy moments of recollection preserve real memories before they are either made into corporate mascots or forgotten altogether, as the *n+1* audience member proposed. Likewise, aging hipster Annie Lin waxed nostalgic, heading home after a concert:

> We somehow ended up with a large group of people on a rooftop. We all lay down on the steps with our beers and looked at the stars. Nate and I played a vigorous match of rock-paper-scissors; I won. Over the course of the evening, we debated the merits of vinyl versus digital, acoustic versus electric, and New Williamsburg versus Old . . .[11]

Wistfully remembering and preserving newly obsolete cultural objects, productions, games, and gestures is a way to say no, to resist the new, to turn back from what feels like a forward movement into an increasingly dark future.

A sincere remembrance of things past, however commodified or cheesy or kitschy or campy or embarrassing, remains real and small and beautiful because otherwise these old things are about to be discarded by a culture that bulldozes content once it has exhausted its economic utility. And so we get all these things: *Charles in Charge*, Nickelodeon, jelly bracelets, Teddy Ruxpin, cassette tapes, *Teenage Mutant Ninja Turtles, He-Man*, shoulder pads, Swatches, Shamrock Shakes, parachute pants, Ray-Ban shades, *Alf,* Rubik's Cube, Trapper Keepers,* jean jackets, and feathered hair. They are ridiculous, but they serve as quaint reminders of a younger, easier, warmer, more sincere life, particularly set against the hardships of adulthood and responsibility in difficult economic times. This remembrance, this yearning for the objects and symbols of a purer youth, recapitulates the entire history of the Protestant-Romantic-rebellious ethos that has aimed for five hundred years to jam a stick into the endlessly turning spokes of time, culture, and consumption and yell, "Stop! I want to get off."

* The cover of Katy Perry's single "Last Friday Night (T.G.I.F.)" offers the overkill message of 1980s'-looking nostalgia: an overwhelmingly pink Trapper-Keeper-like design (*Tron*-ish, actually) overlaid a photo of Perry wearing enormous black-framed glasses, braces with headgear, zits, and donning a general-anxiety-disorder glare, replete with eyes a-poppin' and '80s crazy neon. The cover altogether screams, "I'm Still in Eighth Grade!!" It's hard to imagine how much further outside of cool one could actually go to be, as Katy Perry is, in the middle of cool. Peeing in your pants? Puking in your schoolbag? The only way something like Perry's album cover makes any sense as cool is that it combines, almost photorealistically, all the outsider tropes of Romanticism into one garish montage that leaps at the eyes in an overwhelming attack.

Hipster Semiotic Appendix

The following entries attempt to unpack some popular hipster fashions to reveal the tight knot of sincerity and irony they contain. I pray no offense but fear otherwise.

The Trucker Hat: From *Jackass* to Ashton Kutcher to *Jersey Shore,* the foam-and-mesh cap has made its rounds. It has become so tired that even to talk about how tiresome it is has itself become tiresome. Nevertheless: what once evidenced an occupation (truck driving) tied to low social standing (average national salary as of September 2011, $57,000) now invests its college-educated wearer (average national salary as of September 2011, $50,034) with a bragging (and misinformed) defiance of bourgeois standards. Reminding the cosmopolitan public that there is actual dirty work to get done, the trucker hat stresses class roots rather than class aspirations, reversing the nominal arc of the American dream. It thumbs its nose at bourgeois upward mobility, which it finds worthless but of which it is secretly jealous. This false point of class disdain is shoved into high relief when it is worn by Nicole Richie, Paris Hilton, Lindsay Lohan, Miley Cyrus, or sold at Barney's and Bergdorf Goodman. The trucker hat thus carries on its brim a glow of phantom integrity: imparting a strong, don't-take-no-shit attitude to the blue-collar guys with whom it originates, the hat now dishonestly transmits that myth to whoever wears it. Downward mobility and class resentment as character-builders.

The hat had already debuted on skateboarders, Johnny Knoxville, and *Jackass* in the early 1990s, just like baggy pants, thrift-shop aesthetics, and retro had done. The trucker-hat-as-agricultural-reference has an even more preppy precedent: after the 1987 credit crunch, J. Crew barn jackets and denim shirts became farmy urban chic and blue-collar styles as weekend wear for Wall Street traders grounded the wearer's identity as stable and reliable, forging a fashion solidarity with the workers whose jobs they were obliterating. Trends that reference the "blue-collar life" perform a handy alchemy of class via the ease of the mail-order catalogue. But the trucker hat's popularity re-boomed amidst social and economic conditions that would warrant it: the 1999 dissolution of wealth following the dot-com crash and 9/11. These two events were the last back-to-basics moments prior to the 2008–09 economic recession, which had the multiple effects of reanimating blue-collar styles, stern brows, pursed lips, and grim admissions. These crises swept away superficialities and urged a cultural return to serious things, for which the hat is a symbol. It now conveys both the jokey unlawfulness of *Jackass* and the seriousness of post-9/11, leading to a dense knot of ironic tension: it caricatures the working class but admits that their experiences are more real than the wearer's own. Unraveled further, however, the hipster trucker hat craps upon its origins, thumbing its nose at the lives from which it originates, admitting that they are mere synecdoche ripe for the taking.

The Beard: This common trend suggests that the clean-shaven, well-groomed man is overly civilized, untrustworthy, wimpy, and cunning. Men with beards are real and rugged, but, because of the beard, they don't have to act it. Without effort on the part of their owners, beards display irrefutable maleness and a bold promotion of one's own authenticity. The hipster beard wants to convey a sense of dominant character and personality, uniqueness, impatience with silly games, and a clear-eyed, worldly realism, like a late-nineteenth-century frigate captain in enemy waters. But because the beard took on a soft, Jesus-y feel beginning in the 1960s that flowed into the early 1970s, the hipster beard now bears both crosses in uncomfortable tension: a tough, straightforward character who still understands your feelings. The beard has returned, in this sense, to its Romantic roots as evidence of its wearer's proximity to nature. It connects the contemporary Romantic to his inner animalism, his hormonal tether to the wild and biological self, his opposition to civilized, bourgeois society: no tricks, no cunning, no fake, polite crap. Just *mano a mano.* The beard thus resolutely evidences its opposition to the white-collar world's prohibition of it, conveying a sense of trendy insubordination. Indeed, "recession beards" have arrived: unemployed investment bankers now have the freedom to grow one in their retreat from trickery and re-entrance into the world of humans. The mass-market-hip clothing company H & M, too, employed blue-eyed, bearded men wearing cardigans and thick wool scarves for their fall 2009 billboard campaign. This combination of the genteel and wild brings the rugged into civilized society. The singer Sting, at his December 2008 Christmas concert at the Cathedral Church of St. John the Divine, wore frock coattails, a top hat, high collar, and cane along with his beard, completing the sense that the nineteenth century has returned to a culture that wants to go back to a time before global warming and digital overload. "Sting looked like quite the 19th-century Victorian gentleman when he performed a concert of winter songs," wrote Jon Pareles of the *New York Times*. "He wore a long frock coat, a white shirt and an antique-style tie. Much of the music originated from even earlier times: 15th-century carols, songs from Purcell operas, traditional English ballads." But the hipster beard, for all its surface commentary, reveals something more fundamental about its wearer's inner life: a sense of inauthenticity he has without one. The hipster beard, unlike the non-hipster beard, rides the coattails of manly ruggedness with a degree of cheekiness, saying, *What this beard appears to be, I am not*. A simple counterexample highlights the point: hipsters with beards are not just normal guys with beards. Hipster beards only look like real-guy beards. Attempting sincere presentation of the brawny, unadorned self, hipsters are weighted down by the transparency of their attempt, preventing them from being what they want to be: unself-conscious outsiders. But the "fringe" New York City Beard and Moustache Championship has grown so enormously that on September 23, 2009, it made its way to the homepage of Yahoo!, the most popular webmail client on planet Earth, right next to a story about baking the best oatmeal muffins.

The Mustache: The hair grown above the upper lip and below the nose performs a similar feat, but differently: by playing in the interstice of the clean-shaven and rugged, the mustache indicates shiftiness of character—not all good, not all bad. It thus imparts a feeling of the charming, risqué deviant, a source of moral inscrutability. Remember: the devil has a mustache. So did Hitler and Stalin, and so do most Middle Eastern men. But so did Albert Einstein, Teddy Roosevelt, Groucho Marx, Gandhi, and Tom Selleck. The mustache is a so-called shifting signifier. Discussed over the past several years in the fashion pages of newspapers and magazines, the hipster mustache trend was pinched from gay, working class, porno, and 1970s' iconography and sitcoms. The *New York Times* fashion section wrote, "youngish cultural provocateurs like the fashion photographer Terry Richardson, Dov Charney, the owner of American Apparel clothing, and Morgan Spurlock, the filmmaker of *Super Size Me,* began sporting mustaches in a statement of retro hip. . . . [Originally] gay icons like Freddie Mercury of Queen brought national attention to the mustache as a gay style."[1] The mustache began its march out of the strictly military realm with the Beatles' *Sgt. Pepper* album and, then, further, after the 1969 Stonewall riots, when it was accompanied by flannel shirts, boots, and bomber jackets. Some gay men in the 1970s were "dressing like the blue-collar men that turned us on," cooed retired professor Arnie Kantrowitz in the *Times* article.[2] By looking blue-collar, they were hoping to decoy the working guys they found hot into switching sides. By the mid-seventies mustaches had slowly migrated back to hetero style: Sonny Bono, Burt Reynolds, Ron Jeremy. They also found their way onto the upper lips of law enforcement officers and firemen, where—along with the Fu Manchu—they have remained ever since. The AIDS epidemic in the early 1980s saw gay and straight men alike go clean-shaven. No hair = no disease.

All this hirsute history—from aviator and fireman and cop facial hair to gay disco style and *Borat*'s chuckling xenophobia—brings in tow a swirl of mixed meanings: sexual ambiguity, caricatured ethnic origins, flagrant gayness, or creepily self-aware sexual potency. Distilled, the hipster mustache, accruing all of these meanings, carries with it an element of deception and protean immutability. Today's hipster mustache calls attention to itself with the heightened self-consciousness of trying not to be self-conscious of its own weighty ambiguity. Yet while mustaches open this Pandora's box of signification, the loudest subtext that accompanies them is this: *Though the hair is real, it is still a joke.* The hipster mustache's strongest motivation is to deliver one overwhelming impression about the man upon whom it grows: *Look, This is a Contemporary Person!*

Pabst Blue Ribbon: Originally a working-class beer, PBR consumption may be done out of pure economic necessity. More likely, though, the beer's deification aims to reach across the class aisle to make amends for—or identify with—the economic woes endured by blue-collar laborers over the last decade, as real wages sank to where they were in the early 1980s, when jobs were sent to Southeast Asia. As hipsters affect a similar condition of downtroddenness, a fist of PBR intones, *I'm like you. Let's keep it simple. Here's to temporary good times. Fancy beer is for Europeans and rich kids. Fuck them.* But in these caricatured working-class-guy sentiments one hears a second voice that whispers, *I'm just not worth anything better.* PBR is a kind of beer-jargon that attempts to turn bitterness into a shared condition with a tippled smirk. In this chummy barroom grunting, PBR-as-idol creates an illusion of class cohesion that distracts its drinkers from actual economic injustices. It's surely better to look working-class than actually to be it. Obama's "beer summit" (between Henry Louis Gates, Jr., and Sgt. James Crowley, on July 30, 2009) attempted to take advantage of beer's frothy class-conflict-smoothing qualities. There was no PBR available. (Obama: Bud Light;

Gates: Sam Adams Light; Crowley: Blue Moon.) Such a summit would never have worked in German-speaking Europe, where politicians drink beer openly and frequently, stripping the beverage of any class specificity.

The Knit Wool Cap: Still clueless.

The Wife-Beater: This symbol serves, too, as a white flag of class apology and identification—and of having muscles. The wife-beater stands for the misogynistic, blue-collar Italian immigrant (just add spaghetti sauce stains), 1980s' Matt Dillon film character, or South Boston construction worker after hours, all tinged with a threatening cue of potential violence. The shirt clarifies, *I am the guardian of this lair, and you will be getting seriously fucked up if you tread into it.* Welcome to the House of Pain.

Youthful Sneakers: Keds, Hush Puppies, Vans, Converse All Stars, 'Roos, Reeboks—all exhibit a self-styled young-at-heartness or, in the case of TOMS, humanitarian generosity (when you buy a pair of these alpargata-based footwear, the company will give a pair to "a person in need."). In either case, there is a sort of brassy opposition to the stringent forms of adult responsibility. Life is for the living, not for nine-to-fivers. Hurrah! *Wir leben!* But hipster shoes look more like longing for youth than the real thing. Wearing the same brands embarrassingly purchased by one's mother over two decades ago shows that you have the confidence to wear them, even when buying big-person shoes is an option. This same logic applies to the super-tight trend in hipster clothing: it acknowledges that though the physical body has grown, one has not had time to buy new clothing or indulge other physical needs due to intense artistic pursuits. Tight clothing remains tethered to one's physical past, saying, *My earlier life was better.* Oversized hip-hop attire, however, bespeaks exactly the opposite: *I am still a child who has not yet grown. The best is yet to come.*

A digression on Reebok: One reason that the brand became an ironic staple of hipster style has surely to do with its retro name and shiny white '80s look, but also because targeted marketing works. In February 2005 Reebok launched the largest global integrated marketing and advertising campaign it had undertaken in nearly a decade called "I Am What I Am." The campaign encouraged young people to embrace their individuality by celebrating contemporary "heroes of authenticity." Featured celebrities included music icons Jay-Z, Daddy

Yankee, and 50 Cent; athletes Iker Casillas, Kelly Holmes, Allen Iverson, Donovan McNabb, Yao Ming, and Curt Schilling; and actors Lucy Liu (whose quote echoes the Romantic urge for escape so devoutly it's satirical: "I want to go back to the feeling of being a child, when the heart told you all you needed to know"), John Leguizamo, and Christina Ricci, and skateboarder Stevie Williams. The ad campaign for "I Am What I Am" created such a significant increase in sales that in 2006 the company adopted it as its entire "brand attitude." For Reebok, the campaign "means being proud of who you are, holding your own views and opinions, and being an authentic individual." The phrase, for better or worse, has a storied history. *"Ehyeh asher ehyeh"* is what God answers to Moses when asked for his name in the Hebraic Bible; it translates as "I am that I am." Samuel Taylor Coleridge first used the term as a Romantic response to Descartes' *"Cogito ergo sum,"* writing that Being is "a repetition in the finite mind of the eternal act of creation in the infinite I AM"; Popeye, of course, yummified the phrase as "I yam what I yam"; and "I Am What I Am" is the name of both a Village People single on their 1978 album *Macho Man* and a Gloria Gaynor 1983 disco hit, penned by Broadway composer Jerry Herman, who wrote the song as a paean to gay pride. No matter, though. Reebok's 2010 campaign saw another run at "I Am What I Am" for the upmarket fifteen-to-twenty demographic. It aimed to promote, Reebok says, the "unique individuality of young elite athletes." Authentic individuality apparently scores big in team sports.

Conspicuously Nerdy Glasses: These would have earned the hipster only painful ridicule in high school, but now they allow him to acknowledge this fact while symbolically giving the middle finger to the bullies who would have kicked his ass. The larger they become—and they have been becoming clownishly Philip Johnson-size over the years—the more aggressive the finger-giving. Nerd glasses show proud defiance of what otherwise would have been a shameful accessory. The more radically dead-center, 1970s' electrical-engineer-dad-with-secrets the glasses, the more suspicious one's interpretation of their wearer, leading to the oft-repeated description, "rapist glasses." But ever since these glasses (accompanied sometimes by the knit-cap-in-summer look) have seeped into the wider culture as a trend with an alternative or Buddy Holly-worshipping tinge (see Anderson Cooper, Scarlett Johansson, Justin Timberlake, Justin Bieber, Demi Moore, David Beckham, Jay-Z), they have taken on the whispered hope that could only have followed the dot-com rush: *Nerds are cool (and most* *likely very rich).* It is no mistake that today's hipster nerd glasses look exactly like the ones Bill Gates wore in 1973. But perhaps over and above all these interpretations, oversized nerd glasses—summoning the entire history of modernity's romance with the outsider—bring one immediate, capital-lettered thought to every one of their onlookers: *Those Glasses Look Insane. Please take them off so I can take you seriously.*

Epilogue

Estrangement shows itself precisely in the elimination of distance between people.

- Theodor Adorno

IMAGINE, JUST FOR A MOMENT, that no one in the world was sincere. Everything everyone said or did had an ulterior motive. You would have no real friends to count on. More broadly, there would not be any justice, because no one would take the law seriously. This would make sense, because the law would not mean what it actually said. Much business would be impossible, as binding contracts would be neither binding nor meaningful. Science would become impossible, because data would be deceptive, which would lead to a whole lot more sick people, as doctors would not give trustworthy advice. A world without any sincerity would embody the *X-Files* motto: Trust no one.

Now imagine the exact opposite, a world where everyone was sincere all the time. Everyone would always say exactly what they were thinking or feeling, regardless of its unwantedness, inappropriateness, inaccuracy, relation to truth, poor entertainment value, or consequences (pick a scene from Ricky Gervais's 2009 film *The Invention of Lying*, where precisely this scenario is imagined). Transparency of motive would be the highest value. There would be no lying, cheating, or stealing, and all the protocols of civilized life would melt away. We would finally just say what was on our minds, all the time. This perfectly sincere world would have no literature, of course, because literature is a pretend reality. No comedy, irony, or sarcasm, because they all function by not saying directly what they mean or require that someone is caught unawares. There would also be no representational painting, drawing, or sculpture, because they all feign to look like real things. No acting, which tries its best to look real; or theater, which stages a fake world. In the more brutish world of geopolitics, there would be no military sneak attacks, midnight raids, or surprise victories, as all parties would have had to reveal their plans to the besieged in advance. A totally sincere world does not mean a world with truth always in plain view, as sincerity does not necessarily correlate to objective truths; it correlates to inward states, which surely are not always aware of the facts.

Either of these worlds would obviously be a miserable place to live.

The world we inhabit, however, allows the sincere and insincere to coexist. The right to privacy means the right to hide your motives from whomever you want. Outside a court of law, where deception can land you in jail, there is no enforceable prohibition against being insincere. We are free to be sincere or not. Only we, alone, can determine which mode to engage, when, and with whom.

Because of this freedom, we think of being sincere as a moral choice, and thus a reflection of moral values, and thus a reflection of moral character. This linkage leads to an interesting predicament: people who consider themselves sincere feel morally superior to people who are insincere. Insincere people, on the other hand, find it easy to make fun of the sincere people for their naïveté, lack of worldliness, and overly trusting natures. The sincere people call the insincere people morally bankrupt; the insincere people call the sincere people foolish.

Of course, no one is sincere all the time, and very few people are always insincere. Satire, which straddles both courts, works because its audience knows what is really—that is, sincerely—being conveyed behind its insincere utterances. When satirists from Jonathan Swift to Jon Stewart offer their words and performances, they do so for an audience that knows that the overt words and sentences do not say what is actually meant. Irony has the task of conveying sincerity. When irony stops conveying sincerity but instead conveys mere complaint or flippancy—for example, in knee-jerk sarcasm, or "ironic" marketing gimmicks—it becomes tedious and hollow, empty of the moral force that made it originally compelling. That's when people start to tire of irony.

Long derided but always present in human societies, hypocrites—indeed, more prevalent in our world than satirists—take an opposite tack to satirists: satirists mean sincere things by saying them insincerely; hypocrites say sincere things but actually mean them insincerely. Satirists and hypocrites are therefore always locking horns. Their contestations make up most of the content of *The Daily Show* and *The Colbert Report*. The concerned satirist, acutely sensitive to accusations of hypocrisy, thinks the hypocrite is morally blameworthy because he pretends to be something he is not. Hypocrites, it seems, don't really seem to care what satirists think of them.

There is a third group of participants in this cultural show: sincerity lovers. They believe the satirist and hypocrite are the same: neither reveals their true intentions openly and therefore neither of them is honest. These unvaryingly sincere people can be the most annoying. Lacking a sense of play, irony, darkness, subtlety, or cynicism, the unfailingly sincere are mostly dull, religiously absolutist, and imaginatively limited. They don't assume enjoyable social roles. They fail to realize that when we play-act, openly take on a disguise, mock ourselves, ironically engage, and take our seriousness less seriously, life is less heavy and death is less foreboding. They fail to realize that being ironic does not mean being insincere, and that satirists, perhaps more than any other group, have been preserving the ideal of sincerity in our culture of spin, jargon, and—as philosopher Harry Frankfurt reminded us—bullshit.

At its origins, the ideal of sincerity was supported by religious or literary figures who often ended up hanged, burned, beheaded, hiding in the forest, going crazy, moving to deserted islands, or otherwise hunted out of society. They all made attempts to eradicate hypocrisy from the world—from religion, from politics, from social life. They wished for a return to natural simplicity, a pure and reformed self, a revolutionary change in human affairs, the perfect Christian. Their calls for reform had many followers and many successes. They forged the value of sincerity that remains in our hearts and heads. Their victories, however, were Pyrrhic.

Society, it turns out, likes to turn sincerity on and off when it wants. It has oscillated between being more sincere and less sincere, depending on what cultural forces were at work. Thucydides and Machiavelli advised capriciousness, and generations of nobility took their advice. Rousseau and Robespierre advised total sincerity, at the ultimate expense of human lives. Legions of artists protested against the fake politeness of modern society, only to eventually join its ranks or be shunned. "I don't think you want too much sincerity in society," remarked W. Somerset Maugham. "It would be like an iron girder in a house of cards." Indeed, sincerity is not a moral demand to place upon states or entire societies or the public; it is a demand to place on private individuals. It is, as our religious and psychosocial history bears out, a characteristic that actually made people into private individuals.

We still take sincerity seriously as a moral choice in part because of this old religious reasoning, despite the hits it takes daily from the onslaught of insincerity. We may not believe in the literal word of the Bible; we may think that much religious belief is born of the basic inability to accept death as final. But we cannot deny that the impact of religion on our inner lives has been enormous and likely permanent. This, I think, is good. Religious values—kindness, generosity, empathy, sincerity—can inspire human beings to lessen the suffering and pain of others, to think less of themselves and more of the common good. They also offer a counterweight to some constant political or consumerist values: domination, deception, envy, greed. The final truth of the world may be that force always wins, that the wish for absolute morality is but a dream; but human values like sincerity and compassion can soften this hard reality and instead offer tender, human consolation, extend good faith and trust, and make us, in the end, better animals to live among. Values are not illusions just because they are man-made. After all, who else would make them?

And thus we are conflicted over the value of sincerity today (Is it cheesy? Brave? Embarrassing?) because we find ourselves lodged between two moral feelings: 1) a privacy-liking tendency that recognizes the social mask as a necessary fiction (allowing for social or civil distance), and 2) the cloying Romanticism that longs to possess the self "underneath" the social mask. If you go too far in the first direction, you get the radically superficial society of late seventeenth-century France, or the American 1950s, where everything was always great! Go too far in the second direction, of removing all social masks, and you get the bloodshed of the French Revolution or the over-self-exposure of our own age of revelation: Oprah, Springer, Facebook, YouTube, Twitter, Dr. Phil, and books like *Be Yourself, Everyone Else Is Already Taken: Transform Your Life with the Power of Authenticity* (2009), by Mike Robbins:

> We live in a culture that is starving for authenticity. We want our leaders, our co-workers, our family members, our friends, and everyone else we interact with to tell us the truth and to be themselves. Most important, we want to have the personal freedom and confidence to say, do, and be who we really are, without worrying so much about how we appear to others and what they might think or say about us.

Playing into this second direction, the business book industry has been taking careful note of the importance of authenticity of late (even though some people are, thankfully, starting to question whether or not the authenticity bug has run its course).* In 2007, Harvard Business School Press published a book called *Authenticity: What Consumers Really Want,* by James H. Gilmore and B. Joseph Pine II. There we learn why companies need to harness the power of authenticity and why it has become so powerful as a "sector strategy." Most people want "what is real," the authors say, because they see so much fakeness and phoniness around them. This thirst makes consumers vulnerable to being convinced that anything can be authentic. As Gilmore and Pine see it, authenticity is not a real quality of things or people. Rather, everything is authentic, and there is "no such thing as inauthentic experience because experiences happen inside of us." (By this logic, all experiences are just as equally inauthentic.) In order to capitalize on this, "businesses . . . can gain the perception of authenticity [and] can render their inauthentic offerings as authentic."

* See, for example, Andrew Potter's *The Authenticity Hoax* (HarperCollins, 2010), and "All That Authenticity Might be Getting Old," by Emily Weinstein, in the *New York Times*, October 26, 2011, D1. See also how the "authenticity" of not knowing much about foreign policy or forgetting critical facts about your own program played poorly for some Republican candidates during the 2011 debate season.

So much for fakeness and phoniness. All you need is a few tricks up your sleeve (stonewash, the worn look, or simply the word "authentic" or "vintage" attached to your product) and presto: all things mass-produced, market-tested, inauthentic, and kitschy (that is, things that lie about what they actually are) can be transformed into authentic products. It's no wonder we doubt the reality of authenticity.

But this lurch toward deception has something to do with the disingenuous thinking of business culture itself. The bestselling self-help manual *The 48 Laws of Power* (1998), by Robert Greene, describes a set of "amoral, cunning, ruthless, and instructive" ancient military strategies for getting ahead in business. Illustrated in part through the stories of "Queen Elizabeth I, Henry Kissinger, [and] P. T. Barnum," some of the maxims from *The 48 Laws of Power* include:

Law 3: Conceal your intentions.
Law 7: Get others to do the work for you, but always take the credit.
Law 12: Use selective honesty and generosity to disarm your victim.
Law 14: Pose as a friend, work as a spy.
Law 17: Keep others in suspended terror: cultivate an air of unpredictability.
Law 20: Do not commit to anyone.
Law 24: Play the perfect courtier.
Law 38: Think as you like but behave like others.
Law 48: Assume formlessness.

If you want real power, it's easy: don't uphold your promises or form any meaningful relationships. Cultivate a protean personality of total deception; pretend to mean what you say but then do the opposite. Discard your sense of ethical responsibility. (The soft-spoken, nerdish-leaning Robert Greene said in several interviews that he does not abide by these rules himself.) From deceptive personality to deceptive product is no big leap.

Nearly fifteen years later, *The 48 Laws of Power* remains among Amazon.com's top 300 bestsellers (ranking number seven in "motivational business books"). Greene's success has put him on the board of the clothing company American Apparel and on the inside with some of hip-hop's megastars. Busta Rhymes said *The 48 Laws* helped him become the man he is today, and Greene's most recent book, *The 50th Law* (2009), was written with 50 Cent, who praised Greene for changing his worldview and contributing to his financial might. Greene says he didn't do a whole lot to deserve the kudos: "I just showed [rappers] how power works," he said in a 2007 interview. "And I think the honesty of it helped them deal with these brutal, ruthless people." (He was referring to music executives, who are also readers of his book.)

Of course, Greene is not alone. Bookstores are packed with similar volumes proclaiming the Machiavellian-Nietzschean-personal-trainer ethos: be all you can be; crush the competition; allow business to set you free; go against the pack; don't play by the rules; embrace your inner ruthlessness. In just over a decade, it seems, "authenticity" has become something of a category for marketing that "companies must grasp, manage, and excel at rendering," as Gilmore and Pine wrote. This trend has enabled businesspeople, motivational speakers, and pop psychologists to both cheapen and falsify what was once an esteemed and hard-won moral quality that our religious, philosophical, and artistic tradition has cultivated over the past five centuries (actually, since Socrates). These kinds of books, written for marketing department managers for weekend patio reading, run fiercely counter to what authenticity actually is. Sincerity and authenticity take a long time to cultivate; you cannot "unleash" them after you read a book. They are real qualities of human beings who repeatedly make deliberate choices to steer away from what is immediate and easy, from what is profitable and efficacious, who instead decide that moral commitments must be real to be meaningful, that remaining true to oneself need not be advertised to be real. Unlike nearly all other qualities that you can market, you cannot actually fake them. Those adjectives are most credible when they are conferred upon you, rather than when you assign them to yourself. As André Gide wrote, "One cannot both be sincere and seem so."

As Lionel Trilling avowed in the early 1970s, sincerity and authenticity may be hard to find and difficult to cultivate; they may be often performed, are sometimes entirely misplaced, and may be on the decline. But the only "hoax" about authenticity and sincerity in our own time is how they have been misappropriated and abused, not whether they are real or not. They deserve to mean more than just falsely faded jeans or rustic Pottery Barn end tables or fake political charm. A misleading road does not mean a misleading map.

In 1947, in a book called *Philosophy of Modern Music,* the German philosopher Theodor Adorno wrote that the private artist, working in seclusion, took the highest road of cultural progress because he resisted the world's attempt to mold him into something else. Adorno celebrated the barely comprehensible atonal music of Arnold Schoenberg precisely because its incomprehensibility (like Adorno's writing) offered resistance to "incorporation" into the culture-as-product industry. In our time, given the prevalence of "fake authenticity" (a tip o' the hat to Joshua Glenn for coining the term in the late 1990s), the act of resistance has itself become a popular suit to don, and has been transformed into a postmodern caricature. Speaking of why she may not seek the GOP nomination in 2012, Sarah Palin reminded her *Fox News* viewers on September 27, 2011, of her trenchant opposition to the status quo: "I'm a maverick, and I do go rogue, and I call it like I see it, and I don't mind stirrin' it up," she told *On the Record's* host Greta Van Susteren. The role of president, Palin said, might hem in her native rebellious authenticity.

When figures like Sarah Palin—cheerleader, sportscaster, local politician, former governor, former candidate for vice president of the United States of America, and *Fox News* TV personality—refer to themselves as mavericks, the very concept of what it means to offer true resistance to incorporation, to do something new and challenging, to create new ways of thinking or being, to seek new ways out of the of crushing present, becomes totally meaningless. Sarah Palin is certainly sincere in her belief that she is a maverick. She's just not right about it.

I was motivated to undertake this study not solely for its intellectual charm but rather because for some instinctual reason I cannot rid myself of the view that feigned sincerity, particularly among adults, is cowardly. It is offensive because it not only fakes what it relays, it also assumes that it goes undetected, which reveals the arrogance of the person who undertakes to achieve it. Insincerity pretends toward a democratic sympathy while engaging in aristocratic deceit. "Weak people cannot be sincere," wrote the aristocynic La Rochefoucauld. He was right—as he was about nearly everything else. Insincerity, while not intrinsically bad, exhibits an avoidance of confronting others and ourselves with uncomfortable frankness. It thrusts forward an image of how things are supposed to be rather than how they actually are. The bolder, more democratic move would be to simply offend. Among the well-bred, at least, it's increasingly hard to imagine a way back to that kind of civil directness. We're all trying to get ahead, and being nice is a big part of the recipe.

Being sincere is not always easy—and it is by no means always good, appropriate, relevant, or even interesting. It means skirting hardened social proprieties and rote reactions in order to express something more real and human, more resonant of what we are actually thinking and feeling; no easy task for any culture, as Allen Ginsberg observed. Timed right, sincerity can give rise to goosebumps and revolutions. Timed wrong, it can lead to uncomfortable silences and ruined careers. True, sincerity is not the best method for forward motion in business, law, entertainment, or politics. But for an individual person to have integrity and moral character—to exist as a being without wax, to feel that his or her inner life is a familiar and comfortable place—it is absolutely necessary.

HERE ENDETH THE LESSON.

Acknowledgments

FIRST AND FOREMOST, I WANT TO THANK ALANE Salierno Mason, Denise Scarfi, Starling Lawrence, and W. W. Norton for their early and enthusiastic support of this project. Alane and Denise have painstakingly helped to make a vague and overly ambitious idea into what we hope has become a compelling and readable book. My gratitude for their care and expertise is immense. Thanks go also to copyeditor Allegra Huston, whose attention to detail and fine suggestions have improved this book significantly.

I have never been entirely certain why one should save the best for last, so I want to thank my wife, Tanja Maka, for her sharp editorial teeth, strategic thinking, and her unflagging love and support throughout a very long year. Our son, Jasper Ely, appeared early on the scene in late 2009, and while he has made life all the more charmed, he has also made writing a book all the more tricky. Tanja: *riesen Dank*. This book would not have been possible without you.

To my family—Mom, Liz, Scott—thanks, once again, for, well, everything. And to our Pop, who was taken from all of us unexpectedly during the writing of this book: I owe my own cocktail of irony and sincerity to you more than anyone.

There are many favors that seemed small by dint of others' true modesty but that in the end really count. Toby Lester was of particular support in navigating the treacherous shoals of book proposals. Diane McWhorter helped wrestle some clearer sentences out of some initially mucky ones. C. Ed Emmer was a constant source of obscure and useful material that I otherwise would have missed. Adam Garfinkle allowed me to try out some early material in *The American Interest*, for which I've been lucky enough to draw caricatures for the last seven years. Ralph Martin and Nicole Busse read some sections of the larval manuscript and offered fine advice for changes and additions. And a few Fellows at the American Academy in Berlin bore kind patience with early conversational forays: Adrian Nicole LeBlanc, Joel Harrington, Nathan Englander, Greg Horowitz, Juliet Koss, Mitchell Merback, and Charles Marsh. Thanks for indulging.

I'd also like to thank my indefatigable colleagues at the American Academy and its tireless executive director, Gary Smith, who, with the support of the staff, benefactors, and trustees, has created an institution for the ages.

Susanna Dulkinys's purist cover and overall book design are the result of her patience, professionalism, and trusting friendship; I am ever grateful for her taking on the project with such enthusiasm. Likewise Erik Spiekermann, who listened excitedly to ideas for this book among other projects; Gunter Klötzer's perfect, inquisitive eye captured the ideal author photograph—no easy task; Solveig Köbernick spent time creatively scheming about how best to reach an audience or two; Sarah Lincoln's magical design sense created a smashing website; and Karl Gutjahr was an enormous help in offering a quiet office in which to work. Thanks, all.

Last, not least, there are a few individuals whose advice, ideas, and love have contributed to this book in a much larger sense: Dan Gluibizzi, Jr., Brett Huggett, Evan Lyon, John and Kristin Luther, Jolie Scena, Kelly Hanlon, Michelle Lamunier, Niko and Claire Günther, Bettina Warburg, Mark Solley, Torsten Maka, and Georg Weizsäcker. Thanks for many years of hilarious and, yes, sincere friendship.

Notes

INTRODUCTION

[1] *The Glenn Beck Program,* Fox News Channel, January 13, 2010.

[2] "Assessing the sincerity of politicians: The case of George W. Bush," *Política* 35 (2007): 69–79. See their work also in "The Bush Doctrine and the Psychology of Alliances," in S. A. Renshon and P. Suedfeld, eds., *Understanding the Bush Doctrine: Psychology and Strategy in the Age of Terrorism* (New York: Routledge, 2007).

[3] David A. Andelman, "America's Most Sincere Candidates," *Forbes.com,* available at: forbes.com/opinions/2007/08/15/forbes-tracker-sincere-oped-cx_daa_0815sincere.html (accessed January 1, 2009).

[4] Ibid.

[5] Machiavelli, *The Prince,* translated by Peter Bondanella (New York: Oxford University Press, 2008), 60. "Sincerity" appears in some of the dozens of translations of *The Prince,* such as this one, but is also translated as "honest principles" or "truthfulness," as it is in the standard translation by George Bull, which I have also used; see bibliography. (Alas, more recent editions do not feature the translation "truthiness.")

[6] Leo Strauss, *Thoughts on Machiavelli,* 6.

[7] Trilling, *Sincerity and Authenticity,* 6.

[8] Patricia M. Ball, "Sincerity: The Rise and Fall of a Critical Term," *Modern Language Review* LIX, no. 1, (January 1964): 1.

[9] hks.harvard.edu/saguaro/press/saguaronews.htm (accessed August 6, 2011).

[10] pewresearch.org/pubs/1398/internet-mobile-phones-impact-american-social-networks (accessed September 6, 2011).

CHAPTER I: REFORM THYSELF!

[1] John Frith is mentioned by scholar Jane Taylor in her essay "Why do you tear me from Myself?", 22–23. Credit is due her for some intriguing thoughts on the conditions that gave rise to sincerity in sixteenth-century Europe. See also Annemieke Bijkerk, "Yours Sincerely and yours affectionately," 116–17.

[2] Thomas More quoted in d'Aubigné, *History of the Reformation,* vol. 6, 206.

[3] Ibid., 209.

[4] Accounts of More's famed execution are plentiful, but *A Complete Collection of State Trials and Proceeding Upon Impeachments for High Treason, etc.*

(London, 1719) recalls the episode with era-appropriate phrasing: "Laying his Head upon the Block, he bid the Executioner stay till he had put his Beard aside, for that had committed no Treason. Thus he suffered with much Cheerfulness; his Head was taken off at one Blow, and was placed upon *London-Bridge,* where, having continued for some Months, and being about to be thrown into the Thames to make room for others, his Daughter *Margaret* bought it, in closed it in a Leaden Box, and kept it for a Relique." Originally from *Hall's Chronicle* (1542), vol. 2, s. 2.

[5] *St. Thomas More: Selected Letters,* 249–53.

[6] *Nicomachean Ethics,* book 4, 1127a, line 4–1127b, line 8.

[7] These examples are from units.muohio.edu/englishtech/eng49502/schoenel/Sincere/sincere.htm (Accessed on November 15, 2009). They are also all listed in the *OED.*

[8] Sir Thomas Wriothesley, *A Chronicle of England During the Reigns of the Tudors, from A.D. 1485 to 1559* (London: Camden Society, 1875), 30.

[9] Ibid.

[10] John Strype, *Ecclesiastical Memorials Relating Chiefly to Religion and the Reformation of It and the Emergencies of the Church of England under King Henry VII,* vol. 2 (1725), 628.

[11] Roberts, *History of the World,* 553.

[12] This recounting of papal indiscretions is found in William Manchester's highly readable *A World Lit Only by Fire,* 74–85.

[13] Luther, *Reformation Writings,* 120; emphasis mine.

[14] Ibid., 110–11.

[15] Ibid., 140.

[16] Erikson, *Young Man Luther,* chapter 2.

[17] For a detailed study of the experience of silent reading in late medieval England, when devotional guides, two centuries before the German Reformation, urged readers to "see themselves," see Jennifer Bryan's *Looking Inward.*

[18] A wide-ranging examination of Lutheranism's effects is found in Seigel, *The Idea of the Self,* 301.

[19] Cited in Peter C. Herman, *Squitter-wits and Muse-haters: Sidney, Spenser, Milton, and Renaissance Antipoetic Sentiment* (Detroit: Wayne State University Press, 2006), 42.

[20] For more on this disturbing yet über-fascinating topic, see Vanderbilt University historian Joel Harrington's work on Franz Schmidt, particularly his translation of Schmidt's journals, wherein the lifelong executioner details each and every killing and torture he performed between 1573 and 1617. An upstanding member of sixteenth-century bourgeois Nuremberg, Schmidt, upon his own death, Harrington writes, "enjoyed

a state funeral and burial in the city's most prominent cemetery, a few paces away from other famous sons, such as Albrecht Dürer and Hans Sachs." Harrington's book on Schmidt is forthcoming, but an excerpt, including a few of Schmidt's creepily clinical diary entries, may be read in the fall 2009 issue of *The Berlin Journal*, published by the American Academy in Berlin, available online at americanacademy.de.

[21] Montaigne, "Of Presumption," in *The Complete Essays*, 487.

[22] Ibid., 491.

[23] Ibid.

[24] Montaigne cited in Taylor, *Sources of the Self*, 178.

[25] Montaigne, in Donald M. Frame, *Montaigne: A Biography* (London: Hamish Hamilton, 1965), 323.

[26] Desiderius Erasmus, *The Manual of A Christian Knight* (1501); translated by William Tyndale.

[27] Machiavelli, *The Prince*, 101.

[28] Ibid.

[29] Ibid., 99.

[30] Ibid., 5-6.

[31] Castiglione, *The Book of the Courtier*, 33.

CHAPTER II : A SAINT'S HEART

[1] For a complete account, see Lodge, *The History of England*.

[2] Gurnall, *The Christian in Complete Armour*, 232.

[3] John Calvin, *Institutes*, vol. 1, 51.

[4] For a brilliant and detailed narrative of this shift in political consciousness, on which I have heavily relied, see Walzer's groundbreaking study, *Revolution of the Saints*. Quote from p. 4.

[5] These and other hilarious examples can be found in George Francis Dow, *Everyday Life in the Massachusetts Bay Colony* (New York: Dover, 1988), particularly the chapter "Crimes and Punishments," 199-226.

[6] http://en.wikiquote.org/wiki/Oliver_Cromwell (accessed January 28, 2011).

[7] John Arrowsmith, *Covenant-Avenging Sword Brandished* (London, 1643), 14.

[8] Thomas Case, *Two Sermons Lately Preached* (London, 1642); quoted in Walzer, 11.

[9] John Bailey (1643-97) quoted in Max Weber, *The Protestant Ethic*, 179.

[10] John Cotton, *The Way of Life*, 280.

[11] Ben Johnson, *The Alchemist* (1610), Act III, sc. 1. Tribulation Wholesome's brother is named Zeal-of-the-Land.

[12] Trilling, *Sincerity and Authenticity*, 21-22.

[13] Delbanco, *The Death of Satan*, 27.

[14] Richard J. Bauckham, "Adding to the Church in the Early American Period," at www.the-highway.com/Early_American_Bauckham.html (accessed November 1, 2010).

[15] John Cotton quoted in Pettit, *The Heart Prepared*, 134.

[16] Richard Baxter, *The Saints' Everlasting Rest* (London, 1654), part I, 121.

[17] Stone, *The Family, Sex and Marriage*, 228.

[18] Taylor, *Sources of the Self*, 184.

[19] When Anglicans and Catholics wrote autobiographies, they were on the whole more objective accounts of religious change rather than stories of inward journey. See Delany, *British Autobiography in the Seventeenth Century*. See also the go-to text on Puritan autobiography: Haller, *The Rise of Puritanism*.

[20] Thomas Hooker quoted in Bercovitch, 18.

[21] Hooker, *A Survey of the Summe of Church Discipline*, 45.

[22] John Bunyan, *Grace Abounding*, 5. After 344 years, *Pilgrim's Progress* has never been out of print.

[23] William Penn, "Truth Exalted," in *Selected Works*.

CHAPTER III: THOSE TRICKY BOURGEOIS GENTLEMEN

[1] La Rochefoucauld, *Maxims*, 83 (number 256).

[2] Ibid., 56 (number 124).

[3] Ibid., 25.

[4] Ibid., 29.

[5] britannica.com/EBchecked/topic/388302/Moliere (accessed September 6, 2011).

[6] According to the philosopher Jürgen Habermas, salons were the basic building block of the bourgeois public sphere that emerged in the seventeenth century and that would lead to the revolutions of the eighteenth. See his hallmark study *The Structural Transformation of the Public Sphere*.

[7] See de Staël, *Ten Years' Exile*, and Berger, ed., *Madame de Staël*.

[8] All examples from Antoine de Courtin, *Nouveau traité de la civilité* (1671), quoted in Elias, *The Civilizing Process*, 75.

[9] Sennett, *The Fall of Public Man*, 70.

[10] Lord Chesterfield to his son, August 21, 1749, *Letters of Chesterfield*, 1382–83.

[11] Swift, "A Modest Proposal."

CHAPTER IV: NATURAL MAN REDEEMED

[1] A minor point, but Rousseau was mistaken about when this earth-shattering, unforgettable walk occurred. He writes that "the summer of

1749 was excessively hot," but scholar Leo Damrosch writes, "Diligent scholarship has established that the event actually occurred in October 1749, not summer, and according to meteorological records the temperature barely reached sixty degrees Fahrenheit." *Jean-Jacques Rousseau*, 212–13. Just after this passage about the event, however, Rousseau writes in the *Confessions* that "many of the details have escaped me since I committed them to paper in one of my four letters to M. de Malesherbes," and then laments how bad his memory is.

[2] Cited in Rolland, et al., *French Thought in the Eighteenth Century*, 9. This incident coincides, Rolland writes, with the eruption of a bladder disease that would slowly poison Rousseau to death. In fact, in 1749 doctors gave Rousseau not more than six months to live. While this diagnosis prompted him to get down the torrent of ideas while he could, Rousseau would slog along for nearly thirty more years, dying of a hemorrhage in 1778, at age sixty-six. Some contemporaries, such as Madame de Staël, suspected that Rousseau had actually committed suicide.

[3] Rousseau, "A Discourse on the Arts and Sciences," in *The Social Contract and Discourses*, 6.

[4] Ibid., 8.

[5] There are always at least two sides to a story. Years later, after Diderot and Rousseau had their falling-out, Diderot, while not the most trustworthy of sources given his patronizing treatment of Rousseau, recounts the following: "I was a prisoner at Vincennes; Rousseau used to come and see me. ... One day, when we were taking a walk together, he told me that the Dijon Academy had just proposed an interesting question, and he wanted to take it up: Has the restoration of the sciences and arts contributed to the purification of morals? 'Which side will you take?' I asked. 'The affirmative,' he answered. 'That's the *pons asinorum*,' I said; 'all the mediocre talents will take that route, and you'll find nothing but commonplaces there. The negative side, on the other hand, offers a new, rich, and fertile field for philosophy and eloquence.' 'You're right,' he said after pondering it a bit, 'and I'm going to follow your advice.'" Quoted in Damrosch, *Jean-Jacques Rousseau*, 213–14.

[6] Rousseau, *Confessions*, 67.

[7] Rolland, *French Thought*, 4.

[8] Rousseau, *Confessions*, 1.

[9] Rousseau quoted in Trilling, *Sincerity and Authenticity*, 59.

[10] Rousseau, *Reveries of the Solitary Walker*, 33–34.

[11] Voltaire quoted in Mazella, *The Making of Modern Cynicism*, 126.

[12] Marmontel quoted ibid., 126.

[13] For the whole exchange, see Horace Walpole, *Reminiscences* (London, 1788), 149.
[14] Boswell, *The Life of Samuel Johnson*, 255.
[15] Arendt, *On Revolution*, 106.
[16] Sennett, *The Fall of Public Man*, 185.
[17] Ibid., 186.
[18] See Wood, *The Idea of America*, 102.
[19] Ibid., 109.
[20] Ibid., 105.

CHAPTER V: ROMANTIC ESCAPES

[1] Emile Faguet quoted in Reardon, *Religion in the Age of Romanticism*, 3.
[2] Peyre, *Literature and Sincerity*, 120.
[3] Chateaubriand and Goethe quoted in Schenck, *The Mind of the European Romantics*, 94-95.
[4] Ibid., 96
[5] Diderot, *Rameau's Nephew*, 35.
[6] Ibid., 80-81.
[7] Ibid., 71.
[8] Hegel, *The Phenomenology of Spirit*, 317.
[9] Caspar David Friedrich quoted in Taylor, *The Ethics of Authenticity*, 86.
[10] Earl Wasserman, *The Subtler Language*, 10-11.
[11] Marchand, *Byron*, 7.
[12] For a more contemporary take on the Catholic stance *vis à vis* Romanticism, see Jesuit philosopher Walter Ong's *Frontiers of American Catholicism* (New York: MacMillan, 1957). Romanticism's complications and its relationship to bifurcated Christianity are discussed as well in, among many others, Mellor, *English Romantic Irony*; Bloom, *Romanticism and Consciousness*; and Behler, *Irony and the Discourse of Modernity*; Jacques Barzun, *Romanticism and the Modern Ego* (New York: Little, Brown, 1943), 4-26; Erich Heller, *The Artist's Journey into the Interior and Other Essays* (New York: Harcourt, 1965); Schenck's *The Mind of the European Romantics*, and Paul Johnson's *Birth of the Modern*.
[13] Berger, ed., *Madame de Staël*, 264.
[14] Schlegel, *Lucinde and the Fragments*, fragment 42, 148.
[15] Schlegel, *Literary Notebooks*, 114, 62.
[16] Schlegel, *The Philosophy of Life and Philosophy of Language*, 392.
[17] Ferguson, *Melancholy and the Critique of Modernity*, 48.
[18] Schlegel quoted in Talmon, *Romanticism and Revolt*, 150.
[19] Emerson, "Self-Reliance," in *Essays and Lectures*, 261.

[20] Mill, *On Liberty*, chapter 3, "Of Individuality, As One of the Elements of Well-Being," in *Classics of Western Philosophy*, 1056.
[21] Emerson, "Friendship," in *Essays and Poems*, 178.
[22] Thoreau quoted in Shi, *The Simple Life*, 149.

CHAPTER VI: CASCADING CYNICISM

[1] Guignon, *On Being Authentic*, 71.
[2] Rainer Maria Rilke, *Letters to A Young Poet*, translated by M. D. Herter Norton (New York: W. W. Norton, 1954), 47.
[3] Nietzsche, *The Joyful Wisdom*, section 130.
[4] Nietzsche, *Thus Spoke Zarathustra*, p. 41.
[5] Nietzsche, *Will to Power*, 132.
[6] Max Horkheimer, *The Eclipse of Reason* (New York: Oxford University Press, 1947), 137–38.
[7] Nietzsche quoted in Erich Heller, *The Importance of Nietzsche: Ten Essays* (Chicago: University of Chicago Press, 1988), 13–14.
[8] Roberts, *History of the World*, 700.
[9] Nietzsche, *Human, All Too Human*, 234 (aphorism 485).
[10] An 1871 letter from Flaubert quoted in Peyre, *Literature and Sincerity*, 147.
[11] *The Times* (London), December 1, 1900.
[12] *New York Times*, December 1, 1900.
[13] Morgenthaler, *Madness and Art*, 21.
[14] Klee quoted in Peiry, *Art Brut*, 30.
[15] Dubuffet quoted ibid., 11.
[16] For a hallmark overview of the event's culture-changing effects, see Fussell, *The Great War and Modern Memory*.
[17] Wassily Kandinsky, *Concerning the Spiritual in Art* (New York: Dover, 1974), 9, 14.
[18] Breton quoted in Peiry, *Art Brut*, 33.
[19] Freud, *Civilization and Its Discontents*, 136–37.
[20] Trilling, *Sincerity and Authenticity*, 142. For a more detailed discussion of Freud's impact on the idea of authenticity, see chapter 6, "The Authentic Unconscious," where Trilling treats the younger and older Freud with careful consideration.
[21] I first heard this quote from art critic and philosopher Donald Kuspit in a class at SUNY-Stony Brook in 1996. Though I have not been able to locate the quotation, Freud's sentiment is deducible from other letters and comments to Breton.
[22] Freud quoted in Lynn Gamwell, *Exploring the Invisible* (Princeton: Princeton University Press, 2002), 248.

[23] Cox, *Concerning Painting*, 7.

[24] Anonymous (assumed by scholars to be Beatrice Wood), "The Richard Mutt Case," *The Blind Man* 2 (1917): 5.

[25] Duchamp quoted in William A. Camfield, "Marcel Duchamp's Fountain: Its History and Aesthetics in the Context of 1917," in Rudolf Kuenzli and Francis M. Naumann (eds.), *Marcel Duchamp: Artist of the Century* (Cambridge, MA: MIT Press, 1989), 81.

[26] Pousette-Dart quoted in Bogart, *Artists, Advertising, and the Borders of Art*, 144.

[27] Ibid., 149-50.

[28] Examples from Marchand, *Advertising the American Dream*, 223-25.

[29] Ibid., 150.

[30] Ibid., 152.

[31] Leland, *Hip*, 66. The Ashanti derivation of the Charleston is the product of Leland's thoroughgoing research, not mine.

[32] Ibid. The section on the 1910s and 1920s, "My Black/White Roots" (57-86), is superbly informative and original.

[33] Frank Haddock quoted in Stivers, *The Culture of Cynicism*, 24-25.

[34] Barton quoted in Brown, *Star-Spangled Kitsch*, 45.

[35] T. S. Eliot quoted in Louis Menand, "Practical Cat," *New Yorker*, September 19, 2011, 79.

[36] Fitzgerald quoted in Leland, *Hip*, 72.

[37] Richard Wright, *Black Boy* (New York: Harper & Row, 1945), 270-72.

[38] Peyre, *Literature and Sincerity*, 240.

[39] Baraka quoted in Leland, *Hip*, 144.

[40] Mailer, "The White Negro," 342.

[41] Ginsberg quoted in Leland, *Hip*, 55-56.

[42] Williams, *Camino Real*, 130-32. My thanks to Adrienne Lamb for pointing me to this play years ago.

[43] Brooks Atkinson, "Theatre: Camino Real," *New York Times*. (March 20, 1953).

[44] Riesman, *The Lonely Crowd*, 194.

[45] Ibid., 195-96.

[46] Ibid., 196.

[47] Mills, *White Collar*, ix.

[48] Ibid., xii.

[49] Ibid., 182.

[50] Ibid., xv.

[51] For the full intellectual biography, see Irving L. Horowitz, *C. Wright Mills: An American Utopian* (New York: Free Press, 1983). Of relevance is that Mills's father was an insurance salesman, and Mills himself was a

researcher in a Columbia University bureaucracy, where he helped cull statistical survey analysis, panel methods, latent structure analysis, and contextual analysis for American sociological research.

[52] Goffman, *The Presentation of Self*, 28.

[53] Ibid.

[54] time.com/time/magazine/article/0,9171,826423,00.html#ixzz1TxqQldaD (accessed August 2, 2011).

[55] Read, *The Contrary Experience*, 342.

[56] Herbert Read quoting himself in *The Cult of Sincerity*, 15.

[57] Ibid.

[58] Barnett Newman, *Selected Writings*, 240-41.

CHAPTER VII: LONG LIVE "SINCERITY"

[1] Warhol, *The Philosophy of Andy Warhol*, 27.

[2] Goodman, *New Reformation*, xi.

[3] Pountain and Robins, *Cool Rules*, 80.

[4] Tom Wolfe, "The 'Me' Decade and the Third Great Awakening," *New York*, August 23, 1976, 6 (accessed May 2011 at www.nymag.com; pagination is from the electronic edition).

[5] Hinckle quoted in Thomas Frank, *The Conquest of Cool* (Chicago: University of Chicago Press, 1997), 30.

[6] Ibid., 6.

[7] Trilling, *Sincerity and Authenticity*, 6.

[8] Wolfe, "The 'Me' Generation," 7.

[9] Warhol, *The Philosophy of Andy Warhol*, 100-1.

[10] Warhol on Canadian public television, 1964. Part of a film in the PBS American Masters series, available at: www.pbs.org/wnet/americanmasters/episodes/andy-warhol/a-documentary-film/44/.

[11] Kuspit, *Signs of Psyche*, 276. Kuspit was a student of Theodor Adorno, whose promotion of the radical avant-garde of figures like Arnold Schoenberg and Alban Berg guaranteed the survival of a strong self who stood against, for aesthetic and philosophical reasons, the crowd-pleasing music of the "culture industry." Donald Kuspit was my mentor and thesis advisor at SUNY-Stony Brook in the mid-1990s. I owe a great debt to his early influence.

[12] Roland Barthes, "The Death of the Author," *Aspen* 5 and 6 (1967), reprinted in *Image-Music-Text*, 142-43.

[13] The full transcript of the Senate hearing on Serrano and the NEA, from May 18, 1989, is available at: www.csulb.edu/~jvancamp/361_r7.html 295 (accessed September 17, 2011).

[14] Ibid., 279.

[15] Jerry Saltz, "Sincerity and Irony Hug It Out," *New York*, May 27, 2010.
[16] www.guardian.co.uk/music/2011/mar/06/michael-stipe-rem-collapse-interview (accessed May 20, 2011).
[17] Archived at http://wowhuh.com/archives/295 (accessed June 3, 2011).
[18] David Foster Wallace, "E Unibus Pluram: Television and U.S. Fiction," in *A Supposedly Fun Thing*, 25-26.

CHAPTER VIII: HIP AFFECTED EARNESTNESS

[1] My personal thanks to Mark Greif for generously sending the transcript of "What Was the Hipster?" to me in Berlin. Also please note that *n+1* has itself been called a hipster rag. The reasoning escapes its editors.
[2] The transcript and subsequent *What Was the Hipster?* book cites the questioner as "Manoah Finston."
[3] Ben Davis, "Was the Hipster All That Bad?" *artinfo.com*, April 14, 2011, 2.
[4] Worm Miller, madatoms.com/site/blog/sincerity-is-the-new-black (accessed April 23, 2009).
[5] See Sasha Frere-Jones, "Summer Jam: My Morning Jacket's hippie shake," *New Yorker,* August 1, 2011, 70.
[6] Sasha Frere-Jones, "Into the Woods," *New Yorker,* January 12, 2009, available online at: newyorker.com/arts/critics/musical/2009/01/12/090112crmu_music_frerejones?currentPage=all (accessed January 12, 2009).
[7] spin.com/articles/beck-sincerity-new-irony (accessed April 17, 2011).
[8] youtube.com/watch?v=2yQBceh4pUY (accessed May 25, 2011).
[9] nytimes.com/2008/03/16/fashion/16farmer.html?pagewanted=1&_r=1 (accessed April 8, 2009).
[10] Nietzsche, *The Will to Power*, 143 (aphorism 247).
[11] nonalignmentpact.com/2009/09/aging-hipster-waxing-nostalgic.html (accessed October 3, 2009).

NOTE TO HIPSTER SEMIOTIC APPENDIX

[1] Nick Burns, "One Hairy Lip, A Mix of Messages," *New York Times*, November 2, 2006, nytimes.com/2006/11/02/fashion/02skin.html (accessed November 2, 2006).

Bibliography

ABRAMS, M. H. *The Mirror and the Lamp: Romantic Theory and the Critical Tradition*. New York: Oxford University Press, 1971.

ADORNO, THEODOR W. *The Jargon of Authenticity*. Translated by Knut Tarnowski and Frederic Will. Evanton, IL: Northwestern University Press, 1973.

ANDERSON, AMANDA. *The Powers of Distance*. Princeton: Princeton University Press, 2001.

ARCHER, RICHARD. *Fissures in the Rock: New England in the Seventeenth Century.* Hanover, NH: University of New Hampshire Press, 2001.

ARENDT, HANNAH. *On Revolution.* New York: Penguin Classics, 2006.

ARISTOTLE. *Nicomachean Ethics*. In *Aristotle in 23 Volumes,* translated by H. Rackham. Cambridge, MA: Harvard University Press, 1934.

ARROWSMITH, JOHN. *The Covenant-Avenging Sword Brandished.* London, 1643.

BARBU, ZEVEDEI. *Problems of Historical Psychology.* New York: Grove Press, 1960.

BARTHES, ROLAND. *Image-Music-Text.* Translated by Stephen Heath. New York: Hill and Wang, 1977.

BAXTER, RICHARD. *The Saints' Everlasting Rest.* London, 1654.

BEHLER, ERNST. *Irony and the Discourse of Modernity.* Seattle: University of Washington Press, 1990.

BELL, DANIEL. *The Cultural Contradictions of Capitalism.* New York: Basic Books, 1996.

BENJAMIN, WALTER. *Illuminations: Essays and Reflections.* New York: Schocken Books, 1968.

BERCOVITCH, SACVAN. *The Puritan Origins of the American Self.* New Haven: Yale University Press, 1975.

BERGER, MORROE, ed. *Madame de Staël, On Politics, Literature and National Character.* London: Sidgwick & Jackson, 1964.

BERMAN, MARSHALL. *The Politics of Authenticity: Radical Individualism and the Emergence of Modern Society.* London: Verso, 2009.

BERNIER, OLIVIER. *The World in 1800.* New York: John Wiley & Sons, 2000.

BIJKERK, ANNEMIEKE. "Yours Sincerely and yours affectionately: On the origin and development of two positive politeness markers." In *Letter Writing,* edited by Terttu Nevalainen and Sanna-Kaisa Tanskanen. Amsterdam: John Benjamins, 2007.

BLOOM, HAROLD. *The American Religion: The Emergence of the Post-Christian Nation.* New York: Simon & Schuster, 1992.

——. *Romanticism and Consciousness.* New York: W. W. Norton, 1970.

BOGART, MICHELE H. *Artists, Advertising, and the Borders of Art.* Chicago: University of Chicago Press, 1995.

BOSWELL, JAMES. *The Life of Samuel Johnson.* Edited by David Womersley. New York: Penguin Classics, 2008.

BRONOWSKI, J., and BRUCE MAZLISH. *The Western Intellectual Tradition: From Leonardo to Hegel.* New York: Harper Torch Books, 1970.

BROWN, CURTIS F. *Star-Spangled Kitsch: An Astounding and Tastelessly Illustrated Exploration of the Bawdy, Gaudy, Shoddy Mass-Art Culture in This Grand Land of Ours.* New York: Universe Books, 1975.

BRYAN, JENNIFER. *Looking Inward: Devotional Reading and the Private Self in Late Medieval England.* University Park, PA: University of Pennsylvania Press, 2007.

BUNYAN, JOHN. *Grace Abounding to the Chief of Sinners.* Edited by R. Sharrock. Oxford: Clarendon Press, 1962.

CALVIN, JOHN. *Institutes of the Christian Religion.* Translated by John Allen. New Haven: Hezekiah Howe, 1816.

CASTIGLIONE, BALDASSARRE. *The Book of the Courtier.* Translated by Charles Singleton. New York: Doubleday, 1959.

CHALOUPKA, WILLIAM. *Everybody Knows: Cynicism in America.* Minneapolis: University of Minnesota Press, 1999.

CHESTERFIELD, LORD. *The Letters of Philip Dormer Stanhope, 4th Earl of Chesterfield.* Edited by Bonamy Dobrée. (London: Eyre & Spottiswoode, 1932).

COATES, WILLSON H., HAYDEN V. WHITE, and J. SALWYN SCHAPIRO. *The Emergence of Liberal Humanism: An Intellectual History of Western Europe.* New York: McGraw-Hill, 1966.

COTTON, JOHN. *The Way of Life.* London, 1641.

COX, KENYON. *Concerning Painting: Considerations Theoretical and Historical.* New York: Scribner & Sons, 1917.

CROW, THOMAS. *Modern Art in the Common Culture.* New Haven: Yale University Press, 1996.

CURTI, MERLE. *The Growth of American Thought.* New Brunswick, NJ: Transaction, 1995.

DAMROSCH, LEO. *Jean-Jacques Rousseau: Restless Genius.* Boston: Houghton Mifflin, 2005.

D'AUBIGNÉ, J. H. MERLE. *History of the Reformation in the Time of Calvin.* London: Religious Tract Society, 1867.

DELANY, PAUL. *British Autobiography in the Seventeenth Century.* London: Routledge & Kegan Paul, 1969.

DELBANCO, ANDREW. *The Death of Satan: How Americans Have Lost the Sense of Evil.* New York: Farrar, Straus & Giroux, 1995.

——. *The Real American Dream: A Meditation on Hope.* Cambridge, MA: Harvard University Press, 1999.

DE STAËL, ANNE-LOUISE-GERMAINE. *Ten Years' Exile.* Introduction by Margaret Crosland. Sussex: Centaur Press, 1968.

DIDEROT, DENIS. *Rameau's Nephew, and Other Works.* Translated by Jacques Barzun and Ralph H. Bowen. Garden City, NY: Doubleday Anchor Books, 1956.

DUBY, GEORGES, ed. *A History of Private Life.* Vol 2, *Revelations of the Medieval World.* Cambridge, MA: Belknap Press of Harvard University Press, 1988.

ELIAS, NORBERT. *The Civilizing Process.* Oxford: Blackwell, 1994.

EMERSON, RALPH WALDO. *The Early Lectures of Ralph Waldo Emerson.* Vol. 3. Cambridge, MA: Harvard University Press, 1972.

——. *Essays and Lectures.* New York: Library of America, 1983.

——. *English Traits.* Edited by Robert E. Burkholder. Cambridge, MA: Harvard University Press, 1994.

——. *Essays and Poems by Ralph Waldo Emerson.* Edited by Peter Norberg. New York: Spark Educational, 2005.

ERIKSON, ERIK H. *Young Man Luther: A Study in Psychoanalysis and History.* New York: W. W. Norton, 1958.

FERGUSON, HARVIE. *Melancholy and the Critique of Modernity: Søren Kiekegaard's Religious Psychology.* New York: Routledge, 1995.

FERGUSON, NIALL. *Civilization: The West and the Rest.* New York: Penguin, 2011.

FOXE, JOHN. *The Book of Martyrs.* London, 1576.

FREUD, SIGMUND. *Civilization and Its Discontents.* Translated by Joan Riviere. London: Hogarth Press, 1949.

——. *The Future of An Illusion.* Translated by W. D. Robson Scott. London: Hogarth Press, 1949.

FRITH, JOHN. *Writings of Tindale, Frith, and Barnes.* London: Religious Tract Society, n.d.

FUSSELL, PAUL. *The Great War and Modern Memory.* New York: Oxford University Press, 1975.

GAMWELL, LYNN. *Dreams 1900–2000: Science, Art, and the Unconscious Mind.* Ithaca, NY: Cornell University Press, 2000.

GILLESPIE, MICHAEL ALLEN. *The Theological Origins of Modernity.* Chicago: University of Chicago Press, 2008.

GILMORE, JAMES H., and B. JOSEPH PINE II. *Authenticity: What Consumers Really Want.* Boston: Harvard Business School Press, 2007.

GOFFMAN, ERVING. *The Presentation of Self in Everyday Life.* New York: Pelican Books, 1971.

GOODMAN, PAUL. *New Reformation: Notes of a Neolithic Conservative.* New York: Random House, 1970.

GREENBERG, CLEMENT. *Art and Culture: Critical Essays.* Boston: Beacon Press, 1961.

GREIF, MARK, CHRISTIAN LORENTZEN, and JACE CLAYTON. *What Was the Hipster? A Sociological Investigation.* Brooklyn, NY: n+1 Foundation, 2010.

GROETHUYSEN, BERNARD. *The Bourgeois: Catholicism versus Capitalism in Eighteenth-Century France.* London: Barrie and Rockliffe, 1968.

GUIGNON, CHARLES. *On Being Authentic.* New York: Routledge, 2004.

GUILHAMET, LEON. *The Sincere Ideal: Studies on Sincerity in Eighteenth-Century Literature.* McGill-Queen's University Press, 1974.

GURNALL, WILLIAM. *The Christian in Complete Armour.* Edited by John Ryle. Edinburgh: Banner of Truth Trust, 1989.

HABERMAS, JÜRGEN. *The Structural Transformation of the Public Sphere: An Inquiry into a Category of Bourgeois Society.* Translated by Thomas Burger with the assistance of Frederick Lawrence. Cambridge, MA: MIT Press, 1989.

HALLER, WILLIAM. *The Rise of Puritanism.* New York: Columbia University Press, 1938.

HARRIS, DANIEL. *Cute, Quaint, Hungry and Romantic: The Aesthetics of Consumerism.* New York: Basic Books, 2000.

HEGEL, G. W. F. *The Phenomenology of Spirit.* Translated by A. V. Miller. Oxford: Oxford University Press, 1977.

HELLER, ERICH. *The Artist's Journey into the Interior, and Other Essays.* New York: Harcourt, 1965.

HERZOG, DON. *Cunning.* Princeton: Princeton University Press, 2006.

HOCHSCHILD, ARLIE RUSSELL. *The Managed Heart: Commercialization of Human Feeling.* Berkeley: University of California Press, 1983.

HOOKER, THOMAS. *A Survey of the Summe of Church Discipline.* London: A. M. for John Bellamy, 1648.

HOUGHTON, WALTER E. *The Victorian Frame of Mind, 1830–1870.* New Haven: Yale University Press, 1985.

HOWE, JOHN. *The Works of the Rev. John Howe, M.A. with Memoirs of His Life.* Edited by Edmund Calamy. New York: John Have, 1838.

HUIZINGA, JOHAN. *Erasmus of Rotterdam.* Translated by F. Hopman. London: Phaidon, 1952.

JAY, MARTIN. *The Virtues of Mendacity: On Lying in Politics.* Charlottesville, VA: University of Virginia Press, 2010.

JOHNSON, PAUL. *The Birth of the Modern: World Society 1815–1830.* New York: HarperCollins, 1991.

KÖNIGSBERGER, H. G., and GEORGE L. MOSSE. *Europe in the Sixteenth Century.* London: Longman, 1968.

KUKLICK, BRUCE. *A History of Philosophy in America, 1720–2000.* New York: Oxford University Press, 2001.

KUSPIT, DONALD. *The Cult of the Avant-Garde Artist.* New York: Cambridge University Press, 1993.

———. *Psychostrategies of Avant-Garde Art.* New York: Cambridge University Press, 2000.

———. *Signs of Psyche in Modern and Postmodern Art.* New York: Cambridge University Press, 1993.

LANHAM, ROBERT. *The Hipster Handbook.* New York: Anchor Books, 2002.

LA ROCHEFOUCAULD, FRANÇOIS, DUC DE. *Maxims.* Translated by Constantine FitzGibbon. London: Wingate, 1957.

LASCH, CHRISTOPHER. *The Culture of Narcissism: American Life in an Age of Diminishing Expectations.* New York: W. W. Norton, 1979.

———. *The Minimal Self: Psychic Survival in Troubled Times.* New York: W. W. Norton, 1984.

LELAND, JOHN. *Hip: The History.* New York: Harper Perennial, 2004.

LODGE, RICHARD. *The History of England from the Restoration to the Death of William III (1660–1702).* London: Longmans, Green and Co., 1910.

LÖWITH, KARL. *From Hegel to Nietzsche: The Revolution in Nineteenth-Century Thought.* Translated by David E. Green. New York: Holt, Rinehart & Winston, 1964.

LUTHER, MARTIN. *Reformation Writings of Martin Luther.* Translated by Bertram Lee Woolf. London: Lutterworth Press, 1952.

LÜTHY, HERBERT. *From Calvin to Rousseau: Tradition and Modernity in Socio-Political Thought from the Reformation to the French Revolution.* New York: Basic Books, 1970.

MACHIAVELLI, NICCOLÒ. *The Prince.* Translated by George Bull. London: Penguin, 1961.

MAILER, NORMAN. "The White Negro." In *Advertisements for Myself.* Cambridge, MA: Harvard University Press, 1992.

MANCHESTER, WILLIAM. *A World Lit Only by Fire: The Medieval Mind and the Renaissance: Portrait of an Age.* New York: Little, Brown, 1993.

MARCHAND, LESLIE A., *Byron: A Biography.* New York: Alfred A. Knopf, 1957.

MARCHAND, ROLAND. *Advertising the American Dream: Making Way for Modernity, 1920–1940.* Berkeley: University of California Press, 1985.

MARKOVITS, ELIZABETH. *The Politics of Sincerity: Plato, Frank Speech, and Democratic Judgment.* University Park, PA: University of Pennsylvania Press, 2008.

MAUSS, MARCELL. "A Category of the Human Mind: The Notion of Person, the Notion of Self." In *The Category of the Person: Anthropology, Philosophy, History,* edited by Michael Carrithers, Steven Collins, and Steven Lukes. New York: Cambridge University Press, 1985.

MAZELLA, DAVID. *The Making of Modern Cynicism.* Charlottesville, VA: University of Virginia Press, 2007.

MCCARRAHER, EUGENE. *Christian Critics: Religion and the Impasse in Modern American Social Thought.* Ithaca, NY: Cornell University Press, 2000.

MCDOUGALL, WALTER A. *Freedom Just Around the Corner: A New American History 1585–1828.* New York: HarperCollins, 2004.

MELCHIOR-BONNET, SABINE. *The Mirror: A History.* New York: Routledge, 2001.

MELLOR, ANNE K. *English Romantic Irony.* Cambridge, MA: Harvard University Press, 1980.

MILL, JOHN STUART. *On Liberty.* In *Classics of Western Philosophy.* Indianapolis: Hackett, 1977.

MILLER, PERRY. *The New England Mind: The Seventeenth Century.* Cambridge, MA: Harvard University Press, 1939.

MILLER, WILLIAM IAN. *Faking It.* New York: Cambridge University Press, 2003.

MILLS, C. WRIGHT. *White Collar: The American Middle Classes.* New York: Oxford University Press, 1956.

MILTON, JOHN. *Paradise Lost.* Rochester, NH: Odyssey Press, 1962.

MOLIÈRE (JEAN-BAPTISTE POQUELIN). *The Misanthrope.* Translated by Henri van Laun. New York: Dover, 1992.

———. *Tartuffe, or The Impostor.* Translated by Richard Wilbur. New York: Mariner, 1968.

MONTAIGNE, MICHEL DE. *The Complete Essays of Montaigne.* Translated by Donald M. Frame. Berkeley: University of California Press, 1976.

MORGENTHALER, WALTER. *Madness and Art: The Life and Works of Adolf Wölfli.* Translated by Aaron H. Esman. Lincoln, NE: University of Nebraska Press, 1992.

NEWMAN, BARNETT. *Selected Writings and Interviews.* Edited by John P. O'Neill. Los Angeles: University of California Press, 1990.

NIETZSCHE, FRIEDRICH. *Human, All Too Human.* Translated by Marion Faber. Lincoln, NE: University of Nebraska Press, 1984.

———. *The Joyful Wisdom.* Translated by Thomas Common. New York: Frederick Ungar, 1971.

———. *Thus Spoke Zarathustra.* Translated by R. J. Hollingdale. New York: Penguin Classics, 1961.

———. *Twilight of the Idols and The Anti-Christ.* Translated by R. J. Hollingdale. New York: Penguin, 1990.

———. *The Will to Power.* In *The Complete Works of Friedrich Nietzsche,* edited by Oscar Levy. New York: MacMillan, 1909–14.

PARKER, PHILIP M., ed. *Sincerity: Webster's Timeline History.* San Diego: ICON Group, 2009.

PARR, CATHERINE. *Lamentations of a Sinner.* In *Writings of Edward the Sixth,*

William Hugh, Queen Catherine Parr, Anne Askew, Lady Jane Grey, Hamilton, and Balnaves. Edinburgh: Religious Tract Society, 1831.

PASCAL, BLAISE. *Pensées.* Translated by W. F. Trotter. Introduction by T. S. Eliot. London: J. M. Dent & Sons, 1932.

PECKHAM, MORSE. *Romanticism: The Culture of the Nineteenth Century.* New York: George Braziller, 1965.

PEIRY, LUCIENNE. *Art Brut: The Origins of Outsider Art.* Translated by James Frank. Paris: Flammarion, 2001.

PENN, WILLIAM. *The Selected Works of William Penn.* London: William Phillips and George Yard, 1825.

PETTIT, NORMAN. *The Heart Prepared: Grace and Conversion in Puritan Spiritual Life.* New Haven: Yale University Press, 1966.

PEYRE, HENRI. *Literature and Sincerity.* New Haven: Yale University Press, 1963.

PHELPS, ROBERT, ed. *Twentieth-Century Culture: The Breaking Up.* New York: George Braziller, 1965.

POTTER, ANDREW. *The Authenticity Hoax: How We Get Lost Finding Ourselves.* New York: HarperCollins, 2010.

POUNTAIN, DICK, and DAVID ROBINS. *Cool Rules: Anatomy of an Attitude.* London: Reaktion, 2000.

READ, HERBERT. *The Contrary Experience: Autobiographies.* London: Secker & Warburg, 1973.

———. *The Cult of Sincerity.* London: Faber & Faber, 1968.

REARDON, BERNARD M. G. *Religion in the Age of Romanticism: Studies in Early Nineteenth-Century Thought.* New York: Cambridge University Press, 1985.

RIESMAN, DAVID, with NATHAN GLAZER and REUEL DENNEY. *The Lonely Crowd.* New Haven: Yale University Press, 1953.

RITTER, GERHARD. *Luther: His Life and Work.* London: Collins, 1963.

ROBBINS, MIKE. *Be Yourself, Everybody Else Is Already Taken: Transform Your Life with the Power of Authenticity.* New York: Wiley, 2009.

ROBERTS, J. M. *History of the World.* New York: Oxford University Press, 1993.

ROGERS, ELIZABETH, ed. *St. Thomas More: Selected Letters.* New Haven: Yale University Press, 1961.

ROLLAND, ROMAIN, ANDRÉ MAUROIS, and EDOUARD HERRIOT. *French Thought in the Eighteenth Century.* London: Cassell, 1953.

ROUSSEAU, JEAN-JACQUES. *Confessions.* Translated by John Grant. New York: Dutton, 1946.

———. *Émile.* Translated by Barbara Foxley. London: J. M. Dent, 1950.

———. *Letter to M. d'Alembert on the Theater.* Translated by Allan Bloom. Glencoe, IL: Free Press, 1960.

———. *Reveries of the Solitary Walker.* Translated by Peter France. New York: Penguin, 1979.

———. *The Social Contract and Discourses.* Translated by E. D. H. Cole. London: Everyman, 1993.

SCHENK, H. G. *The Mind of the European Romantics: An Essay in Cultural History.* London: Constable: 1966.

SCHILLER, FRIEDRICH. *On the Aesthetic Education of Man.* Translated by Reginald Snell. London: Routledge & Kegan Paul, 1954.

SCHLEGEL, FRIEDRICH VON. *Friedrich Schlegel's Lucinde and the Fragments.* Translated by Peter Firchnow. Minneapolis: University of Minnesota Press, 1971.

———. *Literary Notebooks, 1797-1801.* Translated by Hans Eichner. Toronto: University of Toronto Press, 1957.

———. *The Philosophy of Life and Philosophy of Language: In A Course of Lectures.* Translated by A. J. W. Morrison. New York: Harper & Brothers, 1855.

SEIGEL, JERROLD. *The Idea of the Self: Thought and Experience in Western Europe since the Seventeenth Century.* New York: Cambridge University Press, 2005.

SELIGMAN, ADAM B. *The Problem of Trust.* Princeton: Princeton University Press, 1997.

SELIGMAN, ADAM B., ROBERT P. WELLER, MICHAEL J. PUETT, and BENNETT SIMON. *Ritual and Its Consequences: An Essay on the Limits of Sincerity.* New York: Oxford University Press, 2008.

SENNETT, RICHARD. *The Fall of Public Man.* New York: W. W. Norton, 1992.

SHI, DAVID E. *The Simple Life: Plain Living and High Thinking in American Culture.* Athens, GA: University of Georgia Press, 1985.

SLOTERDIJK, PETER. *The Critique of Cynical Reason.* Minneapolis: University of Minnesota Press, 1987.

SPENDER, STEPHEN. *The Struggle of the Modern.* London: Hamish Hamilton, 1963.

STEARNS, PETER N. *American Cool: Constructing a Twentieth-Century Emotional Style.* New York: New York University Press, 1994.

STIVERS, RICHARD. *The Culture of Cynicism: American Morality in Decline.* Oxford: Blackwell, 1994.

STONE, LAWRENCE. *The Family, Sex and Marriage in England 1500-1800.* London: Weidenfeld & Nicolson, 1977.

STRAUSS, GERALD, ed. *Manifestations of Discontent in Germany on the Eve of the Reformation.* Bloomington, IN: University of Indiana Press, 1971.

STRAUSS, LEO. *Thoughts on Machiavelli.* Chicago: University of Chicago Press, 1995.

SWIFT, JONATHAN. "A Modest Proposal." In *The Norton Anthology of English Literature.* New York: W. W. Norton, 1979.

TALMON, J. L. *Romanticism and Revolt: Europe 1815-1848.* London: Thames & Hudson, 1967.

TAYLOR, CHARLES. *The Ethics of Authenticity.* Cambridge, MA: Harvard University Press, 1992.

———. *A Secular Age.* Cambridge, MA: Belknap Press of Harvard University Press, 2007.

———. *Sources of the Self: The Making of the Modern Identity.* Cambridge, MA: Harvard University Press, 1989.

TAYLOR, JANE. "Why do you tear me from Myself?: Torture, Truth, and the Arts of the Counter-Reformation." In *The Rhetoric of Sincerity: Cultural Memory in the Present,* edited by Ernst van Alphen, Mieke Bal, and Carel Smith. Stanford: Stanford University Press, 2009.

TRILLING, LIONEL. *Sincerity and Authenticity.* New York: Oxford University Press, 1971.

WAHL, JEAN. *A Short History of Existentialism.* Translated by Forrest Williams and Stanley Maron. New York: Philosophical Library, 1949.

WALLACE, DAVID FOSTER. *A Supposedly Fun Thing I'll Never Do Again: Essays and Arguments.* Boston: Back Bay Books, 1997.

WALZER, MICHAEL. *The Revolution of the Saints: A Study in the Origins of Radical Politics.* Cambridge, MA: Harvard University Press, 1965.

WARHOL, ANDY. *The Philosophy of Andy Warhol (From A to B and Back Again).* New York: Harcourt Brace Jovanovich, 1975.

WASSERMAN, EARL. *The Subtler Language: Critical Readings of Neoclassic and Romantic Poems.* Baltimore: Johns Hopkins University Press, 1968.

WEBER, MAX. *The Protestant Ethic and the Spirit of Capitalism.* Translated by Talcott Parsons. New York: Routledge, 2004.

WILLIAMS, EDWIN OWEN. "Trials of Conscience: Criminalizing Religious Dissidence in Elizabethan England." Dissertation, University of Pennsylvania, 2003.

WILLIAMS, TENNESSEE. *Camino Real.* New York: New Directions, 1970.

WILSON, CARL. *Let's Talk About Love: A Journey to the End of Taste.* New York: Continuum Press, 2007.

WOOD, GORDON S. *The Idea of America: Reflections on the Birth of the United States.* New York: Penguin, 2011.

Index

Page numbers beginning with 239 refer to endnotes.